Seekers after God

Frederic Farrar

Seekers after God

ISBN: 978-1-64799-344-3

CONTENTS

INTRODUCTORY

On the banks of the Baetis—the modern Guadalquiver,—and under the woods that crown the southern slopes of the Sierra Morena, lies the beautiful and famous city of Cordova. It had been selected by Marcellus as the site of a Roman colony; and so many Romans and Spaniards of high rank chose it for their residence, that it obtained from Augustus the honourable surname of the "Patrician Colony." Spain, during this period of the Empire, exercised no small influence upon the literature and politics of Rome. No less than three great Emperors—Trajan, Hadrian, and Theodosius,—were natives of Spain. Columella, the writer on agriculture, was born at Cadiz; Quintilian, the great writer on the education of an orator, was born at Calahorra; the poet Martial was a native of Bilbilis; but Cordova could boast the yet higher honour of having given birth to the Senecas, an honour which won for it the epithet of "The Eloquent." A ruin is shown to modern travellers which is popularly called the House of Seneca, and the fact is at least a proof that the city still retains some memory of its illustrious sons.

Marcus Annaeus Seneca, the father of the philosopher, was by rank a Roman knight. What causes had led him or his family to settle in Spain we do not know, and the names Annaeus and Seneca are alike obscure. It has been vaguely conjectured that both names may involve an allusion to the longevity of some of the founders of the family, for Annaeus seems to be connected with annus, a year, and Seneca with senex, an old man. The common English composite plant ragwort is called senecio from the white and feathery pappus or appendage of its seeds; and similarly, Isidore says that the first Seneca was so named because "he was born with white hair."

Although the father of Seneca was of knightly rank, his family had never risen to any eminence; it belonged to the class of nouveaux riches, and we do not know whether it was of Roman or of Spanish descent. But his mother Helvia—an uncommon name, which, by a curious coincidence, belonged also to the mother of Cicero—was a Spanish lady; and it was from her that Seneca, as well as his famous nephew, the poet Lucan, doubtless derived many of the traits which mark their intellect and their character. There was in the Spaniard a richness and splendour of imagination, an intensity and warmth, a touch of "phantasy and flame," which we find in these two men of genius, and which was wholly wanting to the Roman temperament.

Of Cordova itself, except in a single epigram, Seneca makes no mention; but this epigram suffices to show that he must have been familiar with its stirring and memorable traditions. The elder Seneca must have been living at Cordova during all the troublous years of civil war, when his native city caused equal offence to Pompey and to Caesar. Doubtless, too, he would have had stories to tell of the noble Sertorius, and of the tame fawn which gained for him the credit of divine assistance; and contemporary reminiscences of that day of desperate disaster when Caesar, indignant that Cordova should have embraced the cause of the sons of Pompey, avenged himself by a massacre of 22,000 of the citizens. From his mother Helvia, Seneca must often have heard about the fierce and gallant struggle in which her country had resisted the iron yoke of Rome. Many a time as a boy must he have been told how long and how heroically Saguntum had withstood the assaults and baffled the triumph of Hannibal; how bravely Viriathus had fought, and how shamefully he fell; and how at length the unequal contest, which reduced Spain to the condition of a province, was closed, when the heroic defenders of Numantia, rather than yield to Scipio, reduced their city to a heap of blood-stained ruins.

But, whatever may have been the extent to which Seneca was influenced by the Spanish blood which flowed in his veins, and the Spanish legends on which his youth was fed, it was not in Spain that his lot was cast. When he was yet an infant in arms his father, with all his family, emigrated from Cordova to Rome. What may have been the special reason for this important step we do not know; possibly, like the father of Horace, the elder Seneca may have sought a better education for his sons than could be provided by even so celebrated a provincial town as Cordova; possibly—for he belonged to a somewhat pushing family—he may have desired to gain fresh wealth and honour in the imperial city.

Thither we must follow him; and, as it is our object not only to depict a character but also to sketch the characteristics of a very memorable age in the world's history, we must try to get a glimpse of the family in the midst of which our young philosopher grew up, of the kind of education which he received, and of the influences which were likely to tell upon him during his childish and youthful years. Only by such means shall we be able to judge of him aright. And it is worth while to try and gain a right conception of the man, not only because he was very eminent as a poet, an author, and a politician, not only because he fills a very prominent place in the pages of the great historian, who has drawn so immortal a picture of Rome under the Emperors; not only because in him we can best study the inevitable signs which mark, even in the works of men of genius, a degraded people and a decaying literature; but because he was, as the title of this volume designates him, a "SEEKER AFTER GOD." Whatever may have been the dark and questionable actions of his life—and in this narrative we shall endeavor to furnish a plain and unvarnished picture of the manner in which he lived,—it is certain that, as a philosopher and as a moralist, he furnishes us with the grandest and most eloquent series of truths to which, unilluminated by Christianity, the thoughts of man have ever attained. The purest and most exalted philosophic sect of antiquity was "the sect of the Stoics;" and Stoicism never found a literary exponent more ardent, more eloquent, or more enlightened than Lucius Annaeus Seneca. So nearly, in fact, does he seem to have arrived at the truths of Christianity, that to many it seemed a matter for marvel that he could have known them without having heard them from inspired lips. He is constantly cited with approbation by some of the most eminent Christian fathers. Tertullian, Lactantius, even St. Augustine himself, quote his words with marked admiration, and St. Jerome appeals to him as "our Seneca." The Council of Trent go further still, and quote him as though he were an acknowledged father of the Church. For many centuries there were some who accepted as genuine the spurious letters supposed to have been interchanged between Seneca and St. Paul, in which Seneca is made to express a wish to hold among the Pagans the same beneficial position which St. Paul held in the Christian world. The possibility of such an intercourse, the nature and extent of such supposed obligations, will come under our consideration hereafter. All that I here desire to say is, that in considering the life of Seneca we are not only dealing with a life which was rich in memorable incidents, and which was cast into an age upon which Christianity dawned as a new light in the darkness, but also the life of one who climbed the loftiest peaks of the moral philosophy of Paganism, and who in many respects may be regarded as the Coryphaeus of what has been sometimes called a Natural Religion.

It is not my purpose to turn aside from the narrative in order to indulge in moral reflections, because such reflections will come with tenfold force if they are naturally suggested to the reader's mind by the circumstances of the biography. But from first to last it will be abundantly obvious to every thoughtful mind that alike the morality and the philosophy of Paganism, as contrasted with the splendour of revealed truth and the holiness of Christian life, are but as moonlight is to sunlight. The Stoical philosophy may be compared to a torch which flings a faint gleam here and there in the dusky recesses of a mighty cavern; Christianity to the sun pouring into the inmost depths of the same cavern its sevenfold illumination. The torch had a value and brightness of its own, but compared with the dawning of that new glory it appears to be dim and ineffectual, even though its brightness was a real brightness, and had been drawn from the same etherial source.

SENECA

"Ce nuage frangé de rayons qui toucbe presqu' à l'immortelle aurore des vérités chrétiennes."

PONTMAOTIN

CHAPTER I

THE FAMILY AND EARLY YEARS OF SENECA

The exact date of Seneca's birth is uncertain, but it took place in all probability about seven years before the commencement of the Christian era. It will give to his life a touch of deep and solemn interest if we remember that, during all those guilty and stormy scenes amid which his earlier destiny was cast, there lived and taught in Palestine the Son of God, the Saviour of the world.

The problems which for many years tormented his mind were beginning to find their solution, amid far other scenes, by men whose creed and condition he despised. While Seneca was being guarded by his attendant slave through the crowded and dangerous streets of Rome on his way to school, St. Peter and St. John were fisher-lads by the shores of Gennesareth; while Seneca was ardently assimilating the doctrine of the stoic Attalus, St. Paul, with no less fervancy of soul, sat learning at the feet of Gamaliel; and long before Seneca had made his way, through paths dizzy and dubious, to the zenith of his fame, unknown to him that Saviour had been crucified through whose only merits he and we can ever attain to our final rest.

Seneca was about two years old when he was carried to Rome in his nurse's arms. Like many other men who have succeeded in attaining eminence, he suffered much from ill-health in his early years. He tells us of one serious illness from which he slowly recovered under the affectionate and tender nursing of his mother's sister. All his life long he was subject to attacks of asthma, which, after suffering every form of disease, he says that he considers to be

1

the worst. At one time his personal sufferings weighed so heavily on his spirits that nothing save a regard for his father's wishes prevented him from suicide: and later in life he was only withheld from seeking the deliverance of death by the tender affection of his wife Paulina. He might have used with little alteration the words of Pope, that his various studies but served to help him

"Through this long disease, my life."

The recovery from this tedious illness is the only allusion which Seneca has made to the circumstances of his childhood. The ancient writers, even the ancient poets, but rarely refer, even in the most cursory manner, to their early years. The cause of this reticence offers a curious problem for our inquiry, but the fact is indisputable. Whereas there is scarcely a single modern poet who has not lingered with undisguised feelings of happiness over the gentle memories of his childhood, not one of the ancient poets has systematically touched upon the theme at all. From Lydgate down to Tennyson, it would be easy to quote from our English poets a continuous line of lyric songs on the subject of boyish years. How to the young child the fir-trees seemed to touch the sky, how his heart leaped up at the sight of the rainbow, how he sat at his mother's feet and pricked into paper the tissued flowers of her dress, how he chased the bright butterfly, or in his tenderness feared to brush even the dust from off its wings, how he learnt sweet lessons and said innocent prayers at his father's knee; trifles like these, yet trifles which may have been rendered noble and beautiful by a loving imagination, have been narrated over and over again in the songs of our poets. The lovely lines of Henry Vaughan might be taken as a type of thousands more:—

"Happy those early days, when I
Shined in my Angel infancy.
Before I understood this place
Appointed for my second race,
Or taught my soul to fancy aught
But a white celestial thought;

"Before I taught my tongue to wound
My conscience with a sinful sound
Or had the black art to dispense
A several sin to every sense;
But felt through all this fleshy dress,
Bright shoots of everlastingness."

2

The memory of every student of English poetry will furnish countless parallels to thoughts like these. How is it that no similar poem could be quoted from the whole range of ancient literature? How is it that to the Greek and Roman poets that morning of life, which should have been so filled with "natural blessedness," seems to have been a blank? How is it that writers so voluminous, so domestic, so affectionate as Cicero, Virgil, and Horace do not make so much as a single allusion to the existence of their own mothers?

To answer this question fully would be to write an entire essay on the difference between ancient and modern life, and would carry me far away from my immediate subject.[1] But I may say generally, that the explanation rests in the fact that in all probability childhood among the ancients was a disregarded, and in most cases a far less happy, period than it is with us. The birth of a child in the house of a Greek or a Roman was not necessarily a subject for rejoicing. If the father, when the child was first shown to him, stooped down and took it in his arms, it was received as a member of the family; if he left it unnoticed then it was doomed to death, and was exposed in some lonely or barren place to the mercy of the wild beasts, or of the first passer by. And even if a child escaped this fate, yet for the first seven or eight years of life he was kept in the gynaeceum, or women's apartments, and rarely or never saw his father's face. No halo of romance or poetry was shed over those early years. Until the child was full grown the absolute power of life or death rested in his father's hands; he had no freedom, and met with little notice. For individual life the ancients had a very slight regard; there was nothing autobiographic or introspective in their temperament. With them public life, the life of the State, was everything; domestic life, the life of the individual, occupied but a small share of their consideration. All the innocent pleasures of infancy, the joys of the hearth, the charm of the domestic circle, the flow and sparkle of childish gaity, were by them but little appreciated. The years before manhood were years of prospect, and in most cases they offered but little to make them worth the retrospect. It is a mark of the more modern character which stamps the writings of Seneca, as compared with earlier authors, that he addresses his mother in terms of the deepest affection, and cannot speak of his darling little son except in a voice that seems to break with tears.

Let us add another curious consideration. The growth of the personal character, the reminiscences of a life advancing into

---

[1] See, however, the same question treated from a somewhat different point of view by M. Nisard, in his charming Études sur les Poëtes de la Décadence, ii. 17, sqq.

perfect consciousness, are largely moulded by the gradual recognition of moral laws, by the sense of mystery evolved in the inevitable struggle between duty and pleasure,—between the desire to do right and the temptation to do wrong. But among the ancients the conception of morality was so wholly different from ours, their notions of moral obligation were, in the immense majority of cases, so much less stringent and so much less important, they had so faint a disapproval for sins which we condemn, and so weak an indignation against vices which we abhor, that in their early years we can hardly suppose them to have often fathomed those "abysmal deeps of personality," the recognition of which is a necessary element of marked individual growth.

We have, therefore, no materials for forming any vivid picture of Seneca's childhood; but, from what we gather about the circumstances and the character of his family, we should suppose that he was exceptionally fortunate. The Senecas were wealthy; they held a good position in society; they were a family of cultivated taste, of literary pursuits, of high character, and of amiable dispositions. Their wealth raised them above the necessity of those mean cares and degrading shifts to eke out a scanty livelihood which mark the career of other literary men who were their contemporaries. Their rank and culture secured them the intimacy of all who were best worth knowing in Roman circles; and the general dignity and morality which marked their lives would free them from all likelihood of being thrown into close intercourse with the numerous class of luxurious epicureans, whose unblushing and unbounded vice gave an infamous notority to the capital of the world.

Of Marcus Annaeus Seneca, the father of our philosopher, we know few personal particulars, except that he was a professional rhetorician, who drew up for the use of his sons and pupils a number of oratorical exercises, which have come down to us under the names of Suasoriae and Controversiae. They are a series of declamatory arguments on both sides, respecting a number of historical or purely imaginary subjects; and it would be impossible to conceive any reading more utterly unprofitable. But the elder Seneca was steeped to the lips in an artificial rhetoric; and these highly elaborated arguments, invented in order to sharpen the faculties for purposes of declamation and debate, were probably due partly to his note-book and partly to his memory. His memory was so prodigious that after hearing two thousand words he could repeat them again in the same order. Few of those who have possessed such extraordinary powers of memory have been men of first-rate talent, and the elder Seneca was no exception. But if his memory did not improve his original genius, it must at any rate have made him a very agreeable member of society, and have furnished him with an abundant store of personal and political anecdotes. In short, Marcus Seneca was a well-to-do, intelligent man of the world, with plenty of common sense, with a turn for public speaking, with a profound dislike and contempt for anything which he considered philosophical or fantastic, and with a keen eye to the main advantage.

His wife Helvia, if we may trust the panegyric of her son, was on the other hand a far less common-place character. But for her husband's dislike to learning and philosophy she would have become a proficient in both, and in a short period of study she had made a considerable advance. Yet her intellect was less remarkable than the nobility and sweetness of her mind; other mothers loved their sons because their own ambition was gratified by their honours, and their feminine wants supplied by their riches; but Helvia loved her sons for their own sakes, treated them with liberal generosity, but refused to reap any personal benefit from their wealth, managed their patrimonies with disinterested zeal, and spent her own money to bear the expenses of their political career. She rose superior to the foibles and vices of her time. Immodesty, the plague-spot of her age, had never infected her pure life. Gems and pearls had little charms for her. She was never ashamed of her children, as though their presence betrayed her own advancing age. "You never stained your face," says her son, when writing to console her in his exile, "with walnut-juice or rouge; you never delighted in dresses indelicately low; your single ornament was a loveliness which no age could destroy; your special glory was a conspicuous chastity." We may well say with Mr. Tennyson—

> "Happy he
> With such a mother! faith in womankind
> Beats with his blood, and trust in all things high
> Comes easy to him, and, though he trip and fall,
> He shall not blind his soul with clay."

Nor was his mother Helvia the only high-minded lady in whose society the boyhood of Seneca was spent. Her sister, whose name is unknown, that aunt who had so tenderly protected the delicate boy, and nursed him through the sickness of his infancy, seems to have inspired him with an affection of unusual warmth. He tells us how, when her husband was Prefect of Egypt, so far was she from acting as was usual with the wives of provincial governors, that she was as much respected and beloved as they were for the most

5

part execrated and shunned. So serious was the evil caused by these ladies, so intolerable was their cruel rapacity, that it had been seriously debated in the Senate whether they should ever be allowed to accompany their husbands. Not so with Helvia's sister. She was never seen in public; she allowed no provincial to visit her house; she begged no favour for herself, and suffered none to be begged from her. The province not only praised her, but, what was still more to her credit, barely knew anything about her, and longed in vain for another lady who should imitate her virtue and self-control. Egypt was the headquarters for biting and loquacious calumny, yet even Egypt never breathed a word against the sanctity of her life. And when during their homeward voyage her husband died, in spite of danger and tempest and the deeply-rooted superstition which considered it perilous to sail with a corpse on board, not even the imminent peril of shipwreck could drive her to separate herself from her husband's body until she had provided for its safe and honorable sepulchre. These are the traits of a good and heroic woman; and that she reciprocated the regard which makes her nephew so emphatic in her praise may be conjectured from the fact that, when he made his début as a candidate for the honours of the State, she emerged from her habitual seclusion, laid aside for a time her matronly reserve, and, in order to assist him in his canvass, faced for his sake the rustic impertinence and ambitious turbulence of the crowds who thronged the Forum and the streets of Rome.

Two brothers, very different from each other in their habits and character, completed the family circle, Marcus Annaeus Novatus and Lucius Annaeus Mela, of whom the former was older the latter younger, than their more famous brother.

Marcus Annaeus Novatus is known to history under the name of Junius Gallio, which he took when adopted by the orator of that name, who was a friend of his father. He is none other than the Gallio of the Acts, the Proconsul of Achaia, whose name has passed current among Christians as a proverb of complacent indifference.[2]

The scene, however, in which Scripture gives us a glimpse of him has been much misunderstood, and to talk of him as "careless Gallio," or to apply the expression that "he cared for none of these things," to indifference in religious matters, is entirely to misapply the spirit of the narrative. What really happened was this. The Jews, indignant at the success of Paul's preaching, dragged him before the tribunal of Gallio, and accused him of introducing illegal modes of worship. When the Apostle was about to defend himself, Gallio contemptuously cut him short by saying to the Jews, "If in truth

---

[2] Acts xxv. 19.

there were in question any act of injustice or wicked misconduct, I should naturally have tolerated your complaint. But if this is some verbal inquiry about mere technical matters of your law, look after it yourselves. I do not choose to be a judge of such matters." With these words he drove them from his judgment-seat with exactly the same fine Roman contempt for the Jews and their religious affairs as was subsequently expressed by Festus to the sceptical Agrippa, and as had been expressed previously by Pontius Pilate[3] to the tumultous Pharisees. Exulting at this discomfiture of the hated Jews and apparently siding with Paul, the Greeks then went in a body, seized Sosthenes, the leader of the Jewish synagogue, and beat him in full view of the Proconsul seated on his tribunal. This was the event at which Gallio looked on with such imperturbable disdain. What could it possibly matter to him, the great Proconsul, whether the Greeks beat a poor wretch of a Jew or not? So long as they did not make a riot, or give him any further trouble about the matter, they might beat Sosthenes or any number of Jews black and blue if it pleased them, for all he was likely to care.

What a vivid glimpse do we here obtain, from the graphic picture of an eye-witness, of the daily life in an ancient provincial forum; how completely do we seem to catch sight for a moment of that habitual expression of contempt which curled the thin lips of a Roman aristocrat in the presence of subject nations, and especially of Jews! If Seneca had come across any of the Alexandrian Jews in his Egyptian travels, the only impression left on his mind was that expressed by Tacitus, Juvenal, and Suetonius, who never mention the Jews without execration. In a passage, quoted by St. Augustine (De Civit. Dei, iv. 11) from his lost book on Superstitions, Seneca speaks of the multitude of their proselytes, and calls them "gens sceleratissima," a "most criminal race." It has been often conjectured—it has even been seriously believed—that Seneca had personal intercourse with St. Paul and learnt from him some lessons of Christianity. The scene on which we have just been gazing will show us the utter unlikelihood of such a supposition. Probably the nearest opportunity which ever occurred to bring the Christian

---

3 Matt. xxvii. 24, "See ye to it." Cf. Acts xiv. 15, "Look ye to it." Toleration existed in the Roman Empire, and the magistrates often interfered to protect the Jews from massacre; but they absolutely and persistently refused to trouble themselves with any attempt to understand their doctrines or enter into their disputes. The tradition that Gallio sent some of St. Paul's writings to his brother Seneca is utterly absurd; and indeed at this time (A.D. 54), St. Paul had written nothing except the two Epistles to the Thessalonians. (See Conybeare and Howson, St. Paul, vol. i. Ch. xii.; Aubertin, Sénèque et St. Paul.)

Apostle into intellectual contact with the Roman philosopher was this occasion, when St. Paul was dragged as a prisoner into the presence of Seneca's elder brother. The utter contempt and indifference with which he was treated, the manner in which he was summarily cut short before he could even open his lips in his own defence, will give us a just estimate of the manner in which Seneca would have been likely to regard St. Paul. It is highly improbable that Gallio ever retained the slightest impression or memory of so every-day a circumstance as this, by which alone he is known to the world. It is possible that he had not even heard the mere name of Paul, and that, if he ever thought of him at all, it was only as a miserable, ragged, fanatical Jew, of dim eyes and diminutive stature, who had once wished to inflict upon him a harangue, and who had once come for a few moments "betwixt the wind and his nobility." He would indeed have been unutterably amazed if anyone had whispered to him that well nigh the sole circumstance which would entitle him to be remembered by posterity, and the sole event of his life by which he would be at all generally known, was that momentary and accidental relation to his despised prisoner.

But Novatus—or, to give him his adopted name, Gallio—presented to his brother Seneca, and to the rest of the world, a very different aspect from that under which we are wont to think of him. By them he was regarded as an illustrious declaimer, in an age when declamation was the most valued of all accomplishments. It was true that there was a sort of "tinkle," a certain falsetto tone in his style, which offended men of robust and severe taste; but this meretricious resonance of style was a matter of envy and admiration when affectation was the rage, and when the times were too enervated and too corrupt for the manly conciseness and concentrated force of an eloquence dictated by liberty and by passion. He seems to have acquired both among his friends and among strangers the epithet of "dulcis," "the charming or fascinating Gallio:" "This is more," says the poet Statius, "than to have given Seneca to the world, and to have begotten the sweet Gallio." Seneca's portrait of him is singularly faultless. He says that no one was so gentle to any one as Gallio was to every one; that his charm of manner won over even the people whom mere chance threw in his way, and that such was the force of his natural goodness that no one suspected his behaviour, as though it were due to art or simulation. Speaking of flattery, in his fourth book of Natural Questions, he says to his friend Lucilius, "I used to say to you that my brother Gallio (whom every one loves a little, even people who cannot love him more) was wholly ignorant of other vices, but even detested this. You might try him in any direction.

8

You began to praise his intellect—an intellect of the highest and worthiest kind,... and he walked away! You began to praise his moderation, he instantly cut short your first words. You began to express admiration for his blandness and natural suavity of manner,... yet even here he resisted your compliments; and if you were led to exclaim that you had found a man who could not be overcome by those insidious attacks which every one else admits, and hoped that he would at least tolerate this compliment because of its truth, even on this ground he would resist your flattery; not as though you had been awkward, or as though he suspected that you were jesting with him, or had some secret end in view, but simply because he had a horror of every form of adulation." We can easily imagine that Gallio was Seneca's favorite brother, and we are not surprised to find that the philosopher dedicates to him his three books on Anger, and his charming little treatise "On a Happy Life."

Of the third brother, L. Annaeus Mela, we have fewer notices; but, from what we know, we should conjecture that his character no less than his reputation was inferior to that of his brothers; yet he seems to have been the favorite of his father, who distinctly asserts that his intellect was capable of every excellence, and superior to that of his brothers.[4] This, however, may have been because Mela, "longing only to long for nothing," was content with his father's rank, and devoted himself wholly to the study of eloquence. Instead of entering into public life, he deliberately withdrew himself from all civil duties, and devoted himself to tranquility and ease. Apparently he preferred to be a farmer-general (publicanus) and not a consul. His chief fame rests in the fact that he was father of Lucan, the poet of the decadence or declining literature of Rome. The only anecdote about him which has come down to us is one that sets his avarice in a very unfavourable light. When his famous son, the unhappy poet, had forfeited his life, as well as covered himself with infamy by denouncing his own mother Attila in the conspiracy of Piso, Mela, instead of being overwhelmed with shame and agony, immediately began to collect with indecent avidity his son's debts, as though to show Nero that he felt no great sorrow for his bereavement. But this was not enough for Nero's malice; he told Mela that he must follow his son, and Mela was forced to obey the order, and to die.

Doubtless Helvia, if she survived her sons and grandsons, must have bitterly rued the day when, with her husband and her young children, she left the quiet retreat of a life in Cordova. Each of the three boys grew up to a man of genius, and each of them grew up to stain his memory with deeds that had been better left undone,

---

4 M. Ann. Senec. Controv. ii. Praef.

and to die violent deaths by their own hands or by a tyrant's will. Mela died as we have seen; his son Lucan and his brother Seneca were driven to death by the cruel orders of Nero. Gallio, after stooping to panic-stricken supplications for his preservation, died ultimately by suicide. It was a shameful and miserable end for them all, but it was due partly to their own errors, partly to the hard necessity of the degraded times in which they lived.

CHAPTER II

THE EDUCATION OF SENECA

For a reason which I have already indicated—I mean the habitual reticence of the ancient writers respecting the period of their boyhood—it is not easy to form a very vivid conception of the kind of education given to a Roman boy of good family up to the age of fifteen, when he laid aside the golden amulet and embroidered toga to assume a more independent mode of life.

A few facts, however, we can gather from the scattered allusions of the poets Horace, Juvenal, Martial, and Persius. From these we learn that the school-masters were for the most part underpaid and despised,[5] while at the same time an erudition alike minute and useless was rigidly demanded of them. We learn also that they were exceedingly severe in the infliction of corporeal punishment; Orbilius, the schoolmaster of Horace, appears to have been a perfect Dr. Busby, and the poet Martial records with indignation the barbarities of chastisement which he daily witnessed.

The things taught were chiefly arithmetic, grammar—both Greek and Latin—reading, and repetition of the chief Latin poets. There was also a good deal of recitation and of theme-writing on all kinds of trite historical subjects. The arithmetic seems to have been mainly of a very simple and severely practical kind, especially the computation of interest and compound interest; and the philology generally, both grammar and criticism, was singularly narrow,

---

[5] For the miseries of the literary class, and especially of schoolmasters, see Juv, Sat. vii.

uninteresting, and useless. Of what conceivable advantage can it have been to any human being to know the name of the mother of Hecuba, of the nurse of Anchises, of the stepmother of Anchemolus, the number of years Acestes lived, and how many casks of wine the Sicilians gave to the Phrygians? Yet these were the dispicable minutiae which every schoolmaster was then expected to have at his fingers' ends, and every boy-scholar to learn at the point of the ferule—trash which was only fit to be unlearned the moment it was known.

For this kind of verbal criticism and fantastic archaeology Seneca, who had probably gone through it all, expresses a profound and very rational contempt. In a rather amusing passage[6] he contrasts the kind of use which would be made of a Virgil lesson by a philosopher and a grammarian. Coming to the lines,

"Each happiest day for mortals speeds the first,
Then crowds disease behind and age accurst,"

the philosopher will point out why and in what sense the early days of life are the best days, and how rapidly the evil days succeed them, and consequently how infinitely important it is to use well the golden dawn of our being. But the verbal critic will content himself with the remark that Virgil always uses fugio of the flight of time, and always joins "old age" with "disease," and consequently that these are tags to be remembered, and plagiarized hereafter in the pupils' "original composition." Similarly, if the book in hand be Cicero's treatise "On the Commonwealth," instead of entering into great political questions, our grammarian will note that one of the Roman kings had no father (to speak of), and another no mother; that dictators used formerly to be called "masters of the people;" that Romulus perished during an eclipse; that the old form of reipsa was reapse, and of se ipse was sepse; that the starting point in the circus which is now called creta, or "chalk," used to be called caix, or carcer; that in the time of Ennuis opera meant not only "work," but also "assistance," and so on, and so on. Is this true education? or rather, should our great aim ever be to translate noble precepts into daily action? "Teach me," he says, "to despise pleasure and glory; afterwards you shall teach me to disentangle difficulties, to distinguish ambiguities, to see through obscurities; now teach me what is necessary." Considering the condition of much which in modern times passes under the name of "education," we may possibly find that the hints of Seneca are not yet wholly obsolete.

---

[6] Ep. cviii.

What kind of schoolmaster taught the little Seneca when under the care of the slave who was called pedagogus, or a "boy-leader" (whence our word pedagogue), he daily went with his brothers to school through the streets of Rome, we do not know. He may have been a severe Orbilius, or he may have been one of those noble-minded tutors whose ideal portraiture is drawn in such beautiful colours by the learned and amiable Quintilian. Seneca has not alluded to any one who taught him during his early days. The only schoolfellow whom he mentions by name in his voluminous writings is a certain Claranus, a deformed boy, whom, after leaving school, Seneca never met again until they were both old men, but of whom he speaks with great admiration. In spite of his hump-back, Claranus appeared even beautiful in the eyes of those who knew him well, because his virtue and good sense left a stronger impression than his deformity, and "his body was adorned by the beauty of his soul."

It was not until mere school-lessons were finished that a boy began seriously to enter upon the studies of eloquence and philosophy, which therefore furnish some analogy to what we should call "a university education." Gallio and Mela, Seneca's elder and younger brothers, devoted themselves heart and soul to the theory and practice of eloquence; Seneca made the rarer and the wiser choice in giving his entire enthusiasm to the study of philosophy.

I say the wiser choice, because eloquence is not a thing for which one can give a receipt as one might give a receipt for making eau-de-Cologne. Eloquence is the noble, the harmonious, the passionate expression of truths profoundly realized, or of emotions intensely felt. It is a flame which cannot be kindled by artificial means. Rhetoric may be taught if any one thinks it worth learning; but eloquence is a gift as innate as the genius from which it springs. "Cujus vita fulgur, ejus verba tonitrua"—"if a man's life be lightning, his words will be thunders." But the kind of oratory to be obtained by a constant practice of declamation such as that which occupied the schools of the Rhetors will be a very artificial lightning and a very imitated thunder—not the artillery of heaven, but the Chinese fire and rolled bladders of the stage. Nothing could be more false, more hollow, more pernicious than the perpetual attempt to drill numerous classes of youths into a reproduction of the mere manner of the ancient orators. An age of unlimited declamation, an age of incessant talk, is a hotbed in which real depth and nobility of feeling runs miserably to seed. Style is never worse than it is in ages which employ themselves in teaching little else. Such teaching produces an emptiness of thought concealed under a plethora of words. This age

12

of countless oratorical masters was emphatically the period of decadence and decay. There is a hollow ring about it, a falsetto tone in its voice; a fatiguing literary grimace in the manner of its authors. Even its writers of genius were injured and corrupted by the prevailing mode. They can say nothing simply; they are always in contortions. Their very indignation and bitterness of heart, genuine as it is, assumes a theatrical form of expression.[7] They abound in unrealities: their whole manner is defaced with would-be cleaverness, with antitheses, epigrams, paradoxes, forced expressions, figures and tricks of speech, straining after originality and profundity when they are merely repeating very commonplace remarks. What else could one expect in an age of salaried declaimers, educated in a false atmosphere of superficial talk, for ever haranguing and perorating about great passions which they had never felt, and great deeds which they would have been the last to imitate? After perpetually immolating the Tarquins and the Pisistratids in inflated grandiloquence, they would go to lick the dust off a tyrant's shoes. How could eloquence survive when the magnanimity and freedom which inspired it were dead, and when the men and books which professed to teach it were filled with despicable directions about the exact position in which the orator was to use his hands, and as to whether it was a good thing or not for him to slap his forehead and disarrange his hair?

The philosophic teaching which even from boyhood exercised a powerful fascination on the eager soul of Seneca was at least something better than this; and more than one of his philosophic teachers succeeded in winning his warm affection, and in moulding the principles and habits of his life. Two of them he mentions with special regard, namely Sotion the Pythagorean, and Attalus the Stoic. He also heard the lectures of the fluent and musical Fabianus Papirius, but seems to have owed less to him than to his other teachers.

Sotion had embraced the views of Pythagoras respecting the transmigration of souls, a doctrine which made the eating of animal food little better than cannibalism or parricide. But, even if any of his followers rejected this view, Sotion would still maintain that the eating of animals, if not an impiety, was at least a cruelty and a waste. "What hardship does my advice inflict on you?" he used to ask. "I do but deprive you of the food of vultures and lions." The ardent boy—for at this time he could not have been more than

---

[7] "Juvénal, élevé dans les cris de l'école
   Poussa jusqu'à l'excès sa mordante hyperbole."—
   BOILEAU

seventeen years old—was so convinced by these considerations that he became a vegetarian. At first the abstinence from meat was painful, but after a year he tells us (and many vegetarians will confirm his experience) it was not only easy but delightful; and he used to believe, though he would not assert it as a fact, that it made his intellect more keen and active. He only ceased to be a vegetarian in obedience to the remonstrance of his unphilosophical father, who would have easily tolerated what he regarded as a mere vagary had it not involved the danger of giving rise to a calumny. For about this time Tiberius banished from Rome all the followers of strange and foreign religions; and, as fasting was one of the rites practiced in some of them, Seneca's father thought that perhaps his son might incur, by abstaining from meat, the horrible suspicion of being a Christian or a Jew!

Another Pythagorean philosopher whom he admired and whom he quotes was Sextius, from whom he learnt the admirable practice of daily self-examination:—"When the day was over, and he betook himself to his nightly rest, he used to ask himself, What evil have you cured to day? What vice have you resisted? In what particular have you improved?" "I too adopt this custom," says Seneca, in his book on Anger, "and I daily plead my cause before myself, when the light has been taken away, and my wife, who is now aware of my habit, has become silent; I carefully consider in my heart the entire day, and take a deliberate estimate of my deeds and words."

It was however the Stoic Attalus who seems to have had the main share in the instruction of Seneca; and his teaching did not involve any practical results which the elder Seneca considered objectionable. He tells us how he used to haunt the school of the eloquent philosopher, being the first to enter and the last to leave it. "When I heard him declaiming," he says, "against vice, and error, and the ills of life, I often felt compassion for the human race, and believed my teacher to be exalted above the ordinary stature of mankind. In Stoic fashion he used to call himself a king; but to me his sovereignty seemed more than royal, seeing that it was in his power to pass his judgments on kings themselves. When he began to set forth the praises of poverty, and to show how heavy and superfluous was the burden of all that exceeded the ordinary wants of life, I often longed to leave school a poor man. When he began to reprehend our pleasures, to praise a chaste body, a moderate table, and a mind pure not from all unlawful but even from all superfluous pleasures, it was my delight to set strict limits to all voracity and gluttony. And these precepts, my Lucilius, have left some permanent results; for I embraced them with impetuous eagerness,

14

and afterwards, when I entered upon a political career, I retained a few of my good beginnings. In consequence of them, I have all my life long renounced eating oysters and mushrooms, which do not satisfy hunger but only sharpen appetite; for this reason I habitually abstain from perfumes, because the sweetest perfume for the body is none at all: for this reason I do without wines and baths. Other habits which I once abandoned have come back to me, but in such a way that I merely substitute moderation for abstinence, which perhaps is a still more difficult task; since there are some things which it is easier for the mind to cut away altogether than to enjoy in moderation. Attalus used to recommend a hard couch in which the body could not sink; and, even in my old age, I use one of such a kind that it leaves no impress of the sleeper. I have told you these anecdotes to prove to you what eager impulses our little scholars would have to all that is good, if any one were to exhort them and urge them on. But the harm springs partly from the fault of preceptors, who teach us how to argue, not how to live; and partly from the fault of pupils, who bring to their teacher a purpose of training their intellect and not their souls. Thus it is that philosophy has been degraded into mere philology."

In another lively passage, Seneca brings vividly before us a picture of the various scholars assembled in a school of the philosophers. After observing that philosophy exercises some influence even over those who do not go deeply in it, just as people sitting in a shop of perfumes carry away with them some of the odour, he adds, "Do we not, however, know some who have been among the audience of a philosopher for many years, and have been even entirely uncoloured by his teaching? Of course I do, even most persistent and continuous hearers; whom I do not call pupils, but mere passing auditors of philosophers. Some come to hear, not to learn, just as we are brought into a theatre for pleasure's sake, to delight our ears with language, or with the voice, or with plays. You will observe a large portion of the audience to whom the philosopher's school is a mere haunt of their leisure. Their object is not to lay aside any vices there, or to accept any law in accordance with which they may conform their life, but that they may enjoy a mere tickling of their ears. Some, however, even come with tablets in their hands, to catch up not things but words. Some with eager countenances and spirits are kindled by magnificent utterances, and these are charmed by the beauty of the thoughts, not by the sound of empty words; but the impression is not lasting. Few only have attained the power of carrying home with them the frame of mind into which they had been elevated."

It was to this small latter class that Seneca belonged. He

15

became a Stoic from very early years. The Stoic philosophers, undoubtedly the noblest and purest of ancient sects, received their name from the fact that their founder Zeno had lectured in the Painted Porch or Stoa Paecile of Athens. The influence of these austere and eloquent masters, teaching high lessons of morality and continence, and inspiring their young audience with the glow of their own enthusiasm for virtue, must have been invaluable in that effete and drunken age. Their doctrines were pushed to yet more extravagant lengths by the Cynics, who were so called from a Greek word meaning "dog," from what appeared to the ancients to be the dog-like brutality of their manners. Juvenal scornfully remarks, that the Stoics only differed from the Cynics "by a tunic," which the Stoics wore and the Cynics discarded. Seneca never indeed adopted the practices of Cynicism, but he often speaks admiringly of the arch-Cynic Diogenes, and repeatedly refers to the Cynic Demetrius, as a man deserving of the very highest esteem. "I take with me everywhere," writes he to Lucilius, "that best of men, Demetrius; and, leaving those who wear purple robes, I talk with him who is half naked. Why should I not admire him? I have seen that he has no want. Any one may despise all things, but no one can possess all things. The shortest road to riches lies through contempt of riches. But our Demetrius lives not as though he despised all things, but as though he simply suffered others to possess them."

These habits and sentiments throw considerable light on Seneca's character. They show that even from his earliest days he was capable of adopting self-denial as a principle, and that to his latest days he retained many private habits of a simple and honourable character, even when the exigencies of public life had compelled him to modify others. Although he abandoned an unusual abstinence out of respect for his father, we have positive evidence that he resumed in his old age the spare practices which in his enthusiastic youth he had caught from the lessons of high-minded teachers. These facts are surely sufficient to refute at any rate those gross charges against the private character of Seneca, venomously retailed by a jealous Greekling like Dio Cassius, which do not rest on a tittle of evidence, and seem to be due to a mere spirit of envy and calumny. I shall not again allude to these scandals because I utterly disbelieve them. A man who in his "History" could, as Dio Cassius has done, put into the mouth of a Roman senator such insane falsehoods as he has pretended that Fufius Calenus uttered in full senate against Cicero, was evidently actuated by a spirit which disentitles his statements to my credence. Seneca was an inconsistent philosopher both in theory and in practice; he fell beyond all question into serious errors, which deeply compromise

16

his character; but, so far from being a dissipated or luxurious man, there is every reason to believe that in the very midst of wealth and splendour, and all the temptations which they involve, he retained alike the simplicity of his habits and the rectitude of his mind. Whatever may have been the almost fabulous value of his five hundred tables of cedar and ivory, they were rarely spread with any more sumptuous entertainment than water, vegetables, and fruit. Whatever may have been the amusements common among his wealthy and noble contemporaries, we know that he found his highest enjoyment in the innocent pleasures of his garden, and took some of his exercise by running races there with a little slave.

CHAPTER III

THE STATE OF ROMAN SOCIETY

We have gleaned from Seneca's own writings what facts we could respecting his early education. But in the life of every man there are influences of a far more real and penetrating character than those which come through the medium of schools or teachers. The spirit of the age; the general tone of thought, the prevalent habits of social intercourse, the political tendencies which were moulding the destiny of the nation,—these must have told, more insensibly indeed but more powerfully, on the mind of Seneca than even the lectures of Sotion and of Attalus. And, if we have had reason to fear that there was much which was hollow in the fashionable education, we shall see that the general aspect of the society by which our young philosopher was surrounded from the cradle was yet more injurious and deplorable.

The darkness is deepest just before the dawn, and never did a grosser darkness or a thicker mist of moral pestilence brood over the surface of Pagan society than at the period when the Sun of Righteousness arose with healing in His wings. There have been many ages when the dense gloom of a heartless immorality seemed to settle down with unusual weight; there have been many places where, under the gaslight of an artificial system, vice has seemed to acquire an unusual audacity; but never probably was there any age or any place where the worst forms of wickedness were practiced with a more unblushing effrontery than in the city of Rome under the government of the Caesars. A deeply-seated corruption seemed to have fastened upon the very vitals of the national existence. It is surely a lesson of deep moral significance that just as they became most polished in their luxury they became most vile in their manner of life. Horace had already bewailed that "the age of our fathers, worse than that of our grandsires, has produced us who are yet baser, and who are doomed to give birth to a still more degraded offspring." But fifty years later it seemed to Juvenal that in his times the very final goal of iniquity had been attained, and he exclaims, in a burst of despair, that "posterity will add nothing to our immorality; our descendents can but do and desire the same crimes as ourselves." He who would see but for a moment and afar off to what the Gentile world had sunk, at the very period when Christianity began to spread, may form some faint and shuddering conception from the picture of it drawn in the Epistle to the Romans.

We ought to realize this fact if we would judge of Seneca aright. Let us then glance at the condition of the society in the midst of which he lived. Happily we can but glance at it. The worst cannot be told. Crimes may be spoken of; but things monstrous and inhuman should for ever be concealed. We can but stand at the cavern's mouth, and cast a single ray of light into its dark depths. Were we to enter, our lamp would be quenched by the foul things which would cluster round it.

In the age of Augustus began that "long slow agony," that melancholy process of a society gradually going to pieces under the dissolving influence of its own vices which lasted almost without interruption till nothing was left for Rome except the fire and sword of barbaric invasions. She saw not only her glories but also her virtues "star by star expire." The old heroism, the old beliefs, the old manliness and simplicity, were dead and gone; they had been succeeded by prostration and superstition by luxury and lust.

> "There is the moral of all human tales,
> 'Tis but the same rehearsal of the past,
> First freedom, and then glory; when that fails,
> Wealth, vice, corruption,—barbarism at last:
> And history, with all her volumes vast,
> Hath but one page; 'tis better written here
> Where gorgeous tyranny hath thus amassed
> All treasures, all delights, that eye or ear,
> Heart, soul could seek, tongue ask."

18

The mere elements of society at Rome during this period were very unpromising. It was a mixture of extremes. There was no middle class. At the head of it was an emperor, often deified in his lifetime, and separated from even the noblest of the senators by a distance of immeasurable superiority. He, was, in the startling language of Gibbon, at once "a priest, an atheist, and a god."[8] Surrounding his person and forming his court were usually those of the nobility who were the most absolutely degraded by their vices, their flatteries, or their abject subservience. But even these men were not commonly the repositories of political power. The people of the greatest influence were the freedmen of the emperors—men who had been slaves, Egyptians and Bithynians who had come to Rome with bored ears and with chalk on their naked feet to show that they were for sale, or who had bawled "sea-urchins all alive" in the Velabrum or the Saburra—who had acquired enormous wealth by means often the most unscrupulous and the most degraded, and whose insolence and baseness had kept pace with their rise to power. Such a man was the Felix before whom St. Paul was tried, and such was his brother Pallas,[9] whose golden statue might have been seen among the household gods of the senator, afterwards the emperor, Vitellius. Another of them might often have been observed parading the streets between two consuls. Imagine an Edward II. endowed with absolute and unquestioned powers of tyranny,—imagine some pestilent Piers Gaveston, or Hugh de le Spenser exercising over nobles and people a hideous despotism of the back stairs,—and you have some faint picture of the government of Rome under some of the twelve Caesars. What the barber Olivier le Diable was under Louis XI., what Mesdames du Barri and Pompadour were under Louis XV., what the infamous Earl of Somerset was under James I., what George Villiers became under Charles I., will furnish

---

[8] "To the sound
            Of fifes and drums they danced, or in the shade
            Sung Caesar great and terrible in war,
            Immortal Caesar! 'Lo, a god! a god!
            He cleaves the yielding skies!' Caesar meanwhile
            Gathers the ocean pebbles, or the gnat
            Enraged pursues; or at his lonely meal
            Starves a wide province; tastes, dislikes, and flings
            To dogs and sycophants. 'A god! a god!'
            The flowery shades and shrines obscene return."
            DYER, Ruins of Rome.
[9] The pride of this man was such that he never deigned to speak a word in the presence of his own slaves, but only made known his wishes by signs!— TACITUS.

us with a faint analogy of the far more exaggerated and detestable position held by the freedman Glabrio under Domitian, by the actor Tigellinus under Nero, by Pallus and Narcissus under Claudius, by the obscure knight Sejanus under the iron tyranny of the gloomy Tiberius.

I. It was an age of the most enormous wealth existing side by side with the most abject poverty. Around the splendid palaces wandered hundreds of mendicants, who made of their mendicity a horrible trade, and even went so far as to steal or mutilate infants in order to move compassion by their hideous maladies. This class was increased by the exposure of children, and by that overgrown accumulation of landed property which drove the poor from their native fields. It was increased also by the ambitious attempt of people whose means were moderate to imitate the enormous display of the numerous millionaires. The great Roman conquests in the East, the plunder of the ancient kingdoms of Antiochus, of Attalus, of Mithridates, had caused a turbid stream of wealth to flow into the sober current of Roman life. One reads with silent astonishment of the sums expended by wealthy Romans on their magnificence or their pleasures. And as commerce was considered derogatory to rank and position, and was therefore pursued by men who had no character to lose, these overgrown fortunes were often acquired by wretches of the meanest stamp—by slaves brought from over the sea, who had to conceal the holes bored in their ears;[10] or even by malefactors who had to obliterate, by artificial means, the three letters[11] which had been branded by the executioner on their foreheads. But many of the richest men in Rome, who had not sprung from this convict origin, were fully as well deserving of the same disgraceful stigma. Their houses were built, their coffers were replenished, from the drained resources of exhausted provincials. Every young man of active ambition or noble birth, whose resources had been impoverished by debauchery and extravagance, had but to borrow fresh sums in order to give magnificent gladiatorial shows, and then, if he could once obtain an aedileship, and mount to the higher offices of the State, he would in time become the procurator or proconsul of a province, which he might pillage almost at his will. Enter the house of a Felix or a Verres. Those splendid pillars of mottled green marble were dug by the forced labour of Phrygians

---

[10] This was a common ancient practice; the very words "thrall," "thralldom," are etymologically connected with the roots "thrill," "trill," "drill," (Compare Exod. xxi. 6; Deut. xv. 17; Plut. Cic. 26; and Juv. Sat. i. 104.)

[11] Fur, "thief." (See Martial, ii. 29.)

from the quarry of Synnada; that embossed silver, those murrhine vases, those jeweled cups, those masterpieces of antique sculpture, have all been torn from the homes or the temples of Sicily or Greece. Countries were pilaged and nations crushed that an Apicius might dissolve pearls[12] in the wine he drank, or that Lollia Paulina might gleam in a second-best dress of emeralds and pearls which had cost 40,000,000 sesterces, or more than 32,000l.[13]

Each of these "gorgeous criminals" lived in the midst of an humble crowd of flatterers, parasites, clients, dependents, and slaves. Among the throng that at early morning jostled each other in the marble atrium were to be found a motley and hetrogeneous set of men. Slaves of every age and nation—Germans, Egyptians, Gauls, Goths, Syrians, Britons, Moors, pampered and consequential freedmen, impudent confidential servants, greedy buffoons, who lived by making bad jokes at other people's tables; Dacian gladiators, with whom fighting was a trade; philosophers, whose chief claim to reputation was the length of their beards; supple Greeklings of the Tartuffe species, ready to flatter and lie with consummate skill, and spreading their vile character like a pollution wherever they went: and among all these a number of poor but honest clients, forced quietly to put up with a thousand forms of contumely[14] and insult, and living in discontented idleness on the sportula or daily largesse which was administered by the grudging liberality of their haughty patrons. The stout old Roman burgher had well-nigh disappeared; the sturdy independence, the manly self-reliance of an industrial population were all but unknown. The insolent loungers who bawled in the Forum were often mere stepsons of Italy, who had been dragged thither in chains,—the dregs of all nations, which had flowed into Rome as into a common sewer,[15] bringing with them no heritage except the specialty of their national vices. Their two wants were bread and the shows of the circus; so long as the sportula of their patron, the occasional donative of an emperor, and the ambition of political candidates supplied these wants, they lived in contented abasement, anxious neither for liberty nor for power.

---

[12] "Dissolved pearls, Apicius' diet 'gainst the epilepsy."—BEN JONSON.
[13] Pliny actually saw her thus arrayed. (Nat. Hist. ix. 35, 36.)
[14] Few of the many sad pictures in the Satires of Juvenal are more pitiable than that of the wretched "Quirites" struggling at their patrons' doors for the pittance which formed their daily dole. (Sat i. 101.)
[15] See Juv. Sat. iii. 62. Scipio, on being interrupted by the mob in the Forum, exclaimed,—"Silence, ye stepsons of Italy! What! shall I fear these fellows now they are free, whom I myself have brought in chains to Rome?" (See Cic. De Orat. ii. 61.)

II. It was an age at once of atheism and superstition. Strange to say, the two things usually go together. Just as Philippe Egalité, Duke of Orleans, disbelieved in God, and yet tried to conjecture his fate from the inspection of coffee-grounds at the bottom of a cup,—just as Louis XI. shrank from no perjury and no crime, and yet retained a profound reverence for a little leaden image which he carried in his cap,—so the Romans under the Empire sneered at all the whole crowd of gods and goddesses whom their fathers had worshipped, but gave an implicit credence to sorcerers, astrologers, spirit-rappers, exorcists, and every species of imposter and quack. The ceremonies of religion were performed with ritualistic splendour, but all belief in religion was dead and gone. "That there are such things as ghosts and subterranean realms not even boys believe," says Juvenal, "except those who are still too young to pay a farthing for a bath."[16] Nothing can exceed the cool impertinence with which the poet Martial prefers the favour of Domitian to that of the great Jupiter of the Capitol. Seneca, in his lost book "Against Superstitions,"[17] openly sneered at the old mythological legends of gods married and gods unmarried, and at the gods Panic and Paleness, and at Cloacina, the goddess of sewers, and at other deities whose cruelty and license would have been infamous even in mankind. And yet the priests, and Salii, and Flamens, and Augurs continued to fulfil their solemn functions, and the highest title of the Emperor himself was that of Pontifex Maximus, or Chief Priest, which he claimed as the recognized head of the national religion. "The common worship was regarded," says Gibbon, "by the people as equally true, by the philosophers as equally false, and by the magistrates as equally useful." And this famous remark is little more than a translation from Seneca, who, after exposing the futility of the popular beliefs, adds: "And yet the wise man will observe them all, not as pleasing to the gods, but as commanded by the laws. We shall so adore all that ignoble crowd of gods which long superstition has heaped together in a long period of years, as to remember that their worship has more to do with custom than with reality." "Because he was an illustrious senator of the Roman people," observes St. Augustine, who has preserved for us this fragment, "he worshipped what he blamed, he did what he refuted, he adored that with which he found fault." Could anything be more hollow or heartless than this? Is there anything which is more certain to sap the very foundations of morality than the public maintenance of a

---

[16] JUV. Sat. ii. 149. Cf. Sen. Ep. xxiv. "Nemo tam puer est at Cerberum timeat, et tenebras," &c.
[17] Fragm. xxxiv.

creed which has long ceased to command the assent, and even the respect of its recognized defenders? Seneca, indeed, and a few enlightened philosophers, might have taken refuge from the superstitions which they abandoned in a truer and purer form of faith. "Accordingly," says Lactantius, one of the Christian Fathers, "he has said many things like ourselves concerning God."[18] He utters what Tertullian finely calls "the testimony of A MIND NATURALLY CHRISTIAN." But, meanwhile, what became of the common multitude? They too, like their superiors, learnt to disbelieve or to question the power of the ancient deities; but, as the mind absolutely requires some religion on which to rest, they gave their real devotion to all kinds of strange and foreign deities,—to Isis and Osiris, and the dog Anubus, to Chaldaean magicians, to Jewish exercisers, to Greek quacks, and to the wretched vagabond priests of Cybele, who infested all the streets with their Oriental dances and tinkling tambourines. The visitor to the ruins of Pompeii may still see in her temple the statue of Isis, through whose open lips the gaping worshippers heard the murmured answers they came to seek. No doubt they believed as firmly that the image spoke, as our forefathers believed that their miraculous Madonnas nodded and winked. But time has exposed the cheat. By the ruined shrine the worshipper may now see the secret steps by which the priest got to the back of the statue, and the pipe entering the back of its head through which he whispered the answers of the oracle.

III. It was an age of boundless luxury,—an age in which women recklessly vied with one another in the race of splendour and extravagance, and in which men plunged headlong, without a single scruple of conscience, and with every possible resource at their command, into the pursuit of pleasure. There was no form of luxury, there was no refinement of vice invented by any foreign nation, which had not been eagerly adopted by the Roman patricians. "The softness of Sybaris, the manners of Rhodes and Antioch, and of perfumed, drunken, flower-crowned Miletus," were all to be found at Rome. There was no more of the ancient Roman severity and dignity and self-respect. The descendants of Aemilius and Gracchus—even generals and consuls and praetors—mixed familiarly with the lowest canaille of Rome in their vilest and most squalid purlieus of shameless vice. They fought as amateur gladiators in the arena. They drove as competing charioteers on the race-course. They even condescended to appear as actors on the stage. They devoted themselves with such frantic eagerness to the excitement of gambling, that we read of their staking hundreds of

---

[18] Lactantius, Divin. Inst. i. 4.

23

pounds on a single throw of the dice, when they could not even restore the pawned tunics to their shivering slaves. Under the cold marble statues, or amid the waxen likenesses of their famous stately ancestors, they turned night into day with long and foolish orgies, and exhausted land and sea with the demands of their gluttony. "Woe to that city," says an ancient proverb, "in which a fish costs more than an ox;" and this exactly describes the state of Rome. A banquet would sometimes cost the price of an estate; shell-fish were brought from remote and unknown shores, birds from Parthia and the banks of the Phasis; single dishes were made of the brains of the peacocks and the tongues of nightingales and flamingoes. Apicius, after squandering nearly a million of money in the pleasures of the table, committed suicide, Seneca tells us, because he found that he had only 80,000l. left. Cowley speaks of—

> "Vitellius' table, which did hold
> As many creatures as the ark of old."

"They eat," said Seneca, "and then they vomit; they vomit, and then they eat." But even in this matter we cannot tell anything like the worst facts about—

> "Their sumptuous gluttonies and gorgeous feasts
> On citron tables and Atlantic stone,
> Their wines of Setia, Gales, and Falerne,
> Chios, and Crete, and how they quaff in gold,
> Crystal, and myrrhine cups, embossed with gems
> And studs of pearl."[19]

Still less can we pretend to describe the unblushing and unutterable degradation of this period as it is revealed to us by the poets and the satirists. "All things," says Seneca, "are full of iniquity and vice; more crime is committed than can be remedied by restraint. We struggle in a huge contest of criminality: daily the passion for sin is greater, the shame in committing it is less.... Wickedness is no longer committed in secret: it flaunts before our eyes, and

> "The citron board, the bowl embossed with gems,
> ... whatever is known
> Of rarest acquisition; Tyrian garbs,
> Neptunian Albion's high testaceous food,

---

[19] Compare the lines in Dyer's little-remembered Ruins of Rome.

And flavoured Chian wines, with incense fumed,
To slake patrician thirst: for these their rights
In the vile atreets they prostitute for sale,
Their ancient rights, their dignities, their laws,
Their native glorious freedom.

has been sent forth so openly into public sight, and has prevailed so completely in the breast of all, that innocence is not rare, but non-existent."

IV. And it was an age of deep sadness. That it should have been so is an instructive and solemn lesson. In proportion to the luxury of the age were its misery and its exhaustion. The mad pursuit of pleasure was the death and degradation of all true happiness. Suicide—suicide out of pure ennui and discontent at a life overflowing with every possible means of indulgence—was extraordinarily prevalent. The Stoic philosophy, especially as we see it represented in the tragedies attributed to Seneca, rang with the glorification of it. Men ran to death because their mode of life had left them no other refuge. They died because it seemed so tedious and so superfluous to be seeing and doing and saying the same things over and over again; and because they had exhausted the very possibility of the only pleasures of which they had left themselves capable. The satirical epigram of Destouches,—

"Ci-gît Jean Rosbif, écuyer,
Qui se pendit pour se désennuyer,"

was literally and strictly true of many Romans during this epoch. Marcellinus, a young and wealthy noble, starved himself, and then had himself suffocated in a warm bath, merely because he was attacked with a perfectly curable illness. The philosophy which alone professed itself able to heal men's sorrows applauded the supposed courage of a voluntary death, and it was of too abstract, too fantastic, and too purely theoretical a character to furnish them with any real or lasting consolations. No sentiment caused more surprise to the Roman world than the famous one preserved in the fragment of Maecenas,—

"Debilem facito manu,
  Debilem pede, coxâ,
Tuber adstrue gibberum,
  Lubricos quate dentes;
Vita dum superest bene est;
  Hanc mihi vel acutâ

25

Si sedeam cruce sustine;"

which may be paraphrased,—

"Numb my hands with palsy,
  Rack my feet with gout,
Hunch my back and shoulder,
  Let my teeth fall out;
Still, if Life be granted,
  I prefer the loss;
Save my life, and give me
  Anguish on the cross."

Seneca, in his 101st Letter, calls this "a most disgraceful and most contemptible wish;" but it may be paralleled out of Euripides, and still more closely out of Homer. "Talk not," says the shade of Achilles to Ulysses in the Odyssey,—

"'Talk not of reigning in this dolorous gloom,
Nor think vain lies,' he cried, 'can ease my doom.
Better by far laboriously to bear
A weight of woes, and breathe the vital air,
Slave to the meanest hind that begs his bread,
Than reign the sceptred monarch of the dead.'"

But this falsehood of extremes was one of the sad outcomes of the popular Paganism. Either, like the natural savage, they dreaded death with an intensity of terror; or, when their crimes and sorrows had made life unsupportable, they slank to it as a refuge, with a cowardice which vaunted itself as courage.

V. And it was an age of cruelty. The shows of gladiators, the sanguinary combats of wild beasts, the not unfrequent spectacle of savage tortures and capital punishments, the occasional sight of innocent martyrs burning to death in their shirts of pitchy fire, must have hardened and imbruted the public sensibility. The immense prevalence of slavery tended still more inevitably to the general corruption. "Lust," as usual, was "hard by hate." One hears with perfect amazement of the number of slaves in the wealthy houses. A thousand slaves was no extravagant number, and the vast majority of them were idle, uneducated and corrupt. Treated as little better than animals, they lost much of the dignity of men. Their masters possessed over them the power of life and death, and it is shocking to read of the cruelty with which they were often treated. An accidental murmur, a cough, a sneeze, was punished with rods.

Mute, motionless, fasting, the slaves had to stand by while their masters supped; A brutal and stupid barbarity often turned a house into the shambles of an executioner, sounding with scourges, chains, and yells.[20] One evening the Emperor Augustus was supping at the house of Vedius Pollio, when one of the slaves, who was carrying a crystal goblet, slipped down, and broke it. Transported with rage Vedius at once ordered the slave to be seized, and plunged into the fish-pond as food to the lampreys. The boy escaped from the hands of his fellow-slaves, and fled to Caesar's feet to implore, not that his life should be spared—a pardon which he neither expected nor hoped—but that he might die by a mode of death less horrible than being devoured by fishes. Common as it was to torment slaves, and to put them to death, Augustus, to his honor be it spoken, was horrified by the cruelty of Vedius, and commanded both that the slave should be set free, that every crystal vase in the house of Vedius should be broken in his presence and that the fish pond should be filled up. Even women inflicted upon their female slaves punishments of the most cruel atrocity for faults of the most venial character. A brooch wrongly placed, a tress of hair ill-arranged, and the enraged matron orders her slave to be lashed and crucified. If her milder husband interferes, she not only justifies the cruelty, but asks in amazement: "What! is a slave so much of a human being?" No wonder that there was a proverb, "As many slaves, so many foes." No wonder that many masters lived in perpetual fear, and that "the tyrant's devilish plea, necessity," might be urged in favor of that odious law which enacted that, if a master was murdered by an unknown hand, the whole body of his slaves should suffer death,—a law which more than once was carried into effect under the reigns of the Emperors. Slavery, as we see in the case of Sparta and many other nations, always involves its own retribution. The class of free peasant proprietors gradually disappears. Long before this time Tib. Gracchus, in coming home from Sardinia, had observed that there was scarcely a single freeman to be seen in the fields. The slaves were infinitely more numerous than their owners. Hence arose the constant dread of servile insurrections; the constant hatred of a slave population to which any conspirator revolutionist might successfully appeal; and the constant insecurity of life, which must have struck terror into many hearts.

Such is but a faint and broad outline of some of the features of Seneca's age; and we shall be unjust if we do not admit that much at least of the life he lived, and nearly all the sentiments he uttered,

---

[20] Juv. Sat. i. 219—222.

gain much in grandeur and purity from the contrast they offer to the common life of—

> "That people victor once, now vile and base,
> Deservedly made vassal, who, once just,
> Frugal, and mild, and temperate, conquered well,
> But govern ill the nations under yoke,
> Peeling their provinces, exhausted all
> By lust and rapine; first ambitious grown
> Of triumph, that insulting vanity;
> Then cruel, by their sports to blood inured
> Of fighting beasts, and men to beasts exposed,
> Luxurious by their wealth, and greedier still,
> And from the daily scene effeminate.
> What wise and valient men would seek to free
> These thus degenerate, by themselves enslaved;
> Or could of inward slaves make outward free?"
> MILTON, Paradise Regained, iv. 132-145.

CHAPTER IV

POLITICAL CONDITION OF ROME UNDER TIBERIUS AND CAIUS

The personal notices of Seneca's life up to the period of his manhood are slight and fragmentary. From an incidental expression we conjecture that he visited his aunt in Egypt when her husband was Prefect of that country, and that he shared with her the dangers of shipwreck when her husband had died on board ship during the homeward voyage. Possibly the visit may have excited in his mind that deep interest and curiosity about the phenomena of the Nile which appear so strongly in several passages of his Natural Questions; and, indeed nothing is more likely than that he suggested to Nero the earliest recorded expedition to discover the source of the mysterious river. No other allusion to his travels occur in his writings, but we may infer that from very early days he had felt an interest for physical inquiry, since while still a youth he had written a book on earthquakes; which has not come down to us.

Deterred by his father from the pursuit of philosophy, he entered on the duties of a profession. He became an advocate, and distinguished himself by his genius and eloquence in pleading causes. Entering on a political career, he became a successful candidate for the quaestorship, which was an important step towards the highest offices of the state. During this period of his life he married a lady whose name has not been preserved to us, and to whom we have only one allusion, which is a curious one. As in our own history it has been sometimes the fashion for ladies of rank to have dwarves and negroes among their attendants, so it seems to have been the senseless and revolting custom of the Roman ladies of this time to keep idiots among the number of their servants. The first wife of Seneca had followed this fashion, and Seneca in his fiftieth letter to his friend Lucilius[21] makes the following interesting allusion to the fact. "You know," he says, "that my wife's idiot girl Harpaste has remained in my house as a burdensome legacy. For personally I feel the profoundest dislike to monstrosities of that kind. If ever I want to amuse myself with an idiot, I have not far to look for one. I laugh at myself. This idiot girl has suddenly become blind. Now, incredible as the story seems, it is really true that she is unconscious of her blindness, and consequently begs her attendant to go elsewhere, because the house is dark. But you may be sure that this, at which we laugh in her, happens to us all; no one understands that he is avaricious or covetous. The blind seek for a guide; we wander about without a guide."

This passage will furnish us with an excellent example of Seneca's invariable method of improving every occasion and circumstance into an opportunity for a philosophic harangue.

By this wife, who died shortly before Seneca's banishment to Corsica, he had two sons, one of whom expired in the arms and amid the kisses of Helvia less than a month before Seneca's departure for Corsica. To the other, whose name was Marcus, he makes the following pleasant allusion. After urging his mother Helvia to find consolation in the devotion of his brothers Gallio and Mela, he adds, "From these turn your eyes also on your grandsons—

---

[21] It will be observed that the main biographical facts about the life of Seneca are to be gleaned from his letters to Lucilius, who was his constant friend from youth to old age, and to whom he has dedicated his Natural Questions. Lucilius was a procurator of Sicily, a man of cultivated taste and high principle. He was the author of a poem on Aetna, which in the opinion of many competent judges is the poem which has come down to us, and has been attributed to Varus, Virgil, and others. It has been admirably edited by Mr. Munro. (See Nat. Quaest., iv. ad init. Ep. lxxix.) He also wrote a poem on the fountain Arethusa. (Nat. Quaest. iii, 26.)

to Marcus, that most charming little boy, in sight of whom no melancholy can last long. No misfortune in the breast of any one can have been so great or so recent as not to be soothed by his caresses. Whose tears would not his mirth repress? whose mind would not his prattling loose from the pressure of anxiety? whom will not that joyous manner of his incline to jesting? whose attention, even though he be fixed in thought, will not be attracted and absorbed by that childlike garrulity of which no one can grow tired? God grant that he may survive me: may all the cruelty of destiny be weared out on me!"

Whether the prayer of Seneca was granted we do not know; but, as we do not again hear of Marcus, it is probable that he died before his father, and that the line of Seneca, like that of so many great men, became extinct in the second generation.

It was probably during this period that Seneca laid the foundations of that enormous fortune which excited the hatred and ridicule of his opponents. There is every reason to believe that this fortune was honourably gained. As both his father and mother were wealthy, he had doubtless inherited an ample competency; this was increased by the lucrative profession of a successful advocate, and was finally swollen by the princely donations of his pupil Nero. It is not improbable that Seneca, like Cicero, and like all the wealthy men of their day, increased his property by lending money upon interest. No disgrace attached to such a course; and as there is no proof for the charges of Dio Cassius on this head, we may pass them over with silent contempt. Dio gravely informs us that Seneca excited an insurrection in Britain, by suddenly calling in the enormous sum of 40,000,000 sesterces; but this is in all probability the calumny of a professed enemy. We shall refer again to Seneca's wealth; but we may here admit that it was undoubtedly ungraceful and incongruous in a philosopher who was perpetually dwelling on the praises of poverty, and that even in his own age it attracted unfavourable notice, as we may see from the epithet Proedives, "the over-wealthy," which is applied to him alike by a satiric poet and by a grave historian. Seneca was perfectly well aware that this objection could be urged against him, and it must be admitted that the grounds on which he defends himself in his treatise On a Happy Life are not very conclusive or satisfactory.

The boyhood of Seneca fell in the last years of the Emperor Augustus, when, in spite of the general decorum and amiability of their ruler, people began to see clearly that nothing was left of liberty except the name. His youth and early manhood were spent during those three-and-twenty years of the reign of Tiberius, that reign of terror, during which the Roman world was reduced to a frightful silence and torpor as of death;[22] and, although he was not thrown into personal collision with that "brutal monster," he not unfrequently alludes to him, and to the dangerous power and headlong ruin of his wicked minister Sejanus. Up to this time he had not experienced in his own person those crimes and horrors which fall to the lot of men who are brought into close contact with tyrants. This first happened to him in the reign of Caius Caesar, of whom we are enabled, from the writings of Seneca alone, to draw a full-length portrait.

Caius Caesar was the son of Germanicus and the elder Agrippina. Germanicus was the bravest and most successful general, and one of the wisest and most virtuous men, of his day. His wife Agrippina, in her fidelity, her chastity, her charity, her nobility of mind, was the very model of a Roman matron of the highest and purest stamp. Strange that the son of such parents should have been one of the vilest, cruelest, and foulest of the human race. So, however, it was; and it is a remarkable fact that scarcely one of the six children of this marriage displayed the virtues of their father and mother, while two of them, Caius Caesar and the younger Agrippina, lived to earn an exceptional infamy by their baseness and their crimes. Possibly this unhappy result may have been partly due to the sad circumstances of their early education. Their father, Germanicus, who by his virtue and his successes had excited the suspicious jealousy of his uncle Tiberius, was by his distinct connivance, if not by his actual suggestion, atrociously poisoned in Syria. Agrippina, after being subjected to countless cruel insults, was banished in the extremest poverty to the island of Pandataria. Two of the elder brothers, Nero and Drusus Germanicus, were proclaimed public enemies: Nero was banished to the island Pontia, and there put to death; Drusus was kept a close prisoner in a secret prison of the palace. Caius, the youngest, who is better known by the name Caligula, was summoned by Tiberius to his wicked retirement at Capreae, and there only saved his life by the most abject flattery and the most adroit submission.

Capreae is a little island of surpassing loveliness, forming one extremity of the Bay of Naples. Its soil is rich, its sea bright and limpid, its breezes cool and healthful. Isolated by its position, it is yet within easy reach of Rome. At that time, before Vesuvius had rekindled those wasteful fires which first shook down, and then deluged under lava and scoriae, the little cities of Herculaneum and Pompeii, the scene which it commanded was even more pre-

---

[22] Milton, Paradise Regained, iv. 128. For a picture of Tiberius as he appeared in his old age at Capreae, "hated of all and hating," see Id. 90-97.

eminently beautiful than now. Vineyards and olive-groves clothed the sides of that matchless bay, down to the very line where the bright blue waters seem to kiss with their ripples the many-coloured pebbles of the beach. Over all, with its sides dotted with picturesque villas and happy villages, towered the giant cone of the volcano which for centuries had appeared to be extinct, and which was clothed up to the very crater with luxurious vegetation. Such was the delicious home which Tiberius disgraced for ever by the seclusion of his old age. Here he abandoned himself to every refinement of wickedness, and from hence, being by common consent the most miserable of men, he wrote to the Senate that memorable letter in which he confesses his daily and unutterable misery under the stings of a guilty conscience, which neither solitude nor power enabled him to escape.

Never did a fairer scene undergo a worse degradation; and here, in one or other of the twelve villas which Tiberius had built, and among the azure grottoes which he caused to be constructed, the youthful Caius[23] grew up to manhood. It would have been a terrible school even for a noble nature; for a nature corrupt and bloodthirsty like that of Caius it was complete and total ruin. But, though he was so obsequious to the Emperor as to originate the jest that never had there been a worse master and never a more cringing slave,—though he suppressed every sign of indignation at the horrid deaths of his mother and his brothers,—though he assiduously reflected the looks, and carefully echoed the very words, of his patron,—yet not even by the deep dissimulation which such a position required did he succeed in concealing from the penetrating eye of Tiberius the true ferocity of his character. Not being the acknowledged heir to the kingdom,—for Tiberius Gemellus, the youthful grandson of Tiberius, was living, and Caius was by birth only his grand-nephew,—he became a tool for the machinations of Marco the praetorian praefect and his wife Ennia. One of his chief friends was the cruel Herod Agrippa,[24] who put to death St. James and imprisoned St. Peter, and whose tragical fate is recorded in the 12th chap. of the Acts. On one occasion, when Caius had been

---

[23] We shall call him Caius, because it is as little correct to write of him by the sobriquet Caligula as it would be habitually to write of our kings Edward or John as Longshanks or Lackland. The name Caligula means "a little shoe," and was the pet name given to him by the soldiers of his father, in whose camp he was born.

[24] Josephus adds some curious and interesting particulars to the story of this Herod and his death which are not mentioned in the narrative of St. Luke (Antiq. xix. 7, 8. Jahn, Hebr. Commonwealth, § cxxvi.)

abusing the dictator Sulla, Tiberius scornfully remarked that he would have all Sulla's vices and none of his virtues; and on another, after a quarrel between Caius and his cousin, the Emperor embraced with tears his young grandson, and said to the frowning Caius, with one of those strange flashes of prevision of which we sometimes read in history. "Why are you so eager? Some day you will kill this boy, and some one else will murder you." There were some who believed that Tiberius deliberately cherished the intention of allowing Caius to succeed him, in order that the Roman world might relent towards his own memory under the tyranny of a worse monster than himself. Even the Romans, who looked up to the family of Germanicus with extraordinary affection, seem early to have lost all hopes about Caius. They looked for little improvement under the government of a vicious boy, "ignorant of all things, or nurtured only in the worst," who would be likely to reflect the influence of Macro, and present the spectacle of a worse Tiberius under a worse Sejanus.

At last health and strength failed Tiberius, but not his habitual dissimulation. He retained the same unbending soul, and by his fixed countenance and measured language, sometimes by an artificial affability, he tried to conceal his approaching end. After many restless changes, he finally settled down in a villa at Misenum which had once belonged to the luxurious Lucullus. There the real state of his health was discovered. Charicles, a distinguished physician, who had been paying him a friendly visit on kissing his hand to bid farewell, managed to ascertain the state of his pulse. Suspecting that this was the case Tiberius, concealing his displeasure, ordered a banquet to be spread, as though in honour of his friend's departure, and stayed longer than usual at table. A similar story is told of Louis XIV. who, noticing from the whispers of his courtiers that they believed him to be dying, ate an unusually large dinner on the very day of his death, and sarcastically observed, "Il me semble que pour un homme qui va mourir je ne mange pas mal." But, in spite of the precautions of Tiberius, Charicles informed Macro that the Emperor could not last beyond two days.

A scene of secret intrigue at once began. The court broke up into knots and cliques. Hasty messengers were sent to the provinces and their armies, until at last, on the 16th of March, it was believed that Tiberius had breathed his last. Just as on the death of Louis XV. a sudden noise was heard as of thunder, the sound of courtiers rushing along the corridors to congratulate Louis XVI. in the famous words, "Le roi est mort, vive le roi," so a crowd instantly thronged round Caius with their congratulations, as he went out of

33

the palace to assume his imperial authority. Suddenly a message reached him that Tiberius had recovered voice and sight. Seneca says, that feeling his last hour to be near, he had taken off his ring, and, holding it in his shut left hand, had long lain motionless; then calling his servants, since no one answered his call, he rose from his couch, and, his strength failing him, after a few tottering steps fell prostrate on the ground.

The news produced the same consternation as that which was produced among the conspirators at Adonijah's banquet, when they heard of the measures taken by the dying David. There was a panic-stricken dispersion, and every one pretended to be grieved, or ignorant of what was going on. Caius, in stupified silence, expected death instead of empire. Macro alone did not lose his presence of mind. With the utmost intrepidity, he gave orders that the old man should be suffocated by heaping over him a mass of clothes, and that every one should then leave the chamber. Such was the miserable and unpitied end of the Emperor Tiberius, in the seventy-eighth year of his age. Such was the death, and so miserable had been the life, of the man to whom the Tempter had already given "the kingdoms of the world and the glory of them," when he tried to tempt with them the Son of God. That this man should have been the chief Emperor of the earth at a time when its true King was living as a peasant in his village home at Nazareth, is a fact suggestive of many and of solemn thoughts.

CHAPTER V

THE REIGN OF CAIUS

The poet Gray, in describing the deserted deathbed of our own great Edward III., says:—

> "Low on his funeral couch he lies!
> No pitying heart, no eye afford
> A tear to grace his obsequies!
> "The swarm that in the noontide beam were born?
> Gone to salute the rising Morn.

Fair laughs the Morn, and soft the zephyr blows,
While proudly riding o'er the azure realm,
In gallant trim the gilded vessel goes;
Youth on the prow and Pleasure at the helm;
Regardless of the sweeping Whirlwind's sway,
That, hushed in grim repose, expects his evening prey."

The last lines of this passage would alone have been applicable to Caius Caesar. There was nothing fair or gay even about the beginning of his reign. From first to last it was a reign of fury and madness, and lust and blood. There was an hereditary taint of insanity in this family, which was developed by their being placed on the dizzy pinnacle of imperial despotism, and which usually took the form of monstrous and abnormal crime. If we would seek a parallel for Caius Caesar, we must look for it in the history of Christian VII. of Denmark, and Paul of Russia. In all three we find the same ghastly pallor, the same sleeplessness which compelled them to rise, and pace their rooms at night, the same incessant suspicion; the same inordinate thirst for cruelty and torture. He took a very early opportunity to disembarrass himself of his benefactors, Macro and Ennia, and of his rival, the young Tiberius. The rest of his reign was a series of brutal extravagances. We have lost the portion of those matchless Annals of Tacitus which contained the reign of Caius, but more than enough to revolt and horrify is preserved in the scattered notices of Seneca, and in the narratives of Suetonius in Latin and Dio Cassius in Greek.

His madness showed itself sometimes in gluttonous extravagance, as when he ordered a supper which cost more than 8,000l; sometimes in a bizarre and disgraceful mode of dress, as when he appeared in public in women's stockings, embroidered with gold and pearls; sometimes in a personality and insolence of demeanor towards every rank and class in Rome, which made him ask a senator to supper, and ply him with drunken toasts, on the very evening on which he had condemned his son to death; sometimes in sheer raving blasphemy, as when he expressed his furious indignation against Jupiter for presuming to thunder while he was supping, or looking at the pantomimes; but most of all in a ferocity which makes Seneca apply to him the name of "Bellua," or "wild monster," and say that he seems to have been produced "for the disgrace and destruction of the human race."

We will quote from the pages of Seneca but one single passage to justify his remark "that he was most greedy for human blood, which he ordered to stream in his very presence with such eagerness as though he were going to drink it up with his lips." He says that in one day he scourged and tortured men of consular and quaestorial parentage, knights and senators, not by way of examination, but out of pure caprice and rage; he seriously meditated the butchery of the entire senate; he expressed a wish that the Roman people had but a single neck, that he might strike it off at one blow; he silenced the screams or reproaches of his victims sometimes by thrusting a sponge in their mouths, sometimes by having their mouths gagged with their own torn robes, sometimes by ordering their tongues to be cut out before they were thrown to the wild beasts. On one occasion, rising from a banquet, he called for his slippers, which were kept by the slaves while the guests reclined on the purple couches, and so impatient was he for the sight of death, that, walking up and down his covered portico by lamplight with ladies and senators, he then and there ordered some of his wretched victims to be beheaded in his sight.

It is a singular proof of the unutterable dread and detestation inspired by some of these Caesars, that their mere countenance is said to have inspired anguish. Tacitus, in the life of his father-in-law Agricola, mentions the shuddering recollection of the red face of Domitian, as it looked on at the games. Seneca speaks in one place of wretches doomed to undergo stones, sword, fire, and Caius; in another he says that he had tortured the noblest Romans with everything which could possibly cause the intensest agony,—with cords, plates, rack, fire, and, as though it were the worst torture of all, with his look! What that look was, we learn from Seneca himself, "His face was ghastly pale, with a look of insanity; his fierce, dull eyes were half-hidden under a wrinkled brow; his ill-shaped head was partly bald, partly covered with dyed-hair; his neck covered with bristles, his legs thin, and his feet mis-shapen." Woe to the nation that lies under the heel of a brutal despotism; treble woe to the nation that can tolerate a despot so brutal as this! Yet this was the nation in the midst of which Seneca lived, and this was the despot under whom his early manhood was spent.

> "But what more oft in nations grown corrupt,
>   And by their vices brought to servitude,
>   Than to love bondage more than liberty,
>   Bondage with ease than strenuous liberty?"

It was one of the peculiarities of Caius Caesar that he hated the very existence of any excellence. He used to bully and insult the gods themselves, frowning even at the statues of Apollo and Jupiter of the Capitol. He thought of abolishing Homer, and order the works of Livy and Virgil to be removed from all libraries, because he could not bear that they should be praised. He ordered Julius Graecinus to be put to death for no other reason than this, "That he was a better man than it was expedient for a tyrant that any one should be;" for, as Pliny tells us, the Caesars deliberately preferred that their people should be vicious than that they should be virtuous. It was hardly likely that such a man should view with equanimity the rising splendour of Seneca's reputation. Hitherto, the young man, who was thirty-five years old at the accession of Caius, had not written any of his philosophic works, but in all probability he had published his early, and no longer extant, treatises on earthquakes, on superstitions, and the books On India, and On the Manners of Egypt, which had been the fruit of his early travels. It is probable, too, that he had recited in public some of those tragedies which have come down to us under his name, and in the composition of which he was certainly concerned. All these works, and especially the applause won by the public reading of his poems, would have given him that high literary reputation which we know him to have earned. It was not, however, this reputation, but the brilliancy and eloquence of his orations at the bar which excited the jealous hatred of the Emperor. Caius piqued himself on the possession of eloquence; and, strange to say, there are isolated expressions of his which seem to show that, in lucid intervals, he was by no means devoid of intellectual acuteness. For instance, there is real humour and insight in the nicknames of "a golden sheep" which he gave to the rich and placid Silanus, and of "Ulysses in petticoats," by which he designated his grandmother, the august Livia. The two epigrammetic criticisms which he passed upon the style of Seneca are not wholly devoid of truth; he called his works Commissiones meras, or mere displays.[25] In this expression he hit off, happily enough, the somewhat theatrical, the slightly pedantic and pedagogic and professorial character of Seneca's diction, its rhetorical ornament and antitheses, and its deficiency in stern masculine simplicity and strength. In another remark he showed himself a still more felicitous critic. He called Seneca's writings Arenu sine Calce, "sand without lime," or, as we might say, "a rope of sand." This epigram showed a real critical faculty. It exactly hits off Seneca's short and disjointed sentences, consisting as they often do of detached antitheses. It accords with the amusing comparison of Malebranche, that Seneca's composition, with its perpetual and futile recurrences, calls up to him the image of a dancer who ends where he begins.

But Caius did not confine himself to clever and malignant

---

[25] Suet. Calig. liii.

criticism. On one occasion, when Seneca was pleading in his presence, he was so jealous and displeased at the brilliancy and power of the orator that he marked him out for immediate execution. Had Seneca died at this period he would probably have been little known, and he might have left few traces of his existence beyond a few tragedies of uncertain authenticity, and possibly a passing notice in the page of Dio or Tacitus. But destiny reserved him for a more splendid and more questionable career. One of Caius's favourites whispered to the Emperor that it was useless to extinguish a waning lamp; that the health of the orator was so feeble that a natural death by the progress of his consumptive tendencies would, in a very short time, remove him out of the tyrant's way.

Throughout the remainder of the few years during which the reign of Caius continued, Seneca, warned in time, withdrew himself into complete obscurity, employing his enforced leisure in that unbroken industry which stored his mind with such encyclopaedic wealth. "None of my days," he says, in describing at a later period the way in which he spent his time, "is passed in complete ease. I claim even a part of the night for my studies. I do not find leisure for sleep, but I succumb to it, and I keep my eyes at their work even when they are wearied and drooping with watchfulness. I have retired, not only from men, but from affairs, and especially from my own. I am doing the work for posterity; I am writing out things which may prove of advantage to them. I am intrusting to writing healthful admonitions—compositions, as it were, of useful medicines."

But the days of Caius drew rapidly to an end. His gross and unheard-of insults to Valerius Asiaticus and Cassius Chaereas brought on him condign vengeance. It is an additional proof, if proof were wanting, of the degradation of Imperial Rome, that the deed of retribution was due, not to the people whom he taxed; not to the soldiers, whole regiments of whom he had threatened to decimate; not to the knights, of whom scores had been put to death by his orders; not to the nobles, multitudes of whom had been treated by him with conspicuous infamy; not even to the Senate, which illustrious body he had on all occasions deliberately treated with contumely and hatred,—but to the private revenge of an insulted soldier. The weak thin voice of Cassius Chaereas, tribune of the praetorian cohort, had marked him out for the coarse and calumnious banter of the imperial buffoon; and he determined to avenge himself, and at the same time rid the world of a monster. He engaged several accomplices in the conspiracy, which was nearly frustrated by their want of resolution. For four whole days they hesitated, while day after day, Caius presided in person at the bloody games of the amphitheatre. On the fifth day (Jan. 24, A.D. 41), feeling unwell after one of his gluttonous suppers, he was indisposed to return to the shows, but at last rose to do so at the solicitation of his attendants. A vaulted corridor led from the palace to the circus, and in that corridor Caius met a body of noble Asiatic boys, who were to dance a Pyrrhic dance and sing a laudatory ode upon the stage. Caius wished them at once to practice a rehearsal in his presence, but their leader excused himself on the grounds of hoarseness. At this moment Chaereas asked him for the watchword of the night. He gave the watchword, "Jupiter." "Receive him in his wrath!" exclaimed Chaereas, striking him on the throat, while almost at the same moment the blow of Sabinus cleft the tyrant's jaw, and brought him to his knee. He crouched his limbs together to screen himself from further blows, screaming aloud, "I live! I live!" The bearers of his litter rushed to his assistance, and fought with their poles, but Caius fell pierced with thirty wounds; and, leaving the body weltering in its blood, the conspirators rushed out of the palace, and took measures to concert with the Senate a restoration of the old Republic. On the very night after the murder the consuls gave to Chaereas the long-forgotten watchword of "Liberty." But this little gleam of hope proved delusive to the last degree. It was believed that the unquiet ghost of the murdered madman haunted the palace, and long before it had been laid to rest by the forms of decent sepulchre, a new emperor of the great Julian family was securely seated upon the throne.

CHAPTER VI

THE REIGN OF CLAUDIUS, AND THE BANISHMENT OF SENECA

While the senators were deliberating, the soldiers were acting. They felt a true, though degraded, instinct that to restore the ancient forms of democratic freedom would be alike impossible and useless, and with them the only question lay between the rival claimants for the vacant power. Strange to say that, among these claimants, no one seems ever to have thought of mentioning the prince who became the actual successor.

There was living in the palace at this time a brother of the great Germanicus, and consequently an uncle of the late emperor, whose name was Claudius Caesar. Weakened both in mind and body by the continuous maladies of an orphaned infancy, kept under the cruel tyranny of a barbarous slave, the unhappy youth had lived in despised obscurity among the members of a family who were utterly ashamed of him. His mother Antonia called him a monstrosity, which Nature had begun but never finished; and it became a proverbial expression with her, as is said to have been the case with the mother of the great Wellington, to say of a dull person, "that he was a greater fool than her son Claudius." His grandmother Livia rarely deigned to address him except in the briefest and bitterest terms. His sister Livilla execrated the mere notion of his ever becoming emperor. Augustus, his grandfather by adoption, took pains to keep him as much out of sight as possible, as a wool-gathering[26] and discreditable member of the family, denied him all public honours, and left him a most paltry legacy. Tiberius, when looking out for a successor, deliberately passed him over as a man of deficient intellect. Caius kept him as a butt for his own slaps and blows, and for the low buffoonery of his meanest jesters. If the unhappy Claudius came late for dinner, he would find every place occupied, and peer about disconsolately amid insulting smiles. If, as was his usual custom, he dropped asleep, after a meal, he was pelted with olives and date-stones, or rough stockings were drawn over his hands that he might be seen rubbing his face with them when he was suddenly awaked.

This was the unhappy being who was now summoned to support the falling weight of empire. While rummaging the palace for plunder, a common soldier had spied a pair of feet protruding from under the curtains which shaded the sides of an upper corridor. Seizing these feet, and inquiring who owned them, he dragged out an uncouth, panic-stricken mortal, who immediately prostrated himself at his knees and begged hard for mercy. It was Claudius, who scared out of his wits by the tragedy which he had just beheld, had thus tried to conceal himself until the storm was passed. "Why, this is Germanicus!"[27] exclaimed the soldier, "let's make him emperor." Half joking and half in earnest, they hoisted him on their shoulders—for terror had deprived him of the use of his legs—and hurried him off to the camp of the Praetorians.

---

[26] He calls him [Greek meteoros] which implies awkwardness and constant absence of mind.

[27] The full name of Claudius was Tiberius Claudius Drusus Caesar Germanicus.

Miserable and anxious he reached the camp, an object of compassion to the crowd of passers-by, who believed that he was being hurried off to execution. But the soldiers, who well knew their own interests, accepted him with acclamations, the more so as, by a fatal precedent, he promised them a largess of more than 8ol. apiece. The supple Agrippa (the Herod of Acts xii.), seeing how the wind lay, offered to plead his cause with the Senate, and succeeded partly by arguments, partly by intimidation, and partly by holding out the not unreasonable hopes of a great improvement on the previous reign.

For although Claudius had been accused of gambling and drunkenness, not only were no worse sins laid to his charge, but he had successfully established some claim to being considered a learned man. Had fortune blessed him till death with a private station, he might have been the Lucien Bonaparte of his family—a studious prince, who preferred the charms of literature to the turmoil of ambition. The anecdotes which have been recorded of him show that he was something of an archaeologist, and something of a philologian. The great historian Livy, pitying the neglect with which the poor young man was treated, had encouraged him in the study of history; and he had written memoirs of his own time, memoirs of Augustus, and even a history of the civil wars since the battle of Actium, which was so correct and so candid that his family indignantly suppressed it as a fresh proof of his stupidity.

Such was the man who, at the age of fifty, became master of the civilized world. He offers some singular points of resemblance to our own "most mighty and dread sovereign," King James I. Both were learned, and both were eminently unwise;[28] both of them were authors, and both of them were pedants; both of them delegated their highest powers to worthless favourites, and both of them enriched these favourites with such foolish liberality that they remained poor themselves. Both of them had been terrified into constitutional cowardice by their involuntary presence at deeds of blood. Both of them, though of naturally good dispositions, were misled by selfishness into acts of cruelty; and both of them, though laborious in the discharge of duty, succeeded only in rendering royalty ridiculous. King James kept Sir Walter Raleigh in prison, and Claudius drove Seneca into exile. The parallel, so far as I am aware, has never been noticed, but is susceptible of being drawn out into the minutest particulars.

---

[28] "Knowledge comes, but wisdom lingers," says our own poet. Heraclitus had said the same thing more than two thousand years before him, [Greek: polumaoiae ou didasho].

One of his first acts was to recall his nieces, Julia and Agrippina, from the exile into which their brother had driven them; and both these princesses were destined to effect a powerful influence on the life of our philosopher.

What part Seneca had taken during the few troubled days after the murder of Caius we do not know. Had he taken a leading part—had he been one of those who, like Chaereas, opposed the election of Claudius as being merely the substitution of an imbecile for a lunatic,—or who, like Sabinus, refused to survive the accession of another Caesar,—we should perhaps have heard of it; and we must therefore assume either that he was still absent from Rome in the retirement into which he had been driven by the jealousy of Caius, or that he contented himself with quietly watching the course of events. It will be observed that his biography is not like that of Cicero, with whose life we are acquainted in most trifling details; but that the curtain rises and falls on isolated scenes, throwing into sudden brilliancy or into the deepest shade long and important periods of his history. Nor are his letters and other writings full of those political and personal allusions which convert them into an autobiography. They are, without exception, occupied exclusively with philosophical questions, or else they only refer to such personal reminiscences as may best be converted into the text for some Stoical paradox or moral declamation. It is, however, certain from the sequel that Seneca must have seized the opportunity of Caius's death to emerge from his politic obscurity, and to occupy a conspicuous and brilliant position in the imperial court.

It would have been well for his own happiness and fame if he had adopted the wiser and manlier course of acting up to the doctrines he professed. A court at most periods is, as the poet says,

"A golden but a fatal circle,
Upon whose magic skirts a thousand devils
In crystal forms sit tempting Innocence,
And beckon early Virtue from its centre;"

but the court of a Caius, of a Claudius, or of a Nero, was indeed a place wherein few of the wise could find a footing, and still fewer of the good. And all that Seneca gained from his career of ambition was to be suspected by the first of these Emperors, banished by the second, and murdered by the third.

The first few acts of Claudius showed a sensible and kindly disposition; but it soon became fatally obvious that the real powers of the government would be wielded, not by the timid and absent-minded Emperor, but by any one who for the time being could acquire an ascendency over his well-intentioned but feeble disposition. Now, the friends and confidents of Claudius had long been chosen from the ranks of his freedmen. As under Louis XI. and Don Miguel, the barbers of these monarchs were the real governors, so Claudius was but the minister rather than the master of Narcissus his private secretary, of Polybius his literary adviser, and of Pallas his accountant. A third person, with whose name Scripture has made us familiar, was a freedman of Claudius. This was Felix, the brother of Pallas, and that Procurator who, though he had been the husband or the paramour of three queens, trembled before the simple eloquence of a feeble and imprisoned Jew.[29] These men became proverbial for their insolence and wealth; and once, when Claudius was complaining of his own poverty, some one wittily replied, "that he would have abundance if two of his freedmen would but admit him into partnership with them."

But these men gained additional power from the countenance and intrigues of the young and beautiful wife of Claudius, Valeria Messalina. In his marriage, as in all else, Claudius had been pre-eminent in misfortune. He lived in an age of which the most frightful sign of depravity was that its women were, if possible, a shade worse than its men; and it was the misery of Claudius, as it finally proved his ruin, to have been united by marriage to the very worst among them all. Princesses like the Berenice, and the Drusilla, and the Salome, and the Herodias of the sacred historians were in this age a familiar spectacle; but none of them were so wicked as two at least of Claudius's wives. He was betrothed or married no less than five times. The lady first destined for his bride had been repudiated because her parents had offended Augustus; the next died on the very day intended for her nuptials. By his first actual wife, Urgulania, whom he had married in early youth, he had two children, Drusus and Claudia; Drusus was accidentally choked in boyhood while trying to swallow a pear which had been thrown up into the air. Very shortly after the birth of Claudia, discovering the unfaithfulness of Urgulania, Claudius divorced her, and ordered the child to be stripped naked and exposed to die. His second wife, Aelia Petina, seems to have been an unsuitable person, and her also he divorced. His third and fourth wives lived to earn a colossal infamy—Valeria Messalina for her shameless character, Agrippina the younger for her unscrupulous ambition.

Messalina, when she married, could scarcely have been fifteen years old, yet she at once assumed a dominant position, and secured it by means of the most unblushing wickedness.

---

[29] Acts xix.

But she did not reign so absolutely undisturbed as to be without her own jealousies and apprehensions; and these were mainly kindled by Julia and Agrippina, the two nieces of the Emperor. They were, no less than herself, beautiful, brilliant, and evil-hearted women, quite ready to make their own coteries, and to dispute, as far as they dared, the supremacy of a bold but reckless rival. They too, used their arts, their wealth, their rank, their political influence, their personal fascinations, to secure for themselves a band of adherents, ready, when the proper moment arrived, for any conspiracy. It is unlikely that, even in the first flush of her husband's strange and unexpected triumph, Messalina should have contemplated with any satisfaction their return from exile. In this respect it is probable that the Emperor succeeded in resisting her expressed wishes; so that the mere appearance of the two daughters of Germanicus in her presence was a standing witness of the limitations to which her influence was subjected.

At this period, as is usual among degraded peoples, the history of the Romans degenerates into mere anecdotes of their rulers. Happily, however, it is not our duty to enter on the chronique scandaleuse of plots and counterplots, as little tolerable to contemplate as the factions of the court of France in the worst periods of its history. We can only ask what possible part a philosopher could play at such a court? We can only say that his position there is not to the credit of his philosophical professions; and that we can contemplate his presence there with as little satisfaction as we look on the figure of the worldly and frivolous bishop in Mr. Frith's picture of "The Last Sunday of Charles II. at Whitehall."

And such inconsistencies involve their own retribution, not only in loss of influence and fair fame, but even in direct consequences. It was so with Seneca. Circumstances—possibly a genuine detestation of Messalina's exceptional infamy—seem to have thrown him among the partisans of her rivals. Messalina was only waiting her opportunity to strike a blow. Julia, possibly as being the younger and the less powerful of the two sisters, was marked out as the first victim, and the opportunity seemed a favourable one for involving Seneca in her ruin. His enormous wealth, his high reputation, his splendid abilities, made him a formidable opponent to the Empress, and a valuable ally to her rivals. It was determined to get rid of both by a single scheme. Julia was accused of an intrigue with Seneca, and was first driven into exile and then put to death. Seneca was banished to the barren and pestilential shores of the island of Corsica.

Seneca, as one of the most enlightened men of his age, should have aimed at a character which would have been above the possibility of suspicion: but we must remember that charges such as those which were brought against him were the easiest of all to make, and the most impossible to refute. When we consider who were Seneca's accusers, we are not forced to believe his guilt; his character was indeed deplorably weak, and the laxity of the age in such matters was fearfully demoralising; but there are sufficient circumstances in his favour to justify us in returning a verdict of "Not guilty." Unless we attach an unfair importance to the bitter calumny of his open enemies, we may consider that the general tenor of his life has sufficient weight to exculpate him from an unsupported accusation.

Of Julia, Suetonius expressly says that the crime of which she was accused was uncertain, and that she was condemned unheard. Seneca, on the other hand, was tried in the Senate and found guilty. He tells us that it was not Claudius who flung him down, but rather that, when he was falling headlong, the Emperor supported him with the moderation of his divine hand; "he entreated the Senate on my behalf; he not only gave me life, but even begged it for me. Let it be his to consider," adds Seneca, with the most dulcet flattery, "in what light he may wish my cause to be regarded; either his justice will find, or his mercy will make, it a good cause. He will alike be worthy of my gratitude, whether his ultimate conviction of my innocence be due to his knowledge or to his will."

This passage enables us to conjecture how matters stood. The avarice of Messalina was so insatiable that the non-confiscation of Seneca's immense wealth is a proof that, for some reason, her fear or hatred of him was not implacable. Although it is a remarkable fact that she is barely mentioned, and never once abused, in the writings of Seneca, yet there can be no doubt that the charge was brought by her instigation before the senators; that after a very slight discussion, or none at all, Claudius was, or pretended to be convinced of Seneca's culpability; that the senators, with their usual abject servility, at once voted him guilty of high treason, and condemned him to death, and the confiscation of his goods; and that Claudius, perhaps from his own respect for literature, perhaps at the intercession of Agrippina, or of some powerful freedman, remitted part of his sentence, just as King James I. remitted all the severest portions of the sentence passed on Francis Bacon.

Neither the belief of Claudius nor the condemnation of the Senate furnish the slightest valid proofs against him. The Senate at this time were so base and so filled with terror, that on one occasion a mere word of accusation from the freedman of an Emperor was sufficient to make them fall upon one of their number and stab him to death upon the spot with their iron pens. As for poor Claudius, his administration of justice, patient and laborious as it was, had already grown into a public joke. On one occasion he wrote down and delivered the wise decision, "that he agreed with the side which had set forth the truth." On another occasion, a common Greek whose suit came before him grew so impatient at his stupidity as to exclaim aloud, "You are an old fool." We are not informed that the Greek was punished. Roman usage allowed a good deal of banter and coarse personality. We are told that on one occasion even the furious and bloody Caligula, seeing a provincial smile, called him up, and asked him what he was laughing at. "At you," said the man, "you look such a humbug." The grim tyrant was so struck with the humour of the thing that he took no further notice of it. A Roman knight against whom some foul charge had been trumped up, seeing Claudius listening to the most contemptible and worthless evidence against him, indignantly abused him for his cruel stupidity, and flung his pen and tablets in his face so violently as to cut his cheek. In fact, the Emperor's singular absence of mind gave rise to endless anecdotes. Among other things, when some condemned criminals were to fight as gladiators, and addressed him before the games in the sublime formula—"Ave, Imperator, morituri te salutamus!" ("Hail, Caesar! doomed to die, we salute thee!") he gave the singularly inappropriate answer, "Avete vos!" ("Hail ye also!") which they took as a sign of pardon, and were unwilling to fight until they were actually forced to do so by the gestures of the Emperor.

The decision of such judges as Claudius and his Senate is worth very little in the question of a man's innocence or guilt; but the sentence was that Seneca should be banished to the island of Corsica.

CHAPTER VII

SENECA IN EXILE

So, in A.D. 41, in the prime of life and the full vigour of his faculties, with a name stained by a charge of which he may have been innocent, but of which he was condemned as guilty, Seneca bade farewell to his noble-minded mother, to his loving aunt, to his brothers, the beloved Gallio and the literary Mela, to his nephew, the ardent and promising young Lucan, and, above all—which cost him the severest pang—to Marcus, his sweet and prattling boy. It was a calamity which might have shaken the fortitude of the very noblest soul, and it had by no means come upon him single handed. Already he had lost his wife, he had suffered from acute and chronic ill-health, he had been bereaved but three weeks previously of another little son. He had been cut short by the jealousy of one emperor from a career of splendid success; he was now banished by the imbecile subservience of another from all that he held most dear.

We are hardly able to conceive the intensity of anguish with which an ancient Roman generally regarded the thought of banishment. In the long melancholy wail of Ovid's "Tristia;" in the bitter and heart-rending complaints of Cicero's "Epistles," we may see something of that intense absorption in the life of Rome which to most of her eminent citizens made a permanent separation from the city and its interests a thought almost as terrible as death itself. Even the stoical and heroic Thrasea openly confessed that he should prefer death to exile. To a heart so affectionate, to a disposition so social, to a mind so active and ambitious as that of Seneca, it must have been doubly bitter to exchange the happiness of his family circle, the splendour of an imperial court, the luxuries of enormous wealth, the refined society of statesmen, and the ennobling intercourse of philosophers for the savage wastes of a rocky island and the society of boorish illiterate islanders, or at the best, of a few other political exiles, all of whom would be as miserable as himself, and some of whom would probably have deserved their fate.

The Mediteranean rocks selected for political exiles—Gyaros, Seriphos, Scyathos, Patmos, Pontia, Pandataria—were generally rocky, barren, fever-stricken places, chosen by design as the most wretched conceivable spots in which human life could be maintained at all. Yet these islands were crowded with exiles, and in them were to be found not a few princesses of Caesarian origin. We must not draw a parallel to their position from that of an Eleanor, the wife of Duke Humphrey, immured in Peel Castle in the Isle of Man, or of a Mary Stuart in the Isle of Loch Levin—for it was something incomparably worse. No care was taken even to provide for their actual wants. Their very lives were not secure. Agrippa Posthumus and Nero, the brothers of the Emperor Caligula, had been so reduced by starvation that both of the wretched youths had been driven to support life by eating the materials with which their beds were stuffed. The Emperor Caius had once asked an exile, whom he had recalled from banishment, in what manner he had been accustomed to employ his time on the island. "I used," said the flatterer, "to pray that Tiberius might die, and that you might succeed." It immediately struck Caius that the exiles whom he had banished might be similarly employed, and accordingly he sent centurions round the islands to put them all to death. Such were the miserable circumstances which might be in store for a political outlaw.[30] If we imagine what must have been the feelings of a d'Espréménil, when a lettee de cachet consigned him to a prison in the Isle d'Hières; or what a man like Burke might have felt, if he had been compelled to retire for life to the Bermudas; we may realize to some extent the heavy trial which now befel the life of Seneca.

Corsica was the island chosen for his place of banishment, and a spot more uninviting could hardly have been selected. It was an island "shaggy and savage," intersected from north to south by a chain of wild, inaccessible mountains, clothed to their summits with gloomy and impenetrable forests of pine and fir. Its untamable inhabitants are described by the geographer Strabo as being "wilder than the wild beasts." It produced but little corn, and scarcely any fruit-trees. It abounded, indeed, in swarms of wild bees, but its very honey was bitter and unpalatable, from being infected with the acrid taste of the box-flowers on which they fed. Neither gold nor silver were found there; it produced nothing worth exporting, and barely sufficient for the mere necessaries of its inhabitants; it rejoiced in no great navigable rivers, and even the trees, in which it abounded, were neither beautiful nor fruitful. Seneca describes it in more than one of his epigrams, as a

"Terrible isle, when earliest summer glows
Yet fiercer when his face the dog-star shows;"

and again as a

"Barbarous land, which rugged rocks surround,
Whose horrent cliffs with idle wastes are crowned,
No autumn fruit, no tilth the summer yields,
Nor olives cheer the winter-silvered fields:

---

[30] Among the Jews the homicides who had fled to a city of refuge were set free on the high priest's death, and, in order to prevent them from praying for his death, the mother and other relatives of the high priest used to supply them with clothes and other necessaries. See the author's article on "Asylum" in Kitto's Encyclopedia (ed. Alexander.)

Nor joyous spring her tender foliage lends,
Nor genial herb the luckless soil befriends;
Nor bread, nor sacred fire, nor freshening wave;—
Nought here—save exile, and the exile's grave!"

In such a place, and under such conditions, Seneca had ample need for all his philosophy. And at first it did not fail him. Towards the close of his first year of exile he wrote the "Consolation to his mother Helvia," which is one of the noblest and most charming of all his works.

He had often thought, he said, of writing to console her under this deep and wholly unlooked-for trial, but hitherto he had abstained from doing so, lest, while his own anguish and hers were fresh, he should only renew the pain of the wound by his unskilful treatment. He waited, therefore till time had laid its healing hand upon her sorrows, especially because he found no precedent for one in his position condoling with others when he himself seemed more in need of consolation, and because something new and admirable would be required of a man who, as it were, raised his head from the funeral pyre to console his friends. Still he now feels impelled to write to her, because to alleviate her regrets will be to lay aside his own. He does not attempt to conceal from her the magnitude of the misfortune, because so far from being a mere novice in sorrow, she has tasted it from her earliest years in all its varieties; and because his purpose was to conquer her grief, not to extenuate its causes. Those many miseries would indeed have been in vain, if they had not taught her how to bear wretchedness. He will prove to her therefore that she has no cause to grieve either on his account, or on her own. Not on his—because he is happy among circumstances which others would think miserable and because he assures her with his own lips that not only is he not miserable, but that he can never be made so. Every one can secure his own happiness, if he learns to seek it, not in external circumstances, but in himself. He cannot indeed claim for himself the title of wise, for, if so, he would be the most fortunate of men, and near to God Himself; but, which is the next best thing, he has devoted himself to the study of wise men, and from them he has learnt to expect nothing and to be prepared for all things. The blessings which Fortune had hitherto bestowed on him,—wealth, honours, glory,—he had placed in such a position that she might rob him of them all without disturbing him. There was a great space between them and himself, so that they could be taken but not torn away. Undazzled by the glamour of prosperity, he was unshaken by the blow of adversity. In circumstances which were the envy of all men he had never seen any

49

real or solid blessing, but rather a painted emptiness, a gilded deception; and similarly he found nothing really hard or terrible in ills which the common voice has so described.

What, for instance, was exile? it was but a change of place, an absence from one's native land; and, if you looked at the swarming multitudes in Rome itself, you would find that the majority of them were practically in contented and willing exile, drawn thither by necessity, by ambition, or by the search for the best opportunities of vice. No isle so wretched and so bleak which did not attract some voluntary sojourners; even this precipitous and naked rock of Corsica, the hungriest, roughest, most savage, most unhealthy spot conceivable, had more foreigners in it than native inhabitants. The natural restlessness and mobility of the human mind, which arose from its aetherial origin, drove men to change from place to place. The colonies of different nations, scattered all over the civilized and uncivilized world even in spots the most chilly and uninviting, show that the condition of place is no necessary ingredient in human happiness. Even Corsica had often changed its owners; Greeks from Marseilles had first lived there, then Ligurians and Spaniards, then some Roman colonists, whom the aridity and thorniness of the rock had not kept away.

"Varro thought that nature, Brutus that the consciousness of virtue, were sufficient consolations for any exile. How little have I lost in comparison with those two fairest possessions which I shall everywhere enjoy—nature and my own integrity! Whoever or whatever made the world—whether it were a deity, or disembodied reason, or a divine interfusing spirit, or destiny, or an immutable series of connected causes—the result was that nothing, except our very meanest possessions, should depend on the will of another. Man's best gifts lie beyond the power of man either to give or to take away. This Universe, the grandest and loveliest work of nature, and the Intellect which was created to observe and to admire it, are our special and eternal possessions, which shall last as long as we last ourselves. Cheerful, therefore, and erect, let us hasten with undaunted footsteps whithersoever our fortunes lead us.

"There is no land where man cannot dwell,—no land where he cannot uplift his eyes to heaven; wherever we are, the distance of the divine from the human remains the same. So then, as long as my eyes are not robbed of that spectacle with which they cannot be satiated, so long as I may look upon the sun and moon, and fix my lingering gaze on the other constellations, and consider their rising and setting and the spaces between them and the causes of their less and greater speed,—while I may contemplate the multitude of stars glittering throughout the heaven, some stationary, some revolving, some suddenly blazing forth, others dazzling the gaze with a flood of fire as though they fell, and others leaving over a long space their trails of light; while I am in the midst of such phenomena, and mingle myself, as far as a man may, with things celestial,—while my soul is ever occupied in contemplations so sublime as these, what matters it what ground I tread?

"What though fortune has thrown me where the most magnificent abode is but a cottage? the humblest cottage, if it be but the home of virtue, may be more beautiful than all temples; no place is narrow which can contain the crowd of glorious virtues; no exile severe into which you may go with such a reliance. When Brutus left Marcellus at Mitylene, he seemed to be himself going into exile because he left that illustrious exile behind him. Caesar would not land at Mitylene, because he blushed to see him. Marcellus therefore, though he was living in exile and poverty, was living a most happy and a most noble life.

> "'One self-approving hour whole worlds outweighs
> Of stupid starers and of loud huzzas;
> And more true joy Marcellus exiled feels,
> Than Caesar with a senate at his heels.'

"And as for poverty every one who is not corrupted by the madness of avarice and luxury know that it is no evil. How little does man need, and how easily can he secure that! As for me, I consider myself as having lost not wealth, but the trouble of looking after it. Bodily wants are few—warmth and food, nothing more. May the gods and goddesses confound that gluttony which sweeps the sky, and sea and land for birds, and animals, and fish; which eats to vomit and vomits to eat, and hunts over the whole world for that which after all it cannot even digest! They might satisfy their hunger with little, and they excite it with much. What harm can poverty inflict on a man who despises such excesses? Look at the god-like and heroic poverty of our ancestors, and compare the simple glory of a Camillus with the lasting infamy of a luxurious Apicius! Even exile will yield a sufficiency of necessaries, but not even kingdoms are enough for superfluities. It is the soul that makes us rich or poor: and the soul follows us into exile, and finds and enjoys its own blessings even in the most barren solitudes.

"But it does not even need philosophy to enable us to despise poverty. Look at the poor: are they not often obviously happier than the rich? And the times are so changed that what we would now consider the poverty of an exile would then have been regarded as the patrimony of a prince. Protected by such precedents as those of

51

Homer, and Zeno, and Menenius Agrippa, and Regulus, and Scipio, poverty becomes not only safe but even estimable.

"And if you make the objection that the ills which assail me are not exile only, or poverty only, but disgrace as well, I reply that the soul which is hard enough to resist one wound is invulnerable to all. If we have utterly conquered the fear of death, nothing else can daunt us. What is disgrace to one who stands above the opinion of the multitude? what was even a death of disgrace to Socrates, who by entering a prison made it cease to be disgraceful? Cato was twice defeated in his candidature for the praetorship and consulship: well, this was the disgrace of those honours, and not of Cato. No one can be despised by another until he has learned to despise himself. The man who has learned to triumph over sorrow wears his miseries as though they were sacred fillets upon his brow, and nothing is so entirely admirable as a man bravely wretched. Such men inflict disgrace upon disgrace itself. Some indeed say that death is preferable to contempt; to whom I reply that he who is great when he falls is great in his prostration, and is no more an object of contempt than when men tread on the ruins of sacred buildings, which men of piety venerate no less than if they stood.

"On my behalf therefore, dearest mother; you have no cause for endless weeping: nor have you on your own. You cannot grieve for me on selfish grounds, in consequence of any personal loss to yourself; for you were ever eminently unselfish, and unlike other women in all your dealings with your sons, and you were always a help and a benefactor to them rather than they to you. Nor should you give way out of a regret and longing for me in my absence. We have often previously been separated, and, although it is natural that you should miss that delightful conversation, that unrestricted confidence, that electrical sympathy of heart and intellect that always existed between us, and that boyish glee wherewith your visits always affected me, yet, as you rise above the common herd of women in virtue, the simplicity, the purity of your life, you must abstain from feminine tears as you have done from all feminine follies. Consider how Cornelia, who had lost ten children by death, instead of wailing for her dead sons, thanked fortune that had made her sons Gracchi. Rutilia followed her son Cotta into exile so dearly did she love him, yet no one saw her shed a tear after his burial. She had shown her affection when it was needful, she restrained her sorrow when it was superflous. Imitate the example of these great women as you have imitated their virtues. I want you not to beguile your sorrow by amusements or occupations, but to conquer it. For you may now return to those philosophical studies in which you once showed yourself so apt a proficient, and which formerly my father checked. They will gradually sustain and comfort you in your hour of grief.

"And meanwhile consider how many sources of consolation already exist for you. My brothers are still with you; the dignity of Gallio, the leisure of Mela, will protect you; the ever-sparkling mirth of my darling little Marcus will cheer you up; the training of my little favourite Novatilla will be a duty which will assuage your sorrow. For your father's sake, too, though he is absent from you, you must moderate your lamentations. Above all, your sister—that truly faithful, loving, and high-souled lady, to whom I owe so deep a debt of affection for her kindness to me from my cradle until now,— she will yield you the fondest sympathy and the truest consolation.

"But since I know that after all your thoughts will constantly revert to me, and that none of your children will be more frequently before your mind than I,—not because they are less dear to you than I, but because it is natural to lay the hand most often upon the spot which pains,—I will tell you how you are to think of me. Think of me as happy and cheerful, as though I were in the midst of blessings; as indeed I am, while my mind, free from every care, has leisure for its own pursuits, and sometimes amuses itself with lighter studies, sometimes, eager for truth, soars upwards to the contemplation of its own nature, and the nature of the universe. It inquires first of all about the lands and their situation; then into the condition of the surrounding sea, its ebbings and flowings; then it carefully studies all this terror-fraught interspace between heaven and earth, tumultuous with thunders and lightnings, and the blasts of winds, and the showers of rain, and snow and hail; then, having wandered through all the lower regions, it bursts upwards to the highest things, and revels in the most lovely—spectacle of that which is divine, and, mindful of its own eternity, passes into all that hath been and all that shall be throughout all ages."

Such in briefest outline, and without any of that grace of language with which Seneca has invested it, is a sketch of the little treatise which many have regarded as among the most delightful of Seneca's works. It presents the picture of that grandest of all spectacles—

"A good man struggling with the storms of fate."

So far there was something truly Stoical in the aspect of Seneca's exile. But was this grand attitude consistently maintained? Did his little raft of philosophy sink under him, or did it bear him safely over the stormy waves of this great sea of adversity.

53

CHAPTER VIII

SENECA'S PHILOSOPHY GIVES WAY

There are some misfortunes of which the very essence consists in their continuance. They are tolerable so long as they are illuminated by a ray of hope. Seclusion and hardship might even come at first with some charm of novelty to a philosopher who, as was not unfrequent among the amateur thinkers of his time, occasionally practised them in the very midst of wealth and friends. But as the hopeless years rolled on, as the efforts of friends proved unavailing, as the loving son, and husband, and father felt himself cut off from the society of those whom he cherished in such tender affection, as the dreary island seemed to him ever more barbarous and more barren, while season after season added to its horrors without revealing a single compensation, Seneca grew more and more disconsolate and depressed. It seemed to be his miserable destiny to rust away, useless, unbefriended, and forgotten. Formed to fascinate society, here there were none for him to fascinate; gifted with an eloquence which could keep listening senates hushed, here he found neither subject nor audience; and his life began to resemble a river which, long before it has reached the sea, is lost in dreary marshes and choking sands.

Like the brilliant Ovid, when he was banished to the frozen wilds of Tomi, Seneca vented his anguish in plaintive wailing and bitter verse. In his handful of epigrams he finds nothing too severe for the place of his exile. He cries—

"Spare thou thine exiles, lightly o'er thy dead,
Alive, yet buried, be thy dust bespread."

And addressing some malignant enemy—

"Whoe'er thou art,—thy name shall I repeat?—
Who o'er mine ashes dar'st to press thy feet,
And, uncontented with a fall so dread,
Draw'st bloodstained weapons on my darkened head,
Beware! for nature, pitying, guards the tomb,
And ghosts avenge th' invaders of their gloom,
Hear, Envy, hear the gods proclaim a truth,
Which my shrill ghost repeats to move thy ruth,
WRETCHES ARE SACRED THINGS,—thy hands refrain:
E'en sacrilegious hands from TOMBS abstain."

The one fact that seems to have haunted him most was that his abode in Corsica was a living death.

But the most complete picture of his state of mind, and the most melancholy memorial of his inconsistency as a philosopher, is to be found in his "Consolation to Polybius." Polybius was one of those freedmen of the Emperor whose bloated wealth and servile insolence were one of the darkest and strangest phenomena of the time. Claudius, more than any of his class, from the peculiar imbecility of his character, was under the powerful influence of this class of men; and so dangerous was their power that Messalina herself was forced to win her ascendency over her husband's mind by making these men her supporters, and cultivating their favour. Such were "the most excellent Felix," the judge of St. Paul, and the slave who became a husband to three queens,—Narcissus, in whose household (which moved the envy of the Emperor) were some of those Christians to whom St. Paul sends greetings from the Christians of Corinth,[31]—Pallas, who never deigned to speak to his own slaves, but gave all his commands by signs, and who actually condescended to receive the thanks of the Senate, because he, the descendant of Etruscan kings, yet condescended to serve the Emperor and the Commonwealth; a preposterous and outrageous compliment, which appears to have been solely due to the fact of his name being identical with that of Virgil's young hero, the son of the mythic Evander!

Among this unworthy crew a certain Polybius was not the least conspicuous. He was the director of the Emperor's studies,—a worthy Alcuin to such a Charlemagne. All that we know about him is that he was once the favourite of Messalina, and afterwards her victim, and that in the day of his eminence the favour of the Emperor placed him so high that he was often seen walking between the two consuls. Such was the man to whom, on the occasion of his brother's death, Seneca addressed this treatise of consolation. It has come down to us as a fragment, and it would have been well for Seneca's fame if it had not come down to us at all. Those who are enthusiastic for his reputation would gladly prove it spurious, but we believe that no candid reader can study it without perceiving its genuineness. It is very improbable that he ever intended it to be published, and whoever suffered it to see the light was the successful enemy of its illustrious author.

Its sad and abject tone confirms the inference, drawn from an allusion which it contains, that it was written towards the close of the third year of Seneca's exile. He apologises for its style by saying

---

[31] Rom. xvi. 11.

that if it betrayed any weakness of thought or inelegance of expression this was only what might be expected from a man who had so long been surrounded by the coarse and offensive patois of barbarians. We need hardly follow him into the ordinary topics of moral philosophy with which it abounds, or expose the inconsistency of its tone with that of Seneca's other writings. He consoles the freedman with the "common common-places" that death is inevitable; that grief is useless; that we are all born to sorrow; that the dead would not wish us to be miserable for their sakes. He reminds him that, owing to his illustrious position, all eyes are upon him. He bids him find consolation in the studies in which he has always shown himself so pre-eminent, and lastly he refers him to those shining examples of magnanimous fortitude, for the climax of which, no doubt, the whole piece of interested flattery was composed. For this passage, written in a crescendo style, culminates, as might have been expected, in the sublime spectacle of Claudius Caesar. So far from resenting his exile, he crawls in the dust to kiss Caesar's beneficent feet for saving him from death; so far from asserting his innocence—which, perhaps, was impossible, since to do so might have involved him in a fresh charge of treason—he talks with all the abjectness of guilt. He belauds the clemency of a man, who, he tells us elsewhere, used to kill men with as much sang froid as a dog eats offal; the prodigious powers of memory of a divine creature who used to ask people to dice and to dinner whom he had executed the day before, and who even inquired as to the cause of his wife's absence a few days after having given the order for her execution; the extraordinary eloquence of an indistinct stutterer, whose head shook and whose broad lips seemed to be in contortions whenever he spoke.[32] If Polybius feels sorrowful, let him turn his eyes to Caesar; the splendour of that most great and radiant deity will so dazzle his eyes that all their tears will be dried up in the admiring gaze. Oh that the bright occidental star which has beamed on a world which, before its rising, was plunged in darkness and deluge, would only shed one little beam upon him!

No doubt these grotesque and gorgeous flatteries, contrasting strangely with the bitter language of intense hatred and scathing contempt which Seneca poured out on the memory of Claudius after his death, were penned with the sole purpose of being repeated in those divine and benignant ears. No doubt the superb freedman, who had been allowed so rich a share of the flatteries lavished on his

---

[32] These slight discrepancies of description are taken from counter passages of Consol, ad Polyb.. and the Ludus de Morte Caesaris.

master, would take the opportunity—if not out of good nature, at least out of vanity,—to retail them in the imperial ear. If the moment were but favourable, who knows but what at some oblivious and crapulous moment the Emperor might be induced to sign an order for our philosopher's recall?

Let us not be hard on him. Exile and wretchedness are stern trials, and it is difficult for him to brave a martyr's misery who has no conception of a martyr's crown. To a man who, like Seneca, aimed at being not only a philosopher, but also a man of the world—who in this very treatise criticises the Stoics for their ignorance of life—there would not have seemed to be even the shadow of disgrace in a private effusion of insincere flattery intended to win the remission of a deplorable banishment. Or, if we condemn Seneca, let us remember that Christians, no less than philosophers, have attained a higher eminence only to exemplify a more disastrous fall. The flatteries of Seneca to Claudius are not more fulsome, and are infinitely less disgraceful, than those which fawning bishops exuded on his counterpart, King James. And if the Roman Stoic can gain nothing from a comparison with the yet more egregious moral failure of the greatest of Christian thinkers—-Francis Bacon, Viscount St. Alban's—let us not forget that a Savonarola and a Cranmer recanted under torment, and that the anguish of exile drew even from the starry and imperial spirit of Dante Alighieri words and sentiments for which in his noblest moments he might have blushed.

CHAPTER IX

SENECA'S RECALL FROM EXILE

Of the last five years of Seneca's weary exile no trace has been preserved to us. What were his alternations of hope and fear, of devotion to philosophy and of hankering after the world which he had lost, we cannot tell. Any hopes which he may have entertained respecting the intervention of Polybius in his favour must have been utterly quenched when he heard that the freedman, though formerly powerful with Messalina, had forfeited his own life in consequence of her machinations. But the closing period of his days in Corsica must have brought him thrilling news, which would save him from falling into absolute despair.

For the career of Messalina was drawing rapidly to a close. The life of this beautiful princess, short as it was, for she died at a very early age, was enough to make her name a proverb of everlasting infamy. For a time she appeared irresistible. Her personal fascination had won for her an unlimited sway over the facile mind of Claudius, and she had either won over by her intrigues, or terrified by her pitiless severity, the noblest of the Romans and the most powerful of the freedmen. But we see in her fate, as we see on every page of history, that vice ever carries with it the germ of its own ruin, and that a retribution, which is all the more inevitable from being often slow, awaits every violation of the moral law.

There is something almost incredible in the penal infatuation which brought about her fall. During the absence of her husband at Ostia, she wedded in open day with C. Silius, the most beautiful and the most promising of the young Roman nobles. She had apparently persuaded Claudius that this was merely a mock-marriage, intended to avert some ominous auguries which threatened to destroy "the husband of Messalina;" but, whatever Claudius may have imagined, all the rest of the world knew the marriage to be real, and regarded it not only as a vile enormity, but also as a direct attempt to bring about a usurpation of the imperial power.

It was by this view of the case that the freedman Narcissus roused the inert spirit and timid indignation of the injured Emperor. While the wild revelry of the wedding ceremony was at its height, Vettius Valens, a well-known physician of the day, had in the license of the festival struggled up to the top of a lofty tree, and when they asked him what he saw, he replied in words which, though meant for jest, were full of dreadful significance, "I see a fierce storm approaching from Ostia." He had scarcely uttered the words when first an uncertain rumour, and then numerous messengers brought the news that Claudius knew all, and was coming to take vengeance. The news fell like a thunderbolt on the assembled guests. Silius, as though nothing had happened, went to transact his public duties in the Forum; Messalina instantly sending for her children, Octavia and Britannicus, that she might meet her husband with them by her side, implored the protection of Vibidia, the eldest of the chaste virgins of Vesta, and, deserted by all but three companions, fled on foot and unpitied, through the whole breadth of the city, until she reached the Ostian gate, and mounted the rubbish-cart of a market gardener which happened to be passing. But Narcissus absorbed both the looks and the attention of the Emperor by the proofs and the narrative of her crimes, and, getting rid of the Vestal by promising her that the cause of Messalina should be tried, he hurried Claudius forward, first to the house of Silius, which abounded with the proofs of his guilt, and then to the camp of the Praetorians, where swift vengeance was taken on the whole band of those who had been involved in Messalina's crimes. She meanwhile, in alternative paroxysms of fury and abject terror, had taken refuge in the garden of Lucullus, which she had coveted and made her own by injustice. Claudius, who had returned home, and had recovered some of his facile equanimity in the pleasures of the table, showed signs of relenting; but Narcissus knew that delay was death, and on his own authority sent a tribune and centurions to despatch the Empress. They found her prostrate on the ground at the feet of her mother Lepida, with whom in her prosperity she had quarrelled, but who now came to pity and console her misery, and to urge her to that voluntary death which alone could save her from imminent and more cruel infamy. But the mind of Messalina, like that of Nero afterwards, was so corrupted by wickedness that not even such poor nobility was left in her as is implied in the courage of despair. While she wasted the time in tears and lamentations, a noise was heard of battering at the doors, and the tribune stood by her in stern silence, the freedman with slavish vituperation. First she took the dagger in her irresolute hand, and after she had twice stabbed herself in vain, the tribune drove home the fatal blow, and the corpse of Messalina, like that of Jezebel, lay weltering in its blood in the plot of ground of which her crimes had robbed its lawful owner. Claudius, still lingering at his dinner, was informed that she had perished, and neither asked a single question at the time, nor subsequently displayed the slightest sign of anger, of hatred, of pity, or of any human emotion.

The absolute silence of Seneca respecting the woman who had caused him the bitterest anguish and humiliation of his life is, as we have remarked already, a strange and significant phenomenon. It is clearly not due to accident, for the vices which he is incessantly describing and denouncing would have found in this miserable woman their most flagrant illustration, nor could contemporary history have furnished a more apposite example of the vindication by her fate of the stern majesty of the moral law. But yet, though Seneca had every reason to loathe her character and to detest her memory, though he could not have rendered to his patrons a more welcome service than by blackening her reputation, he never so much as mentions her name. And this honourable silence gives us a favourable insight into his character. For it can only be due to his pitying sense of the fact that even Messalina, bad as she

59

undoubtedly was, had been judged already by a higher Power, and had met her dread punishment at the hand of God. It has been conjectured, with every appearance of probability, that the blackest of the scandals which were believed and circulated respecting her had their origin in the published autobiography of her deadly enemy and victorious successor. The many who had had a share in Messalina's fall would be only too glad to poison every reminiscence of her life; and the deadly implacable hatred of the worst woman who ever lived would find peculiar gratification in scattering every conceivable hue of disgrace over the acts of a rival whose young children it was her dearest object to supplant. That Seneca did not deign to chronicle even of an enemy what Agrippina was not ashamed to write,—that he spared one whom it was every one's interest and pleasure to malign,—that he regarded her terrible fall as a sufficient claim to pity, as it was a sufficient Nemesis upon her crimes,—is a trait in the character of the philosopher which has hardly yet received the credit which it deserves.

CHAPTER X

AGRIPPINA, THE MOTHER OF NERO

Scarcely had the grave closed over Messalina when the court was plunged into the most violent factions about the appointment of her successor. There were three principal candidates for the honour of the aged Emperor's hand. They were his former wife, Aelia Petina, who had only been divorced in consequence of trivial disagreements, and who was supported by Narcissus; Lollia Paulina, so celebrated in antiquity for her beauty and splendour, and who for a short time had been the wife of Caius; and Agrippina the younger, the daughter of the great Germanicus, and the niece of Claudius himself. Claudius, indeed, who had been as unlucky as Henry VIII. himself in the unhappiness which had attended his five experiments of matrimony, had made the strongest possible asseverations that he would never again submit himself to such a yoke. But he was so completely a tool in the hands of his own courtiers that no one attached the slightest importance to anything which he had said.

The marriage of an uncle with his own niece was considered a violation of natural laws, and was regarded with no less horror among the Romans than it would be among ourselves. But Agrippina, by the use of means the most unscrupulous, prevailed over all her rivals, and managed her interests with such consummate skill that, before many months had elapsed, she had become the spouse of Claudius and the Empress of Rome.

With this princess the destinies of Seneca were most closely intertwined, and it will enable us the better to understand his position, and his writings, if we remember that all history discloses to us no phenomenon more portentous and terrible than that presented to us in the character of Agrippina, the mother of Nero.

Of the virtues of her great parents she, like their other children, had inherited not one; and she had exaggerated their family tendencies into passions which urged her into every form of crime. Her career from the very cradle had been a career of wickedness, nor had any one of the many fierce vicissitudes of her life called forth in her a single noble or amiable trait. Born at Oppidum Ubiorum (afterwards called in her honour Colonia Agrippina, and still retaining its name in the form Cologne), she lost her father at the age of three, and her mother (by banishment) at the age of twelve. She was educated with bad sisters, with a wild and wicked brother, and under a grandmother whom she detested. At the age of fourteen she was married to Cnaeus Domitius Ahenobarbus, one of the most worthless and ill-reputed of the young Roman nobles of his day. The gossiping biographies of the time still retain some anecdotes of his cruelty and selfishness. They tell us how he once, without the slightest remorse, ran over a poor boy who was playing on the Appian Road; how on another occasion he knocked out the eye of a Roman knight who had given him a hasty answer; and how, when his friend congratulated him on the birth of his son (the young Claudius Domitius, afterwards the Emperor Nero), he brutally remarked that from people like himself and Agrippina could only be born some monster destined for the public ruin.

Domitius was forty years old when he married Agrippina, and the young Nero was not born till nine years afterwards. Whatever there was of possible affection in the tigress-nature of Agrippina was now absorbed in the person of her child. For that child, from its cradle to her own death by his means, she toiled and sinned. The fury of her own ambition, inextricably linked with the uncontrollable fierceness of her love for this only son, henceforth directed every action of her life. Destiny had made her the sister of one Emperor; intrigue elevated her into the wife of another; her own crimes made her the mother of a third. And at first sight her career might have seemed unusually successful, for while still in the prime of life she was wielding, first in the name of her husband, and then in that of her son, no mean share in the absolute government of the Roman world. But meanwhile that same unerring retribution, whose stealthy footsteps in the rear of the triumphant criminal we can track through page after page of history, was stealing nearer and nearer to her with uplifted hand. When she had reached the dizzy pinnacle of gratified love and pride to which she had waded through so many a deed of sin and blood, she was struck down into terrible ruin and violent shameful death, by the hand of that very son for whose sake she had so often violated the laws of virtue and integrity, and spurned so often the pure and tender obligations which even the heathen had been taught by the voice of God within their conscience to recognize and to adore.

Intending that her son should marry Octavia, the daughter of Claudius, her first step was to drive to death Silanus, a young nobleman to whom Octavia had already been betrothed. Her next care was to get rid of all rivals possible or actual. Among the former were the beautiful Calpurnia and her own sister-in-law, Domitia Lepida. Among the latter was the wealthy Lollia Paulina, against whom she trumped up an accusation of sorcery and treason, upon which her wealth was confiscated, but her life spared by the Emperor, who banished her from Italy. This half-vengeance was not enough for the mother of Nero. Like the daughter of Herodias in sacred history, she despatched a tribune with orders to bring her the head of her enemy; and when it was brought to her, and she found a difficulty in recognizing those withered and ghastly features of a once-celebrated beauty, she is said with her own hand to have lifted one of the lips, and to have satisfied herself that this was indeed the head of Lollia. To such horrors may a woman sink, when she has abandoned the love of God; and a fair face may hide a soul "leprous as sin itself." Well may Adolf Stahr observe that Shakespeare's Lady Macbeth and husband-murdering Gertrude are mere children by the side of this awful giant-shape of steely feminine cruelty.

Such was the princess who, in the year A.D. 49, recalled Seneca from exile.[33] She saw that her cruelties were inspiring horror even into a city that had long been accustomed to blood, and Tacitus expressly tells us that she hoped to counterbalance this feeling by a stroke of popularity in recalling from the waste solitudes of Corsica

---

[33] Gallio was Proconsul of Achaia about A.D. 53, when St. Paul was brought before his tribunal. Very possibly his elevation may have been due to the restoration of Seneca's influence.

the favourite philosopher and most popular author of the Roman world. Nor was she content with this public proof of her belief in his innocence of the crime which had been laid to his charge, for she further procured for him the Praetorship, and appointed him tutor and governor to her youthful son. Even in taking this step she did not forget her ambitious views; for she knew that Seneca cherished a secret indignation against Claudius, and that Nero could have no more wise adviser in taking steps to secure the fruition of his imperial hopes. It might perhaps have been better for Seneca's happiness if he had never left Corsica, or set his foot again in that Circean and bloodstained court. Let it, however, be added in his exculpation, that another man of undoubted and scrupulous honesty,—Afranius Burrus—a man of the old, blunt, faithful type of Roman manliness, whom Agrippina had raised to the Prefectship of the Praetorian cohorts, was willing to share his danger and his responsibilities. Yet he must have lived from the first in the very atmosphere of base and criminal intrigues. He must have formed an important member of Agrippina's party, which was in daily and deadly enmity against the party of Narcissus. He must have watched the incessant artifices by which Agrippina secured the adoption of her son Nero by an Emperor whose own son Britannicus was but three years his junior. He must have seen Nero always honoured, promoted, paraded before the eyes of the populace as the future hope of Rome, whilst Britannicus, like the young Edward V. under the regency of his uncle, was neglected, surrounded with spies, kept as much as possible out of his father's sight, and so completely thrust into the background from all observation that the populace began seriously to doubt whether he were alive or dead. He must have seen Agrippina, who had now received the unprecedented honour of the title "Augusta" in her lifetime, acting with such haughty insolence that there could be little doubt as to her ulterior designs upon the throne. He must have known that his splendid intellect was practically at the service of a woman in whom avarice, haughtiness, violence, treachery, and every form of unscrupulous criminality had reached a point hitherto unmatched even in a corrupt and pagan world. From this time forth the biography of Seneca must assume the form of an apology rather than of a panegyric.

The Emperor could not but feel that in Agrippina he had chosen a wife even more intolerable than Messalina herself. Messalina had not interfered with the friends he loved, had not robbed him of the insignia of empire, had not filled his palace with a hard and unfeminine tyranny, and had of course watched with a mother's interest over the lives and fortunes of his children. Narcissus would not be likely to leave him long in ignorance that, in addition to her other plots and crimes, Agrippina had been as little true to him as his former unhappy wife. The information sank deep into his heart, and he was heard to mutter that it had been his destiny all along first to bear, and then to avenge, the enormities of his wives. Agrippina, whose spies filled the palace, could not long remain uninformed of so significant a speech; and she probably saw with an instinct quickened by the awful terrors of her own guilty conscience that the Emperor showed distinct signs of his regret for having married his niece, and adopted her child to the prejudice, if not to the ruin, of his own young son. If she wanted to reach the goal which she had held so long in view no time was to be lost. Let us hope that Seneca and Burrus were at least ignorant of the means which she took to effect her purpose.

Fortune favoured her. The dreaded Narcissus, the most formidable obstacle to her murderous plans, was seized with an attack of the gout. Agrippina managed that his physician should recommend him the waters of Sinuessa in Campania by way of cure. He was thus got out of the way, and she proceeded at once to her work of blood. Entrusting the secret to Halotus, the Emperor's praegustator—the slave whose office it was to protect him from poison by tasting every dish before him—and to his physician, Xenophon of Cos, she consulted Locusta, the Mrs. Turner of the period of this classical King James, as to the poison best suited to her purpose. Locusta was mistress of her art, in which long practice had given her a consummate skill. The poison must not be too rapid, lest it should cause suspicion; nor too slow, lest it should give the Emperor time to consult for the interests of his son Britannicus; but it was to be one which should disturb his intellect without causing immediate death. Claudius was a glutton, and the poison was given him with all the more ease because it was mixed with a dish of mushrooms, of which he was extravagantly fond. Agrippina herself handed him the choicest mushroom in the dish, and the poison at once reduced him to silence. As was too frequently the case, Claudius was intoxicated at the time, and was carried off to his bed as if nothing had happened. A violent colic ensued, and it was feared that this, with a quantity of wine which he had drunk, would render the poison innocuous. But Agrippina had gone too far for retreat, and Xenophon, who knew that great crimes if frustrated are perilous, if successful are rewarded, came to her assistance. Under pretence of causing him to vomit, he tickled the throat of the

Emperor with a feather smeared with a swift and deadly poison. It did its work, and before morning the Caesar was a corpse.[34]

As has been the case not unfrequently in history, from the times of Tarquinius Priscus to those of Charles II., the death was concealed until everything had been prepared for the production of a successor. The palace was carefully watched; no one was even admitted into it except Agrippina's most trusty partisans. The body was propped up with pillows; actors were sent for "by his own desire" to afford it some amusement; and priests and consuls were bidden to offer up their vows for the life of the dead. Giving out that the Emperor was getting better, Agrippina took care to keep Britannicus and his two sisters, Octavia and Antonia, under her own immediate eye. As though overwhelmed with sorrow she wept, and embraced them, and above all kept Britannicus by her side, kissing him with the exclamation "that he was the very image of his father," and taking care that he should on no account leave her room. So the day wore on till it was the hour which the Chaldaeans declared would be the only lucky hour in that unlucky October day.

Noon came; the palace doors were suddenly thrown open: and Nero with Burrus at his side went out to the Praetorian cohort which was on guard. By the order of their commandant, they received him with cheers. A few only hesitated, looking round them and asking "Where was Britannicus?" Since, however, he was not to be seen, and no one stirred in his favour, they followed the multitude. Nero was carried in triumph to the camp, made the soldiers a short speech, and promised to each man of them a splendid donative. He was at once saluted Emperor. The Senate followed the choice of the soldiers, and the provinces made no

---

[34] There is usually found among the writings of Seneca a most remarkable burlesque called Ludus de Morte Caesaris. As to its authorship opinions will always vary, but it is a work of such undoubted genius, so interesting, and so unique in its character, that I have thought it necessary to give in an Appendix a brief sketch of its argument. We may at least hope that this satire, which overflows with the deadliest contempt of Claudius, is not from the same pen which wrote for Nero his funeral oration. It has, however, been supposed (without sufficient grounds) to be the lost [Greek: Apokolokuntoois] which Seneca is said to have written on the apotheosis of Claudius. The very name is a bitter satire. It imagines the Emperor transformed, not into a God, but into a gourd—one of those "bloated gourds which sun their speckled bellies before the doors of the Roman peasants." "The Senate decreed his divinity; Seneca translated it into pumpkinity" (Merivale, Rom. Emp. v. 601). The Ludus begins by spattering mud on the memory of the divine Claudius; it ends with a shower of poetic roses over the glory of the diviner Nero!

demur. Divine honors were decreed to the murdered man, and preparations made for a funeral which was to rival in its splendour the one which Livia had ordered for Augustus. But the will—which beyond all doubt had provided for the succession of Britannicus—was quietly done away with, and its exact provisions were never known.

And on the first evening of his imperial power, Nero, well aware to whom he owed his throne, gave to the sentinel who came to ask him the pass for the night the grateful and significant watchword of "Optima Mater,"—"the best of mothers!"

CHAPTER XI

NERO AND HIS TUTOR

The imperial youth, whose destinies are now inextricably mingled with those of Seneca, was accompanied to the throne by the acclamations of the people. Wearied by the astuteness of an Augustus, the sullen wrath of a Tiberius, the mad ferocity of a Caius, the senile insensibility of a Claudius, they could not but welcome the succession of a bright and beautiful youth, whose fair hair floated over his shoulders, and whose features displayed the finest type of Roman beauty. There was nothing in his antecedents to give a sinister augury to his future development, and all classes alike dreamt of the advent of a golden age. We can understand their feelings if we compare them with those of our own countrymen when the sullen tyranny of Henry VIII. was followed by the youthful virtue and gentleness of Edward VI. Happy would it have been for Nero if his reign, like that of Edward, could have been cut short before the thick night of many crimes had settled down upon the promise of its dawn. For the first five years of Nero's reign—the famous Quinquennium Neronis—were fondly regarded by the Romans as a period of almost ideal happiness. In reality, it was Seneca who was ruling in Nero's, name. Even so excellent an Emperor as Trajan is said to have admitted "that no other prince had nearly equalled the praise of that period." It is indeed probable that those years appeared to shine with an exaggerated splendour from the intense gloom which succeeded them; yet we can see in them abundant circumstances which were quite sufficient to inspire an enthusiasm of hope and joy. The young Nero was at first modest and docile. His opening speeches, written with all the beauty of thought and language which betrayed the style of Seneca no less than his habitual sentiments, were full of glowing promises. All those things which had been felt to be injurious or oppressive he promised to eschew. He would not, he said, reserve to himself, as Claudius had done, the irresponsible decision in all matters of business; no office or dignity should be won from him by flattery or purchased by bribes; he would not confuse his own personal interests with those of the commonwealth; he would respect the ancient prerogatives of the Senate; he would confine his own immediate attention to the provinces and the army.

Nor were such promises falsified by his immediate conduct. The odious informers who had flourished in previous reigns were frowned upon and punished. Offices of public dignity were relieved from unjust and oppressive burdens. Nero prudently declined the gold and silver statues and other extravagant honours which were offered to him by the corrupt and servile Senate, but he treated that body, which, fallen as it was, continued still to be the main representative of constitutional authority, with favour and respect. Nobles and officials begun to breathe more freely, and the general sense of an intolerable tyranny was perceptibly relaxed. Severity was reserved for notorious criminals, and was only inflicted in a regular and authorized manner, when no one could doubt that it had been deserved. Above all, Seneca had disseminated an anecdote about his young pupil which tended more than any other circumstance to his wide spread popularity. England has remembered with gratitude and admiration the tearful reluctance of her youthful Edward to sign the death-warrant of Joan Boucher; Rome, accustomed to a cruel indifference to human life, regarded with something like transport the sense of pity which had made Nero, when asked to affix his signature to an order for execution, exclaim, "How I wish that I did not know how to write!"

It is admitted that no small share of the happiness of this period was due to the firmness of the honest Burrus, and the wise, high-minded precepts of Seneca. They deserve the amplest gratitude and credit for this happy interregnum, for they had no easy task to perform. Besides the difficulties which arose from the base and frivolous character of their pupil, besides the infinite delicacy which was requisite for the restraint of a youth who was absolute master of such gigantic destinies, they had the task of curbing the wild and imperious ambition of Agrippina, and of defeating the incessant intrigues of her many powerful dependents.

Agrippina had no doubt persuaded herself that her crimes had been mainly committed in the interest of her son; but her conduct showed that she wished him to be a mere instrument in her hands. She wished to govern him, and had probably calculated on doing so by the assistance of Seneca, just as our own Queen Caroline completely managed George II. with the aid of Sir Robert Walpole. She rode in a litter with him; without his knowledge she ordered the poisoning of M. Silanus, a brother of her former victim, she goaded Narcissus to death, against his will; through her influence the Senate was sometimes assembled in the palace, and she took no pains to conceal from the senators that she was herself seated behind a curtain where she could hear every word of their deliberations;—nay, on one occasion, when Nero was about to give audience to an important Armenian legation, she had the audacity to enter the audience-chamber, and advance to take her seat by the side of the Emperor. Every one else was struck dumb with amazement, and even terror, at a proceeding so unusual; but Seneca, with ready and admirable tact, suggested to Nero that he should rise and meet his mother, thus obviating a public scandal under the pretext of filial affection.

But Seneca from the very first had been guilty of a fatal error in the education of his pupil. He had governed him throughout on the ruinous principle of concession. Nero was not devoid of talent; he had a decided turn for Latin versification, and the few lines of his composition which have come down to us, bizarre and effected as they are, yet display a certain sense of melody and power of language. But his vivid imagination was accompained by a want of purpose; and Seneca, instead of trying to train him in habits of serious attention and sustained thought, suffered him to waste his best efforts in pursuits and amusements which were considered partly frivolous and partly disreputable, such as singing, painting, dancing, and driving. Seneca might have argued that there was, at any rate, no great harm in such employments, and that they probably kept Nero out of worse mischief. But we respect Nero the less for his indifferent singing and harp-twanging just as we respect Louis XVI. less for making very poor locks; and, if Seneca had adopted a loftier tone with his pupil from the first, Rome might have been spared the disgraceful folly of Nero's subsequent buffooneries in the cities of Greece and the theatres of Rome. We may lay it down as an invariable axiom in all high education, that it is never sensible to permit what is bad for the supposed sake of preventing what is worse. Seneca very probably persuaded himself that with a mind like Nero's—the innate worthlessness of which he must early have recognised—success of any high description would be simply impossible. But this did not absolve him from attempting the only noble means by which success could, under any circumstances, be attainable. Let us, however, remember that his concessions to his pupil were mainly in matters which he regarded as indifferent—or, at the worst, as discreditable—rather than as criminal; and that his mistake probably arose from an error in judgment far more than from any deficiency in moral character.

Yet it is clear that, even intellectually, Nero was the worse for this laxity of training. We have already seen that, in his maiden-speech before the Senate, every one recognized the hand of Seneca, and many observed with a sigh that this was the first occasion on which an Emperor had not been able, at least to all appearance, to address the Senate in his own words and with his own thoughts. Tiberius, as an orator, had been dignified and forcible; Claudius had been learned and polished; even the disturbed reason of Caligula had not been wanting in a capacity for delivering forcible and eloquent harangues; but Nero's youth had been frittered away in paltry and indecorus accomplishments, which had left him neither time nor inclination for weightier and nobler pursuits.

The fame of Seneca has, no doubt, suffered grieviously from the subsequent infamy of his pupil; and it is obvious that the dislike of Tacitus to his memory is due to his connexion with Nero. Now, even though the tutor's system had not been so wise as, when judged by an inflexible standard, it might have been, it is yet clearly unjust to make him responsible for the depravity of his pupil; and it must be remembered, to Seneca's eternal honour, that the evidence of facts, the testimony of contemporaries, and even the grudging admission of Tacitus himself, establishes in his favour that whatever wisdom and moderation characterized the earlier years of Nero's reign were due to his counsels; that he enjoyed the cordial esteem of the virtuous Burrus; that he helped to check the sanguinary audacities of Agrippina; that the writings which he addressed to Nero, and the speeches which he wrote for him, breathed the loftiest counsels; and that it was not until he was wholly removed from power and influence that Nero, under the fierce impulses of despotic power, developed those atrocious tendencies of which the seeds had long been latent in his disposition. An ancient writer records the tradition that Seneca very early observed in Nero a savagery of disposition which he could not wholly eradicate; and that to his intimate friends he used to observe that, "when once the lion tasted human blood, his innate cruelty would return."

But while we give Seneca this credit, and allow that his intentions were thoroughly upright, we cannot but impugn his judgment for having thus deliberately adopted the morality of expedience; and we believe that to this cause, more than to any other, was due the extent of his failure and the misery of his life. We may, indeed, be permitted to doubt whether Nero himself—a vain and loose youth, the son of bad parents, and heir to boundless expectations—would, under any circumstances, have grown up much better than he did; but it is clear that Seneca might have been held in infinitely higher honour but for the share which he had in his education. Had Seneca been as firm and wise as Socrates, Nero in all probability would not have been much worse than Alcibiades. If the tutor had set before his pupil no ideal but the very highest, if he had inflexibly opposed to the extent of his ability every tendency which was dishonourable and wrong, he might possibly have been rewarded by success, and have earned the indelible gratitude of mankind; and if he had failed he would at least have failed nobly, and have carried with him into a calm and honourable retirement the respect, if not the affection, of his imperial pupil. Nay, even if he had failed completely, and lost his life in the attempt, it would have been infinitely better both for him and for mankind. Even Homer might have taught him that "it is better to die than live in sin." At any rate he might have known from study and observation that an education founded on compromise must always and necessarily fail. It must fail because it overlooks that great eternal law of retribution for and continuity in evil, which is illustrated by every single history of individuals and of nations. And the education which Seneca gave to Nero—noble as it was in many respects, and eminent as was its partial and temporary success—was yet an education of compromises. Alike in the studies of Nero's boyhood and the graver temptations of his manhood, he acted on the foolishly-fatal principle that

> "Had the wild oat not been sown,
> The soil left barren scarce had grown,
> The grain whereby a man may live."

Any Christian might have predicted the result; one would have thought that even a pagan philosopher might have been enlightened enough to observe it. We often quote the lines—

> "The child is father of the man,"

and

> "Just as the twig is bent the tree inclines."

70

But the ancients were quite as familiar with the same truth under other images. "The cask," wrote Horace, "will long retain the odour of that which has once been poured into it when new." Quintilian, describing the depraved influences which surrounded even the infancy of a Roman child, said, "From these arise first familiarity, then nature."

No one has laid down the principle more emphatically than Seneca himself. Take, for instance, the following passage from his Letters, on evil conversation. "The conversation," he says, "of these men is very injurious; for, even if it does no immediate harm, it leaves its seeds in the mind, and follows us even when we have gone from the speakers,—a plague sure to spring up in future resurrection. Just as those who have heard a symphony carry in their ears the tune and sweetness of the song which entangles their thoughts, and does not suffer them to give their whole energy to serious matters; so the conversation of flatterers and of those who praise evil things, lingers longer in the mind than the time of hearing it. Nor is it easy to shake out of the soul a sweet sound; it pursues us, and lingers with us, and at perpetual intervals recurs. Our ears therefore must be closed to evil words, and that to the very first we hear. For when they have once begun and been admitted, they acquire more and more audacity;" and so he adds a little afterwards, "our days flow on, and irreparable life passes beyond our reach." Yet he who wrote these noble words was not only a flatterer to his imperial pupil, but is charged with having deliberately encouraged him in a foolish passion for a freedwoman named Acte, into which Nero fell. It was of course his duty to recall the wavering affections of the youthful Emperor to his betrothed Octavia, the daughter of Claudius, to whom he had been bound by every tie of honour and affection, and his union with whom gave some shadow of greater legitimacy to his practical usurpation. But princes rarely love the wives to whom they owe any part of their elevation. Henry VII. treated Elizabeth of York with many slights. The union of William III. with Mary was overshadowed by her superior claim to the royal power; and Nero from the first regarded with aversion, which ended in assassination, the poor young orphan girl who recalled to the popular memory his slender pretensions to hereditary empire, and whom he regarded as a possible rival, if her cowed and plastic nature should ever become a tool in the hands of more powerful intriguers. But we do not hear of any attempt on Seneca's part to urge upon Nero the fulfillment of this high duty, and we find him sinking into the degraded position of an accomplice with young profligates like Otho, as the confident of a dishonourable love. Such conduct, which would have done discredit

71

to a mere courtier, was to a Stoic disgraceful. But the principle which led to it is the very principle to which we have been pointing,—the principle of moral compromise, the principle of permitting and encouraging what is evil in the vain hope of thereby preventing what is worse. It is hardly strange that Seneca should have erred in this way, for compromise was the character of his entire life. He appears to have set before himself the wholly impossible task of being both a genuine philosopher and a statesman under the Caesars. He prided himself on being not only a philosopher, but also a man of the world, and the consequence was, that in both capacities he failed. It was as true in Paganism as it is in Christianity, that a man must make his choice between duty and interest—between the service of Mammon and the service of God. No man ever gained anything but contempt and ruin by incessantly halting between two opinions.

And by not taking that lofty line of duty which a Zeno or an Antisthenes would have taken, Seneca became more or less involved in some of the most dreadful events of Nero's reign. Every one of the terrible doubts under which his reputation has suffered arose from his having permitted the principle of expedience to supercede the laws of virtue. One or two of these events we must briefly narrate.

We have already pointed out that the Nemesis which for so many years had been secretly dogging the footsteps of Agrippina made her tremble under the weight of its first cruel blows when she seemed to have attained the highest summit of her ambition. Very early indeed Nero began to be galled and irritated by the insatiate assumption and swollen authority of "the best of mothers." The furious reproaches which she heaped upon him when she saw in Acte a possible rival to her power drove him to take refuge in the facile and unphilosophic worldliness of Seneca's concessions, and goaded him almost immediately afterwards into an atrocious crime. He naturally looked on Britannicus, the youthful son of Claudius, with even more suspicion and hatred than that with which he regarded Octavia. Kings have rarely been able to abstain from acts of severity against those who might become claimants to the throne. The feelings of King John towards Prince Arthur, of Henry IV. towards the Earl of March, of Mary towards Lady Jane Grey, of Elizabeth towards Mary Stuart, of King James towards Lady Arabella Stuart, resembled, but probably by no means equalled in intensity, those of Nero towards his kinsman and adoptive brother. To show him any affection was a dangerous crime, and it furnished a sufficient cause for immediate removal if any attendant behaved towards him with fidelity. Such a line of treatment foreshadowed the catastrophe which was hastened by the rage of Agrippina. She would go, she said, and take with her to the camp the noble boy who was now of full age to undertake those imperial duties which a usurper was exercising in virtue of crimes which she was now prepared to confess. Then let the mutilated Burrus and the glib-tongued Seneca see whether they could be a match for the son of Claudius and the daughter of Germanicus. Such language, uttered with violent gestures and furious imprecations, might well excite the alarm of the timid Nero. And that alarm was increased by a recent circumstance, which showed that all the ancestral spirit was not dead in the breast of Britannicus. During the festivities of the Saturnalia, which were kept by the ancients with all the hilarity of the modern Christmas, Nero had been elected by lot as "governor of the feast," and, in that capacity, was entitled to issue his orders to the guests. To the others he issued trivial mandates which would not make them blush; but Britannicus in violation of every principle of Roman decorum, was ordered to stand up in the middle and sing a song. The boy, inexperienced as yet even in sober banquets, and wholly unaccustomed to drunken convivialities, might well have faltered; but he at once rose, and with a steady voice began a strain—probably the magnificent wail of Andromache over the fall of Troy, which has been preserved to us from a lost play of Ennius—in which he indicated his own disgraceful ejection from his hereditary rights. His courage and his misfortunes woke in the guests a feeling of pity which night and wine made them less careful to disguise. From that moment the fate of Britannicus was sealed. Locusta, the celebrated poisoner of ancient Rome, was summoned to the councils of Nero to get rid of Britannicus, as she had already been summoned to those of his mother when she wished to disembarrass herself of Britannicus's father. The main difficulty was to avoid discovery, since nothing was eaten or drunk at the imperial table till it had been tasted by the praegustator. To avoid this difficulty a very hot draught was given to Britannicus, and when he wished for something cooler a swift and subtle poison was dropped into the cold water with which it was tempered. The boy drank, and instantly sank from his seat, gasping and speechless. The guests started up in consternation, and fixed their eyes on Nero. He with the utmost coolness assured them that it was merely a fit of epilepsy, to which his brother was accustomed, and from which he would soon recover. The terror and agitation of Agrippina showed to every one that she at least was guiltless of this dark deed; but the unhappy Octavia, young as she was, and doubly terrible on every ground as the blow must have been to her, sat silent and motionless, having already learnt by her misfortunes the awful necessity for suppressing under an impassive exterior her affections and sorrows, her hopes and fears. In the dead of night, amid storms and murky rain, which were thought to indicate the wrath of heaven, the last of the Claudii was hastily and meanly hurried into a dishonourable grave.

We may believe that in this crime Seneca had no share whatever, but we can hardly believe that he was ignorant of it after it had been committed, or that he had no share in the intensely hypocritical edict in which Nero bewailed the fact of his adoptive brother's death, excused his hurried funeral, and threw himself on the additional indulgence and protection of the Senate. Nero showed the consciousness of guilt by the immense largesses which he distributed to the most powerful of his friends, "Nor were there wanting men," says Tacitus, in a most significant manner, "who accused certain people, notorious for their high professions, of having at that period divided among them villas and houses as though they had been so much spoil." There can hardly be a doubt that the great historian intends by this remark to point at Seneca, to whom he tries to be fair, but whom he could never quite forgive for his share in the disgraces of Nero's reign. That avarice was one of Seneca's temptations is too probable; that expediency was a guiding principle of his conduct is but too evident; and for a man with such a character to rebut an innuendo is never an easy task. Nay more, it was after this foul event, at the close of Nero's first year, that Seneca addressed him in the extravagant and glowing language of his treatise on Clemency. "The quality of mercy," and the duty of princes to practise it, has never been more eloquently extolled; but it is accompanied by a fulsome flattery which has in it something painfully grotesque as addressed by a philosopher to one whom he knew to have been guilty, that very year, of an inhuman fratricide. Imagine some Jewish Pharisee,—a Nicodemus or a Gamaliel—pronouncing an eulogy on the tenderness of a Herod, and you have some picture of the appearance which Seneca's consistency must have worn in the eyes of his contemporaries.

This event took place A.D. 55, in the first year of Nero's Quinquennium, and the same year was nearly signalized by the death of his mother. A charge of pretended conspiracy was invented against her, and it is probable that but for the intervention of Burrus, who with Seneca was appointed to examine into the charge, she would have fallen a very sudden victim to the cowardly credulity and growing hatred of her son. The extraordinary and eloquent audacity of her defence created a reaction in her favour, and secured the punishment of her accusers. But the ties of affection could not long unite two such wicked and imperious natures as those of

Agrippina and her son. All history shows that there can be no real love between souls exceptionally wicked, and that this is still more impossible when the alliance between them has been sealed by a complicity in crime. Nero had now fallen into a deep infatuation for Poppaea Sabina, the beautiful wife of Otho, and she refused him her hand so long as he was still under the control of his mother. At this time Agrippina, as the just consequence of her many crimes, was regarded by all classes with a fanaticism of hatred which in Poppaea Sabina was intensified by manifest self-interest. Nero, always weak, had long regarded his mother with real terror and disgust, and he scarcely needed the urgency of constant application to make him long to get rid of her. But the daughter of Germanicus could not be openly destroyed, while her own precautions helped to secure her against secret assassination. It only remained to compass her death by treachery. Nero had long compelled her to live in suburban retirement, and had made no attempt to conceal the open rapture which existed between them. Anicetus, admiral of the fleet at Misenum, and a former instructor of Nero, suggested the expedient of a pretended public reconciliation, in virtue of which Agrippina should be invited to Baiae, and on her return should be placed on board a vessel so constructed as to come to pieces by the removal of bolts. The disaster might then be attributed to a mere naval accident, and Nero might make the most ostentatious display of his affection and regret.

The invitation was sent, and a vessel specially decorated was ordered to await her movements. But, either from suspicion or from secret information, she declined to avail herself of it, and was conveyed to Baiae in a litter. The effusion of hypocritical affection with which she was received, the unusual tenderness and honour with which she was treated, the earnest gaze, the warm embrace, the varied conversation, removed her suspicions, and she consented to return in the vessel of honour. As though for the purpose of revealing the crime, the night was starry and the sea calm. The ship had not sailed far, and Crepereius Gallus, one of her friends, was standing near the helm, while a lady named Acerronia was seated at her feet as she reclined, and both were vieing with each other in the warmth of their congratulations upon the recent interview, when a crash was heard, and the canopy above them which had been weighted with a quantity of lead, was suddenly let go. Crepereius was crushed to death upon the spot; Agrippina and Acerronia were saved by the projecting sides of the couch on which they were resting; in the hurry and alarm, as accomplices were mingled with a greater number who were innocent of the plot, the machinery of the treacherous vessel failed. Some of the rowers rushed to one side of

75

the ship, hoping in that manner to sink it, but here too their councils were divided and confused. Acerronia, in the selfish hope of securing assistance, exclaimed that she was Agrippina, and was immediately despatched with oars and poles; Agrippina, silent and unrecognized, received a wound upon the shoulder, but succeeded in keeping herself afloat till she was picked up by fishermen and carried in safety to her villa.

The hideous attempt from which she had been thus miraculously rescued did not escape her keen intuition, accustomed as it was to deeds of guilt; but, seeing that her only chance of safety rested in dissimulation and reticense, she sent her freedman Agerinus to tell her son that by the mercy of heaven she had escaped from a terrible accident, but to beg him not to be alarmed, and not to come to see her because she needed rest.

The news filled Nero with the wildest terror, and the expectation of an immediate revenge. In horrible agitation and uncertainty he instantly required the presence of Burrus and Seneca. Tacitus doubts whether they may not have been already aware of what he had attempted, and Dion, to whose gross calumnies, however, we need pay no attention, declares that Seneca had frequently urged Nero to the deed, either in the hope of overshadowing his own guilt, or of involving Nero in a crime which should hasten his most speedy destruction at the hands of gods and men. In the absence of all evidence we may with perfect confidence acquit the memory of these eminent men from having gone so far as this.

It must have been a strange and awful scene. The young man, for Nero was but twenty-two years old, poured into the ears their tumult of his agitation and alarm. White with fear, weak with dissipation, and tormented by the furies of a guilty conscience, the wretched youth looked from one to another of his aged ministers. A long and painful pause ensued. If they dissuaded him in vain from the crime which he meditated their lives would have been in danger; and perhaps they sincerely thought that things had gone so far that, unless Agrippina were anticipated, Nero would be destroyed. Seneca was the first to break that silence of anguish by inquiring of Burrus whether the soldiery could be entrusted to put her to death. His reply was that the praetorians would do nothing against a daughter of Germanicus and that Anicetus should accomplish what he had promised. Anicetus showed himself prompt to crime, and Nero thanked him in a rapture of gratitude. While the freedman Agerinus was delivering to Nero his mother's message, Anicetus dropped a dagger at his feet, declared that he had caught him in the very act of attempting the Emperor's assassination, and hurried off with a band of soldiers to punish Agrippina as the author of the crime.

The multitude meanwhile were roaming in wild excitement along the shore; their torches were seen glimmering in evident commotion about the scene of the calamity, where some were wading into the water in search of the body, and others were shouting incoherent questions and replies. At the rumour of Agrippina's escape they rushed off in a body to her villa to express their congratulations, where they were dispersed by the soldiers of Anicetus, who had already token possession of it. Scattering or seizing the slaves who came in their way, and bursting their passage from door to door, they found the Empress in a dimly-lighted chamber, attended only by a single handmaid. "Dost thou too desert me?" exclaimed the wretched woman to her servant, as she rose to slip away. In silent determination the soldiers surrounded her couch, and Anicetus was the first to strike her with a stick. "Strike my womb," she cried to him faintly, as he drew his sword, "for it bore Nero." The blow of Anicetus was the signal for her immediate destruction: she was dispatched with many wounds, and was buried that night at Misenum on a common couch and with a mean funeral. Such an end, many years previously, this sister, and wife, and mother of emperors had anticipated and despised; for when the Chaldaeans had assured her that her son would become Emperor, and would murder her, she is said to have exclaimed, "Occidat dum imperet," "Let him slay me if he but reign."

It only remained to account for the crime, and offer for it such lying defences as were most likely to gain credit. Flying to Naples from a scene which had now become awful to him,—for places do not change as men's faces change, and, besides this, his disturbed conscience made him fancy that he heard from the hill of Misenum the blowing of a ghostly trumpet and wailings about his mother's tomb in the hours of night,—he sent from thence a letter to the Senate, saying that his mother had been punished for an attempt upon his life, and adding a list of her crimes, real and imaginary, the narrative of her accidental shipwreck, and his opinion that her death was a public blessing. The author of this shameful document was Seneca, and in composing it he reached the nadir of his moral degradation. Even the lax morality of a most degenerate age condemned him for calmly sitting down to decorate with the graces of rhetoric and antithesis an atrocity too deep for the powers of indignation. A Seneca could stoop to write what a Thrasea Paetus could scarcely stoop to hear; for in the meeting of the Senate at which the letter was recited, Thrasea rose in indignation, and went straight home rather than seem to sanction by his presence the adulation of a matricide.

And the composition of that guily, elaborate, shameful letter was the last prominent act of Seneca's public life.

CHAPTER XII

THE BEGINNING OF THE END

Nor was it unnatural that it should be. Moral precepts, philosophic guidance were no longer possible to one whose compliances or whose timidity had led him so far as first to sanction matricide, and then to defend it. He might indeed be still powerful to recommend principles of common sense and political expediency, but the loftier lessons of Stoicism, nay, even the better utterances of a mere ordinary Pagan morality, could henceforth only fall from his lips with something of a hollow ring. He might interfere, as we know he did, to render as innocuous as possible the pernicious vanity which made Nero so ready to degrade his imperial rank by public appearances on the orchestra or in the race-course, but he could hardly address again such noble teachings as that of the treatise on Clemency to one whom, on grounds of political expediency, he had not dissuaded from the treacherous murder of a mother, who, whatever her enormities, yet for his sake had sold her very soul.

Although there may have been a strong suspicion that foul play had been committed, the actual facts and details of the death of Agrippina would rest between Nero and Seneca as a guilty secret, in the guilt of which Seneca himself must have his share. Such a position of things was the inevitable death-blow, not only to all friendship, but to all confidence, and ultimately to all intercourse. We see in sacred history that Joab's participation in David's guilty secret gave him the absolute mastery over his own sovereign; we see repeatedly in profane history that the mutual knowledge of some crime is the invariable cause of deadly hatred between a subject and a king. Such feelings as King John may be supposed to have had to Hubert de Burgh, or King Richard III. to Sir James Tyrrel, or King James I. to the Earl of Somerset, such probably, in still more virulent intensity, were the feelings of Nero towards his whilome "guide, philosopher, and friend."

For Nero very soon learnt that Seneca was no longer

necessary to him. For a time he lingered in Campania, guiltily dubious as to the kind of reception that awaited him in the capital. The assurances of the vile crew which surrounded him soon made that fear wear off, and when he plucked up the courage to return to his palace, he might himself have been amazed at the effusion of infamous loyalty and venal acclamation with which he was received. All Rome poured itself forth to meet him; the Senate appeared in festal robes with their wives and girls and boys in long array; seats and scaffoldings were built up along the road by which he had to pass, as though the populace had gone forth to see a triumph. With haughty mein, the victor of a nation of slaves, he ascended the Capitol, gave thanks to the gods, and went home to betray henceforth the full perversity of a nature which the reverence for his mother, such as it was, had hitherto in part restrained. But the instincts of the populace were suppressed rather than eradicated. They hung a sack from his statue by night in allusion to the old punishment of parricides, who were sentenced to be flung into the sea, tied up in a sack with a serpent, a monkey, and a cock. They exposed an infant in the Forum with a tablet on which was written, "I refuse to rear thee, lest thou shouldst slay thy mother." They scrawled upon the blank walls of Rome an iambic line which reminded all who read it that Nero, Orestes, and Alcmaeon were murderers of their mothers. Even Nero must have been well aware that he presented a hideous spectacle in the eyes of all who had the faintest shade of righteousness among the people whom he ruled.

All this took place in A.D. 59, and we hear no more of Seneca till the year 62, a year memorable for the death of Burrus, who had long been his honest, friendly, and faithful colleague. In these dark times, when all men seemed to be speaking in a whisper, almost every death of a conspicuous and high-minded man, if not caused by open violence, falls under the suspicion of secret poison. The death of Burrus may have been due (from the description) to diphtheria, but the popular voice charged Nero with having hastened his death by a pretended remedy, and declared that, when the Emperor visited his sick bed, the dying man turned away from his inquiries with the laconic answer, "I am well."

His death was regretted, not only from the memory of his virtues, but also from the fact that Nero appointed two men as his successors, of whom the one, Fenius Rufus, was honorable but indolent; the other and more powerful, Sofonius Tigellinus had won for himself among cruel and shameful associates a pre-eminence of hatred and of shame.

However faulty and inconsistent Seneca may have been, there was at any rate no possibility that he should divide with a Tigellinus

79

the direction of his still youthful master. He was by no means deceived as to the position in which he stood, and the few among Nero's followers in whom any spark of honour was left informed him of the incessant calumnies which were used to undermine his influence. Tigellinus and his friends dwelt on his enormous wealth and his magnificent villas and gardens, which could only have been acquired with ulterior objects, and which threw into the shade the splendour of the Emperor himself. They tried to kindle the inflammable jealousies of Nero's feeble mind by representing Seneca as attempting to rival him in poetry, and as claiming the entire credit of his eloquence, while he mocked his divine singing, and disparaged his accomplishments as a harper and charioteer because he himself was unable to acquire them. Nero, they urged was a boy no longer; let him get rid of his schoolmaster, and find sufficient instruction in the example of his ancestors.

Foreseeing how such arguments must end; Seneca requested an interview with Nero; begged to be suffered to retire altogether from public life; pleaded age and increasing infirmities as an excuse for desiring a calm retreat; and offered unconditionally to resign the wealth and honours which had excited the cupidity of his enemies, but which were simply due to Nero's unexampled liberality during the eight years of his government, towards one whom he had regarded as a benefactor and a friend. But Nero did not choose to let Seneca escape so lightly. He argued that, being still young, he could not spare him, and that to accept his offers would not be at all in accordance with his fame for generosity. A proficient in the imperial art of hiding detestation under deceitful blandishments, Nero ended the interview with embraces and assurances of friendship. Seneca thanked him—the usual termination, as Tacitus bitterly adds, of interviews with a ruler—but nevertheless altered his entire manner of life, forbade his friends to throng to his levees, avoided all companions, and rarely appeared in public—wishing it to be believed that he was suffering from weak health, or was wholly occupied in the pursuit of philosophy. He well knew the arts of courts, for in his book on Anger he has told an anecdote of one who, being asked how he had managed to attain so rare a gift as old age in a palace, replied, "By submitting to injuries, and returning thanks for them." But he must have known that his life hung upon a thread, for in the very same year an attempt was made to involve him in a charge of treason as one of the friends of C. Calpurnius Piso, an illustrious nobleman whose wealth and ability made him an object of jealousy and suspicion, though he was naturally unambitious and devoid of energy. The attempt failed at the time, and Seneca was able triumphantly to refute the charge of any treasonable design.

But the fact of such a charge being made showed how insecure was the position of any man of eminence under the deepening tyranny of Nero, and it precipitated the conspiracy which two years afterwards was actually formed.

Not long after the death of Burrus, when Nero began to add sacrilege to his other crimes, Seneca made one more attempt to retire from Rome; and, when permission was a second time refused, he feigned a severe illness, and confined himself to his chamber. It was asserted, and believed, that about this time Nero made an attempt to poison him by the instrumentality of his freedman Cleonicus, which was only defeated by the confession of an accomplice or by the abstemious habits of the philosopher who now took nothing but bread and fruit, and never quenched his thirst except out of the running stream.

It was during those two years of Seneca's seclusion and disgrace that an event happened of imperishable interest. On the orgies of a shameful court, on the supineness of a degenerate people, there burst—as upon the court of Charles II.—a sudden lightning-flash of retribution. In its character, in its extent, in the devastation and anguish of which it was the cause, in the improvements by which it was followed, in the lying origin to which it was attributed, even in the general circumstances of the period and character of the reign in which it happened, there is a close and singular analogy between the Great Fire of London in 1666 and the Great Fire of Rome in 64. Beginning in the crowded part of the city, under the Palatine and Caelian Hills, it raged, first for six, and then again for three days, among the inflammable material of booths and shops, and driven along by a furious wind, amid feeble and ill-directed efforts to check its course, it burst irresistibly over palaces, temples, and porticoes, and amid the narrow tortuous streets of old Rome, involving in a common destruction the most magnificent works of ancient art, the choicest manuscripts of ancient literature, and the most venerable monuments of ancient superstition. In a few touches of inimitable compression, such as the stern genius of the Latin language permits, but which are too condensed for direct translation, Tacitus has depicted the horror of the scene,—wailing of panic-stricken women, the helplessness of the very aged and the very young, the passionate eagerness for themselves and for others, the dragging along of the feeble or the waiting for them, the lingering and the hurry, the common and inextricable confusion. Many, while they looked backward, were cut off by the flames in front or at the sides; if they sought some neighboring refuge, they found it in the grasp of the conflagration; if they hurried to some more distant spot, that too was found to be involved in the same calamity. At last, uncertain what to seek or what to avoid, they crowded the streets, they lay huddled together in the fields. Some, having lost all their possessions, died from the want of daily food; and others, who might have escaped died of a broken heart from the anguish of being bereaved of those whom they had been unable to rescue; while, to add to the universal horror, it was believed that all attempts to repress the flames were checked by authoritive prohibition; nay more, that hired incendiaries were seen flinging firebrands in new directions, either because they had been bidden to do so, or that they might exercise their rapine undisturbed.

The historians and anecdotists of the time, whose accounts must be taken for what they are worth, attribute to Nero the origin of the conflagration; and it is certain that he did not return to Rome until the fire had caught the galleries of his palace. In vain did he use every exertion to assist the homeless and ruined population; in vain did he order food to be sold to them at a price unprecedentedly low, and throw open to them the monuments of Agrippa, his own gardens, and a multitude of temporary sheds. A rumour had been spread that, during the terrible unfolding of that great "flower of flame," he had mounted to the roof of his distant villa, and delighted with the beauty of the spectacle, exulting in the safe sensation of a new excitement, had dressed himself in theatrical attire, and sung to his harp a poem on the burning of Troy. Such a heartless mixture of buffoonery and affectation had exasperated the people too deeply for forgiveness, and Nero thought it necessary to draw off the general odium into a new channel, since neither his largesses nor any other popular measures succeeded in removing from himself the ignominy of this terrible suspicion. What follows is so remarkable, and, to a Christian reader, so deeply interesting, that I will give it in the very words of that great historian whom I have been so closely following.

"Therefore, to get rid of this report, Nero trumped up an accusation against a sect, detested for their atrocities, whom the common people called Christians, and inflicted on them the most recondite punishments. Christ, the founder of this sect, had been capitally punished by the Procurator Pontius Pilate, in the reign of Tiberius; and this damnable superstition, repressed for the present, was again breaking out, not only through Judaea, where the evil originated, but even through the City, whither from all regions all things that are atrocious or shameful flow together and gain a following. Those, therefore, were first arrested who confessed their religion, and then on their evidence a vast multitude were condemned, not so much on the charge of incendiarism, as for their hatred towards the human race. And mockery was added to their death; for they were covered in the skins of wild beasts and were torn to death by dogs, or crucified, or set apart for burning, and after the close of the day were reserved for the purpose of nocturnal illumination. Nero lent his own gardens for the spectacle, and gave a chariot-race, mingling with the people in the costume of a charioteer, or driving among them in his chariot; by which conduct he raised a feeling of commiseration towards the sufferers, guilty though they were, and deserving of the extremest penalties, as though they were being exterminated, not for the public interests, but to gratify the savage cruelty of one man."

Such are the brief but deeply pathetic particulars which have come down to us respecting the first great persecution of the Christians, and such must have been the horrid events of which Seneca was a contemporary, and probably an actual eye-witness, in the very last year of his life. Profoundly as in all likelihood he must have despised the very name of Christian, a heart so naturally mild and humane as his must have shuddered at the monstrous cruelties devised against the unhappy votaries of this new religion. But to the relations of Christianity with the Pagan world we shall return in a subsequent chapter and we must now hasten to the end of our biography.

CHAPTER XIII

THE DEATH OF SENECA

The false charge which had been brought against Seneca, and in which the name of Piso had been involved, tended to urge that nobleman and his friends into a real and formidable conspiracy. Many men of influence and distinction joined in it, and among others Annaeus Lucanus, the celebrated poet-nephew of Seneca, and Fenius Rufus the colleague of Tigellinus in the command of the imperial guards. The plot was long discussed, and many were admitted into the secret, which was nevertheless marvellously well kept. One of the most eager conspirators was Subrius Flavus, an officer of the guards, who suggested the plan of stabbing Nero as he sang upon the stage, or of attacking him as he went about without guards at night in the galleries of his burning palace. Flavus is even said to have cherished the design of subsequently murdering Piso likewise, and of offering the imperial power to Seneca, with the full cognisance of the philosopher himself.[35] However this may have been—and the story has no probability—many schemes were discussed and rejected, from the difficulty of finding a man sufficiently bold and sufficiently in earnest to put his own life to such imminent risk. While things were still under discussion, the plot was nearly ruined by the information of Volusius Proculus, an admiral of the fleet, to whom it had been mentioned by a freedwoman of the name of Ephicharis. Although no sufficient evidence could be adduced against her, the conspirators thought it advisable to hasten matters, and one of them, a senator named Scaevinus, undertook the dangerous task of assassination. Plautius Lateranus, the cousul-elect, was to pretend to offer a petition, in which he was to embrace the Emperor's knees and throw him to the ground, and then Scaevinus was to deal the fatal blow. The theatrical conduct of Scaevinus—who took an antique dagger from the Temple of Safety, made his will, ordered the dagger to be sharpened, sat down to an unusually luxurious banquet, manumitted or made presents to his slaves, showed great agitation, and finally ordered ligaments for wounds to be prepared,—awoke the suspicions of one of his freedmen named Milichus, who hastened to claim a reward for revealing his suspicions. Confronted with Milichus, Scaevinus met and refuted his accusations with the greatest firmness; but when Milichus mentioned among other things that, the day before, Scaevinus had held a long and secret conversation with another friend of Piso named Natalis, and when Natalis, on being summoned, gave a very different account of the subject of this conversation from that which Scaevinus had given, they were both put in chains; and, unable to endure the threats and the sight of tortures, revealed the entire conspiracy. Natalis was the first to mentioned the name of Piso, and he added the hated name of Seneca, either because he had been the confidential messenger between the two, or because he knew that he could not do a greater favour to Nero than by giving him the opportunity of injuring a man whom he had long sought every possible opportunity to crush. Scaevinus, with equal weakness, perhaps because he thought that Natalis had left nothing to reveal, mentioned the names of the others, and among them of Lucan, whose complicity in the plot would undoubtedly tend to give greater probability to the supposed guilt of Seneca. Lucan, after long denying all knowledge of the design, corrupted by the promise of impunity, was guilty of the

---

[35] See Juv. Sat. viii. 212.

incredible baseness of making up for the slowness of his confession by its completeness, and of naming among the conspirators his chief friend Gallus and Pollio, and his own mother Atilla. The woman Ephicharis, slave though she had once been, alone showed the slightest constancy, and, by her brave unshaken reticence under the most excruciating and varied tortures, put to shame the pusillanimous treachery of senators and knights. On the second day, when, with limbs too dislocated to admit of her standing, she was again brought to the presence of her executioners, she succeeded, by a sudden movement, in strangling herself with her own girdle.

In the hurry and alarm of the moment the slightest show of resolution would have achieved the object of the conspiracy. Fenius Rufus had not yet been named among the conspirators, and as he sat by the side of the Emperor, and presided over the torture of his associates, Subrius Flavus made him a secret sign to inquire whether even then and there he should stab Nero. Rufus not only made a sign of dissent, but actually held the hand of Subrius as it was grasping the hilt of his sword. Perhaps it would have been better for him if he had not done so, for it was not likely that the numerous conspirators would long permit the same man to be at once their accomplice and the fiercest of their judges. Shortly afterwards, as he was urging and threatening, Scaevinus remarked, with a quiet smile, "that nobody knew more about the matter than he did himself, and that he had better show his gratitude to so excellent a prince by telling all he knew." The confusion and alarm of Rufus betrayed his consciousness of guilt; he was seized and bound on the spot, and subsequently put to death.

Meanwhile the friends of Piso were urging to take some bold and sudden step, which, if it did not succeed in retrieving his fortunes, would at least shed lustre on his death. But his somewhat slothful nature, weakened still further by a luxurious life, was not to be aroused, and he calmly awaited the end. It was customary among the Roman Emperors at this period to avoid the disgrace and danger of public executions by sending a messenger to a man's house, and ordering him to put himself to death by whatever means he preferred. Some raw recruits—for Nero dared not intrust any veterans with the duty—brought the mandate to Piso, who proceeded to make a will full of disgraceful adulation towards Nero, opened his veins, and died. Plautius Lateranus was not even allowed the poor privilege of choosing his own death, but, without time even to embrace his children, was hurried off to a place set apart for the punishment of slaves, and there died, without a word, by the sword of a tribune whom he knew to be one his own accomplices.

85

Lucan, in the prime of his life and the full bloom of his genius, was believed to have joined the plot from his indignation at the manner in which Nero's jealousy had repressed his poetic fame, and forbidden him the opportunity of public rectitations. He too opened his veins; and as he felt the deathful chill creeping upwards from the extremities of his limbs, he recited some verses from his own "Pharsalia," in which he had described the similar death of the soldier Lycidas. They were his last words. His mother Atilla, whom to his everlasting infamy, he had betrayed, was passed over as a victim too insignificant for notice, and was neither pardoned nor punished.

But, of all the many deaths which were brought about by this unhappy and ill-managed conspiracy, none caused more delight to Nero than that of Seneca, whom he was now able to dispatch by the sword, since he had been unable to do so by secret poison. What share Seneca really had in the conspiracy is unknown. If he were really cognisant of it, he must have acted with consummate tact, for no particle of convincing evidence was adduced against him. All that even Natalis could relate was, that when Piso had sent him to complain to Seneca of his not admitting Piso to more of his intercourse, Seneca had replied "that it was better for them both to hold aloof from each other, but that his own safety depended on that of Piso." A tribune was sent to ask Seneca as to the truth of this story, and found,—which was in itself regarded as a suspicious circumstance,—that on that very day he had returned from Campania to a villa four miles from the city. The tribune arrived in the evening, and surrounded the villa with soldiers. Seneca was at supper, with his wife Paulina and two friends. He entirely denied the truth of the evidence, and said that "the only reason which he had assigned to Piso for seeing so little of him was his weak health and love of retirement. Nero, who knew how little prone he was to flattery, might judge whether or no it was likely that he, a man of consular rank, would prefer the safety of a man of private station to his own." Such was the message which the tribune took back to Nero, whom he found sitting with his dearest and most detestable advisers, his wife Poppaea and his minister Tigellinus. Nero asked "whether Seneca was preparing a voluntary death." On the tribune replying that he showed no gloom or terror in his language or countenance, Nero ordered that he should at once be bidden to die. The message was taken, and Seneca, without any sign of alarm, quietly demanded leave to revise his will. This was refused him, and he then turned to his friends with the remark that, as he was unable to reward their merits as they had deserved, he would bequeath to them the only, and yet the most precious, possession left to him, namely, the example of his life, and if they were mindful of it they would win the reputation alike for integrity and for faithful friendship. At the same time he checked their tears, sometimes by his conversation, and sometimes with serious reproaches, asking them "where were their precepts of philosophy, and where the fortitude under trials which should have been learnt from the studies of many years? Did not every one know the cruelty of Nero? and what was left for him to do but to make an end of his master and tutor after the murder of his mother and his brother?" He then embraced his wife Paulina, and, with a slight faltering of his lofty sternness, begged and entreated her not to enter on an endless sorrow, but to endure the loss of her husband by the aid of those noble consolations which she must derive from the contemplation of his virtuous life. But Paulina declared that she would die with him, and Seneca, not opposing the deed which would win her such permanent glory, and at the same time unwilling to leave her to future wrongs, yielded to her wish. The veins of their arms were opened by the same blow; but the blood of Seneca, impoverished by old age and temperate living, flowed so slowly that it was necessary also to open the veins of his legs. This mode of death, chosen by the Romans as comparatively painless, is in fact under certain circumstances most agonizing. Worn out by these cruel tortures, and unwilling to weaken his wife's fortitude by so dreadful a spectacle, glad at the same time to spare himself the sight of her sufferings, he persuaded her to go to another room. Even then his eloquence did not fail. It is told of Andrè Chénier, the French poet, that on his way to execution he asked for writing materials to record some of the strange thoughts which filled his mind. The wish was denied him, but Seneca had ample liberty to record his last utterances. Amanuenses were summoned, who took down those dying admonitions, and in the time of Tacitus they still were extant. To us, however, this interesting memorial of a Pagan deathbed is irrevocably lost.

Nero, meanwhile, to whom the news of these circumstances was taken, having no dislike to Paulina, and unwilling to incur the odium of too much bloodshed, ordered her death to be prohibited and her wounds to be bound. She was already unconscious, but her slaves and freedmen succeeded in saving her life. She lived a few years longer, cherishing her husband's memory, and bearing in the attenuation of her frame, and the ghastly pallor of her countenance, the lasting proofs of that deep affection which had characterised their married life.

Seneca was not yet dead, and, to shorten these protracted and useless sufferings, he begged his friend and physician Statius

Annaeus to give him a draught of hemlock, the same poison by which the great philosopher of Athens had been put to death. But his limbs were already cold, and the draught proved fruitless. He then entered a bath of hot water, sprinkling the slaves who stood nearest to him, with the words that he was pouring a libation to Jupiter the Liberator.[36] Even the warm water failed to make the blood flow more speedily, and he was finally carried into one of those vapour baths which the Romans called sudatoria, and stifled with its steam. His body was burned privately, without any of the usual ceremonies. Such had been his own wish, expressed, not after the fall of his fortunes, but at a time when his thoughts had been directed to his latter end, in the zenith of his great wealth and conspicuous power.

So died a Pagan philosopher, whose life must always excite our interest and pity, although we cannot apply to him the titles of great or good. He was a man of high genius, of great susceptibility, of an ardent and generous temperament, of far-sighted and sincere humanity. Some of his sentiments are so remarkable for their moral beauty and profundity that they forcibly remind us of the expressions of St. Paul. But Seneca fell infinitely short of his own high standard, and has contemptuously been called "the father of all them that wear shovel hats." Inconsistency is written on the entire history of his life, and it has earned him the scathing contempt with which many writers have treated his memory. "The business of a philosopher," says Lord Macaulay, in his most scornful strain, "was to declaim in praise of poverty, with two millions sterling out at usury; to meditate epigrammatic conceits about the evils of luxury in gardens which moved the envy of sovereigns; to rant about liberty while fawning on the insolent and pampered freedmen of a tyrant; to celebrate the divine beauty of virtue with the same pen which had just before written a defence of the murder of a mother by a son." "Seneca," says Niebuhr, "was an accomplished man of the world, who occupied himself very much with virtue, and may have considered himself to be an ancient Stoic. He certainly believed that he was a most ingenious and virtuous philosopher; but he acted on the principle that, as far as he himself was concerned, he could dispense with the laws of morality which he laid down for others, and that he might give way to his natural propensities."

In Seneca's life, then, we see as clearly as in those of many professing Christians that it is impossible to be at once worldly and

---

[36] Sicco Polentone, an Italian, who wrote a Life of Seneca (d. 1461), makes Seneca a secret Christian, and represents this as an invocation of Christ, and says that he baptized himself with the water of the bath!

righteous. Seneca's utter failure was due to the vain attempt to combine in his own person two opposite characters—that of a Stoic and that of a courtier. Had he been a true philosopher, or a mere courtier, he would have been happier, and even more respected. To be both was absurd: hence, even in his writings, he was driven into inconsistency. He is often compelled to abandon the lofty utterances of Stoicism, and to charge philosophers with ignorance of life. In his treatise on a Happy Life he is obliged to introduce a sort of indirect autobiographical apology for his wealth and position.[37] In spite of his lofty pretensions to simplicity, in spite of that sort of amateur asceticism which, in common with other wealthy Romans, he occasionally practised, in spite of his final offer to abandon his entire patrimony to the Emperor, we fear that he cannot be acquitted of an almost insatiable avarice. We need not indeed believe the fierce calumnies which charged him with exhausting Italy by a boundless usury, and even stirring up a war in Britain by the severity of his exactions; but it is quite clear that he deserved the title of Proedives, "the over-wealthy," by which he has been so pointedly signalized. It is strange that the most splendid intellects should so often have sunk under the slavery of this meanest vice. In the Bible we read how the "rewards of divination" seduced from his allegiance to God the splendid enchanter of Mesopotamia:

"In outline dim and vast
　　Their fearful shadows cast
The giant form of Empires on their way
　　To ruin:—one by one
　　They tower and they are gone,
Yet in the prophet's soul the dreams of avarice stay.

"No sun or star so bright,
　　In all the world of light,
That they should draw to heaven his downward eye:
　　He hears the Almighty's word,
　　He sees the angel's sword,
Yet low upon the earth his heart and treasure lie."

And in Seneca we see some of the most glowing pictures of the nobility of poverty combined with the most questionable avidity in the pursuit of wealth. Yet how completely did he sell himself for naught. It is the lesson which we see in every conspicuously erring life, and it was illustrated less than three years afterwards in the

---

[37] See Ad. Polyb. 37: Ep. 75; De Vit. Beat. 17, 18, 22.

terrible fate of the tyrant who had driven him to death. For a short period of his life, indeed, Seneca was at the summit of power; yet, courtier as he was, he incurred the hatred, the suspicion, and the punishment of all the three Emperors during whose reigns his manhood was passed. "Of all unsuccessful men," says Mr. Froude, "in every shape, whether divine or human, or devilish, there is none equal to Bunyan's Mr. Facing-both-ways—the fellow with one eye on heaven and one on earth—who sincerely preaches one thing and sincerely does another, and from the intensity of his unreality is unable either to see or feel the contradiction. He is substantially trying to cheat both God and the devil, and is in reality only cheating himself and his neighbours. This of all characters upon the earth appears to us to be the one of which there is no hope at all, a character becoming in these days alarmingly abundant; and the aboundance of which makes us find even in a Reineke an inexpressible relief." And, in point of fact, the inconsistency of Seneca's life was a conscious inconsistency. "To the student," he says, "who professes his wish to rise to a loftier grade of virtue, I would answer that this is my wish also, but I dare not hope it. I am preoccupied with vices. All I require of myself is, not to be equal to the best, but only to be better than the bad." No doubt Seneca meant this to be understood merely for modest depreciation; but it was far truer than he would have liked seriously to confess. He must have often and deeply felt that he was not living in accordance with the light which was in him.

It would indeed be cheap and easy, to attribute the general inferiority and the many shortcomings of Seneca's life and character to the fact that he was a Pagan, and to suppose that if he had known Christianity he would necessarily have attained to a loftier ideal. But such a style of reasoning and inference, commonly as it is adopted for rhetorical purposes, might surely be refused by any intelligent child. A more intellectual assent to the lessons of Christianity would have probably been but of little avail to inspire in Seneca a nobler life. The fact is, that neither the gift of genius nor the knowledge of Christianity are adequate to the ennoblement of the human heart, nor does the grace of God flow through the channels of surpassing intellect or of orthodox belief. Men there have been in all ages, Pagan no less than Christian, who with scanty mental enlightenment and spiritual knowledge have yet lived holy and noble lives: men there have been in all ages, Christian no less than Pagan, who with consummate gifts and profound erudition have disgraced some of the noblest words which ever were uttered by some of the meanest lives which were ever lived. In the twelfth century was there any mind that shone more brightly, was there any eloquence which flowed more mightily, than that of Peter Abelard? Yet Abelard sank beneath the meanest of his scholastic cotemporaries in the degradation of his career as much as he towered above the highest of them in the grandeur of his genius. In the seventeenth century was there any philosopher more profound, any moralist more elevated, than Francis Bacon? Yet Bacon could flatter a tyrant, and betray a friend, and receive a bribe, and be one of the latest of English judges to adopt the brutal expedient of enforcing confession by the exercise of torture. If Seneca defended the murder of Agrippina, Bacon blackened the character of Essex. "What I would I do not; but the thing that I would not, that I do," might be the motto for many a confession of the sins of genius; and Seneca need not blush if we compare him with men who were his equals in intellectual power, but whose "means of grace," whose privileges, whose knowledge of the truth, were infinitely higher than his own. Let the noble constancy of his death shed a light over his memory which may dissipate something of those dark shades which rest on portions of his history. We think of Abelard, humble, silent, patient, God-fearing, tended by the kindly-hearted Peter in the peaceful gardens of Clugny; we think of Bacon, neglected, broken, and despised, dying of the chill caught in a philosophical experiment and leaving his memory to the judgment of posterity; let us think of Seneca, quietly yielding to his destiny without a murmur, cheering the constancy of the mourners round him during the long agonies of his enforced suicide and dictating some of the purest utterances of Pagan wisdom almost with his latest breath. The language of his great contemporary, the Apostle St. Paul, will best help us to understand his position. He was one of those who was seeking the Lord, if haply he might feel after Him, and find Him, though He be not far from every one of us: for in Him we live, and move, and have our being.

CHAPTER XIV

SENECA AND ST. PAUL

In the spring of the year 61, not long after the time when the murder of Agrippina, and Seneca's justifications of it, had been absorbing the attention of the Roman world, there disembarked at Puteoli a troop of prisoners, whom the Procurator of Judaea had sent to Rome under the charge of a centurion. Walking among them, chained and weary, but affectionately tended by two younger companions,[38] and treated with profound respect by little deputations of friends who met him at Appii Forum and the Three Taverns, was a man of mean presence and weather-beaten aspect, who was handed over like the rest to the charge of Burrus, the Praefect of the Praetorian Guards. Learning from the letters of the Jewish Procurator that the prisoner had been guilty of no serious offence,[39] but had used his privilege of Roman citizenship to appeal to Caesar for protection against the infuriated malice of his co-religionists—possibly also having heard from the centurion Julius some remarkable facts about his behaviour and history—Burrus allowed him, pending the hearing of his appeal, to live in his own hired apartments.[40] This lodging was in all probability in that quarter of the city opposite the island in the Tiber, which corresponds to the modern Trastevere. It was the resort of the very lowest and meanest of the populace—that promiscuous jumble of all nations which makes Tacitus call Rome at this time "the sewer of the universe." It was here especially that the Jews exercised some of the meanest trades in Rome, selling matches, and old clothes, and broken glass, or begging and fortune-telling on the Cestian or Fabrican bridges.[41] In one of these narrow, dark, and dirty streets, thronged by the dregs of the Roman populace, St. Mark and St. Peter had in all probability lived when they founded the little Christian Church at Rome. It was undoubtedly in the same despised locality that St. Paul,—the prisoner who had been consigned to the care of Burrus,—hired a room, sent for the principle Jews, and for two years taught to Jews and Christians, to any Pagans who would listen to him, the doctrines which were destined to regenerate the world.

Any one entering that mean and dingy room would have seen a Jew with bent body and furrowed countenance, and with every appearance of age, weakness, and disease chained by the arm to a Roman soldier. But it is impossible that, had they deigned to look

---

[38] Luke and Aristarchus.

[39] Acts xxiv. 23, xxvii. 3.

[40] Acts xxviii. 30, [Greek: en idio misthomati].

[41] MART. Ep. i. 42: JUV. xiv. 186. In these few paragraphs I follow M. Aubertin, who (as well as many other authors) has collected many of the principal passages in which Roman writers allude to the Jews and Christians.

closer, they should not also have seen the gleam of genius and enthusiasm, the fire of inspiration, the serene light of exalted hope and dauntless courage upon those withered features. And though he was chained, "the Word of God was not chained."[42] Had they listened to the words which he occasionally dictated, or overlooked the large handwriting which alone his weak eyesight and bodily infirmities, as well as the inconvenience of his chains, permitted, they would have heard or read the immortal utterances which strengthened the faith of the nascent and struggling Churches in Ephesus, Philippi, and Colossae, and which have since been treasured among the most inestimable possessions of a Christian world.

His efforts were not unsuccessful; his misfortunes were for the furtherance of the Gospel; his chains were manifest "in all the palace, and in all other places;"[43] and many waxing confident by his bonds were much more bold to speak the word without fear. Let us not be misled by assuming a wrong explanation of these words, or by adopting the Middle Age traditions which made St. Paul convert some of the immediate favourites of the Emperor, and electrify with his eloquence an admiring Senate. The word here rendered "palace"[44] may indeed have that meaning, for we know that among the early converts were "they of Caesar's household;"[45] but these were in all probability—if not certainly—Jews of the lowest rank, who were, as we know, to be found among the hundreds of unfortunates of every age and country who composed a Roman familia. And it is at least equally probable that the word "praetorium" simply means the barrack of that detachment of Roman soldiers from which Paul's gaolers were taken in turn. In such labours St. Paul in all probability spent two years (61-63), during which occurred the divorce of Octavia, the marriage with Poppaea, the death of Burrus, the disgrace of Seneca, and the many subsequent infamies of Nero.

It is out of such materials that some early Christian forger thought it edifying to compose the work which is supposed to contain the correspondence of Seneca and St. Paul. The undoubted spuriousness of that work is now universally admitted, and indeed the forgery is too clumsy to be even worth reading. But it is worth while inquiring whether in the circumstances of the time there is

---

[42] 2 Tim. ii. 9.
[43] Phil. i. 12.
[44] [Greek: en olo to praitorio].
[45] Phil. iv. 22.

even a bare possibility that Seneca should ever have been among the readers or the auditors of Paul.

And the answer is, There is absolutely no such probability. A vivid imagination is naturally attracted by the points of contrast and resemblance offered by two such characters, and we shall see that there is a singular likeness between many of their sentiments and expressions. But this was a period in which, as M. Villemain observes, "from one extremity of the social world to the other truths met each other without recognition." Stoicism, noble as were many of its precepts, lofty as was the morality it professed, deeply as it was imbued in many respects with a semi-Christian piety, looked upon Christianity with profound contempt. The Christians disliked the Stoics, the Stoics despised and persecuted the Christians. "The world knows nothing of its greatest men." Seneca would have stood aghast at the very notion of his receiving the lessons, still more of his adopting the religion, of a poor, accused, and wandering Jew. The haughty, wealthy, eloquent, prosperous, powerful philosopher would have smiled at the notion that any future ages would suspect him of having borrowed any of his polished and epigrammatic lessons of philosophic morals or religion from one whom, if he heard of him, he would have regarded as a poor wretch, half fanatic and half barbarian.

We learn from St. Paul himself that the early converts of Christianity were men in the very depths of poverty,[46] and that its preachers were regarded as fools, and weak, and were despised, and naked, and buffeted—persecuted and homeless labourers—a spectacle to the world, and to angels, and to men, "made as the filth of the earth and the off-scouring of all things." We know that their preaching was to the Greeks "foolishness," and that, when they spoke of Jesus and the resurrection, their hearers mocked[47] and jeered. And these indications are more than confirmed by many contemporary passages of ancient writers. We have already seen the violent expressions of hatred which the ardent and high-toned soul of Tacitus thought applicable to the Christians; and such language is echoed by Roman writers of every character and class. The fact is that at this time and for centuries afterwards the Romans regarded the Christians with such lordly indifference that—like Festus, and Felix and Seneca's brother Gallio—they never took the trouble to

---

[46] 2 Cor. viii. 2.
[47] [Greek: Echleuazon], Acts xvii. 32. The word expresses the most profound and unconcealed contempt.

distinguish them from the Jews. The distinction was not fully realized by the Pagan world till the cruel and wholesale massacre of the Christians by the pseudo-Messiah Barchochebas in the reign of Adrian opened their eyes to the fact of the irreconcilable differences which existed between the two religions. And pages might be filled with the ignorant and scornful allusions which the heathen applied to the Jews. They confused them with the whole degraded mass of Egyptian and Oriental impostors and brute-worshippers; they disdained them as seditious, turbulent, obstinate, and avaricious; they regarded them as mainly composed of the very meanest slaves out of the gross and abject multitude; their proselytism they considered as the clandestine initiation into some strange and revolting mystery, which involved as its direct teachings contempt of the gods, and the negation of all patriotism and all family affection; they firmly believed that they worshipped the head of an ass; they thought it natural that none but the vilest slaves and the silliest woman should adopt so misanthropic and degraded a superstition; they characterized their customs as "absurd, sordid, foul, and depraved," and their nation as "prone to superstition, opposed to religion."[48] And as far as they made any distinction between Jews and Christians, it was for the latter that they reserved their choicest and most concentrated epithets of hatred and abuse. A "new," "pernicious," "detestable," "execrable," superstition is the only language with which Suetonius and Tacitus vouchsafe to notice it. Seneca,—though he must have heard the name of Christian during the reign of Claudius (when both they and the Jews were expelled from Rome, "because of their perpetual turbulence, at the instigation of Chrestus," as Suetonius ignorantly observed), and during the Neronian persecution—never once alludes to them, and only mentions the Jews to apply a few contemptuous remarks to the idleness of their sabbaths, and to call them "a most abandoned race."

---

[48] Tac. Hist. i. 13: ib. v. 5: JUV. xiv. 85: Pers. v. 190, &c.
The reader will now judge whether there is the slightest probability that Seneca had any intercourse with St. Paul, or was likely to have stooped from his superfluity of wealth, and pride of power, to take lessons from obscure and despised slaves in the purlieus inhabited by the crowded households of Caesar or Narcissus.

CHAPTER XV

SENECA'S RESEMBLANCES TO SCRIPTURE

And yet in a very high sense of the word Seneca may be called, as he is called in the title of this book, a Seeker after God; and the resemblances to the sacred writings which may be found in the pages of his works are numerous and striking. A few of these will probably interest our readers, and will put them in a better position for understanding how large a measure of truth and enlightenment had rewarded the honest search of the ancient philosophers. We will place a few such passages side by side with the texts of Scripture which they resemble or recall.

1. *God's Indwelling Presence.*

"Know ye not that ye are the temple of God, and that the Spirit of God dwelleth in you?" asks St. Paul (1 Cor. iii. 16).

"God is near you, is with you, is within you," writes Seneca to his friend Lucilius, in the 41st of those Letters which abound in his most valuable moral reflections; "a sacred Spirit dwells within us, the observer and guardian of all our evil and our good ... there is no good man without God."

And again (Ep. 73): "Do you wonder that man goes to the gods? God comes to men: nay, what is yet nearer; He comes into men. No good mind is holy without God."

2. The Eye of God.

"All things are naked and opened unto the eyes of Him with whom we have to do." (Heb. iv. 13.)

"Pray to thy Father which is in secret; and thy Father which seeth in secret shall reward thee openly." (Matt. vi. 6.)

Seneca (On Providence, 1): *"It is no advantage that conscience is shut within us; we lie open to God."*

Letter 83: "What advantage is it that anything is hidden from man? Nothing is closed to God: He is present to our minds, and enters into our central thoughts."

Letter 83: "We must live as if we were living in sight of all men; we must think as though some one could and can gaze into our inmost breast."

3. *God is a Spirit.*

St. Paul, "We ought not to think that the God-head is like unto gold, or silver, or stone, graven by art and man's device." (Acts xvii. 29.)

Seneca *(Letter 31):* *"Even from a corner it is possible to spring up into heaven: rise, therefore, and form thyself into a fashion worthy of God; thou canst not do this, however, with gold and silver: an image like to God cannot be formed out of such materials as these."*

4. *Imitating God.*

"Be ye therefore followers ([Greek: mimaetai], imitators) of God, as dear children." (Eph. v. 1.)

"He that in these things [righteousness, peace, joy in the Holy Ghost] serveth Christ is acceptable to God." (Rom. xiv. 18.)

Seneca *(Letter 95):* *"Do you wish to render the gods propitious? Be virtuous. To honour them it is enough to imitate them."*

Letter 124: *"Let man aim at the good which belongs to him. What is this good? A mind reformed and pure, the imitator of God, raising itself above things human, confining all its desires within itself."*

5. *Hypocrites like whited Sepulchres.*

"Woe unto you, Scribes and Pharisees, hypocrites! for ye are like unto whited sepulchres, which indeed appear beautiful outward, but are within full of dead men's bones, and of all uncleanness." (Matt, xxiii. 27.)

Seneca: *"Those whom you regard as happy, if you saw them, not in their externals, but in their hidden aspect, are wretched, sordid, base; like their own walls adorned outwardly. It is no solid and genuine felicity; it is a plaster, and that a thin one; and so, as long as they can stand and be seen at their pleasure, they shine and impose on us: when anything has fallen which disturbs and uncovers them, it is evident how much deep and real foulness an extraneous splendour has concealed."*

6. *Teaching compared to Seed.*

"But other fell into good ground, and brought forth fruit; some an hundred-fold, some sixty-fold, some thirty-fold." (Matt xiii.8.)

Seneca *(Letter 38):* *"Words must be sown like seed; which, although it be small, when it hath found a suitable ground, unfolds its strength, and from very small size is expanded into the largest increase. Reason does the same.... The things spoken are few; but if the mind have received them well, they gain strength and grow."*

7. *All Men are Sinners.*

"If we say that we have no sin, we deceive ourselves and the truth is not in us." (1 John i. 8.)

Seneca *(On Anger, i. 14, ii. 27):* *"If we wish to be just judges of all things, let us first persuade ourselves of this:—that there is* not one of us without fault.... No man is found who can acquit himself; and he who calls himself innocent does so with reference to a witness, and not to his conscience."

8. *Avarice.*

"The love of money is the root of all evil." (1 Tim. vi. 10.)

Seneca (*On Tranquillity of Soul, 8*): *"Riches ... the greatest source of human trouble."*

"Be content with such things as ye have." (Heb. xiii. 5.)

"Having food and raiment, let us be therewith content." (1 Tim. vi. 8.)

Seneca (*Letter 114*): *"We shall be wise if we desire but little; if each man takes count of himself, and at the same time measures his own body, he will know how little it can contain, and for how short a time."*

Letter 110: *"We have polenta, we have water; let us challenge Jupiter himself to a comparison of bliss!"*

"Godliness with contentment is great gain." (1 Tim. vi. 6.)

Seneca (*Letter 110*): *"Why are you struck with wonder and astonishment? It is all display! Those things are shown, not possessed.... Turn thyself rather to the true riches, learn to be content with little."*

"It is easier for a camel to go through the eye of a needle, than for a rich man to enter into the kingdom of God." (Matt. xix. 24.)

Seneca (*Letter 20*): *"He is a high-souled man who sees riches spread around him, and hears rather than feels that they are his. It is much not to be corrupted by fellowship with riches: great is he who in the midst of wealth is poor, but safer he who has no wealth at all."*

9. *The Duty of Kindness.*

"Be kindly affectioned one to another with brotherly love." (Rom. xii. 10.)

Seneca (*On Anger, i. 5*): *"Man is born for mutual assistance."*

"Thou shalt love thy neighbour as thyself." (Lev. xiv. 18.)

Letter 48: "You must live for another, if you wish to live for yourself."

On Anger, iii. 43: "While we are among men let us cultivate kindness; let us not be to any man a cause either of peril or of fear."

10. *Our common Membership.*

"Ye are the body of Christ, and members in particular." (1 Cor. xii. 27.)

"We being many are one body in Christ, and every one members one of another." (Rom. xii. 5.)

Seneca (*Letter 95*): *"Do we teach that he should stretch his* hand to the shipwrecked, show his path to the wanderer, divide his bread with the hungry?... when I could briefly deliver to him the formula of human duty: all this that you see, in which things divine and human are included, is one: we are members of one great body."

11. *Secrecy in doing Good.*

"Let not thy left hand know what thy right hand doeth." (Matt.vi. 3.)

Seneca (On Benefits, ii. 11): "Let him who hath conferred a favour hold his tongue.... In conferring a favour nothing should be more avoided than pride."

12. *God's impartial Goodness.*

"He maketh His sun to rise on the evil and on the good, and sendeth rain on the just and on the unjust." (Matt. v. 45.)

Seneca *(On Benefits, i. 1): "How many are unworthy of the light! and yet the day dawns."*

Id. vii. 31: "The gods begin to confer benefits on those who recognize them not, they continue them to those who are thankless for them.... They distribute their blessings in impartial tenor through the nations and peoples;... they sprinkle the earth with timely showers, they stir the seas with wind, they mark out the seasons by the revolution of the constellations, they temper the winter and summer by the intervention of a gentler air."

It would be a needless task to continue these parallels, because by reading any treatise of Seneca a student might add to them by scores; and they prove incontestably that, as far as moral illumination was concerned, Seneca "was not far from the kingdom of heaven." They have been collected by several writers; and all of these here adduced, together with many others, may be found in the pages of Fleury, Troplong, Aubertin, and others. Some authors, like M. Fleury, have endeavoured to show that they can only be accounted for by the supposition that Seneca had some acquaintance with the sacred writings. M. Aubertin, on the other hand, has conclusively demonstrated that this could not have been the case. Many words and expressions detached from their context have been forced into a resemblance with the words of Scripture, when the context wholly militates against its spirit; many belong to that great common stock of moral truths which had been elaborated by the conscientious labours of ancient philosophers; and there is hardly one of the thoughts so eloquently enunciated which may not be found even more nobly and more distinctly expressed in the writings of Plato and of Cicero. In a subsequent chapter we shall show that, in spite of them all, the divergences of Seneca from the spirit of Christianity are at least as remarkable as the closest of his resemblances; but it will be more convenient to do this when we have also examined the doctrines of those two other great representatives of spiritual enlightenment in Pagan souls, Epictetus the slave and Marcus Aurelius the emperor.

Meanwhile, it is a matter for rejoicing that writings such as these give us a clear proof that in all ages the Spirit of the Lord has entered into holy men, and made them sons of God and prophets. God "left not Himself without witness" among them. The language of St. Thomas Aquinas, that many a heathen has had an "implicit faith," is but another way of expressing St. Paul's statement that "not having the law they were a law unto themselves, and showed the work of the law written in their hearts."[49] To them the Eternal Power and Godhead were known from the things that do appear, and alike from the voice of conscience and the voice of nature they derived a true, although a partial and inadequate, knowledge. To them "the voice of nature was the voice of God." Their revelation was the law of nature, which was confirmed, strengthened, and extended, but not suspended, by the written law of God.[50]

The knowledge thus derived, i.e. the sum-total of religious impressions resulting from the combination of reason and experience, has been called "natural religion;" the term is in itself a convenient and unobjectionable one, so long as it is remembered that natural religion is itself a revelation. No antithesis is so unfortunate and pernicious as that of natural with revealed religion. It is "a contrast rather of words than of ideas; it is an opposition of abstractions to which no facts really correspond." God has revealed Himself, not in one but in many ways, not only by inspiring the hearts of a few, but by vouchsafing His guidance to all who seek it. "The spirit of man is the candle of the Lord," and it is not religion but apostasy to deny the reality of any of God's revelations of truth to man, merely because they have not descended through a single channel. On the contrary, we ought to hail with gratitude, instead of viewing with suspicion, the enunciation by heathen writers of truths which we might at first sight have been disposed to regard as the special heritage of Christianity. In Pythagoras, and Socrates, and Plato,—in Seneca, Epictetus, and Marcus Aurelius—we see the light of heaven struggling its impeded way through clouds of darkness and ignorance; we thankfully recognize that the souls of men in the Pagan world, surrounded as they were by perplexities and dangers, were yet enabled to reflect, as from the dim surface of silver, some image of what was divine and true; we hail, with the great and

---

[49] Rom. i. 2.
[50] Hooker, Eccl. Pol. iii. 8.

eloquent Bossuet, "THE CHRISTIANITY OF NATURE." "The divine image in man," says St. Bernard, "may be burned, but it cannot be burnt out."

And this is the pleasantest side on which to consider the life and the writings of Seneca. It is true that his style partakes of the defects of his age, that the brilliancy of his rhetoric does not always compensate for the defectiveness of his reasoning; that he resembles, not a mirror which clearly reflects the truth, but "a glass fantastically cut into a thousand spangles;" that side by side with great moral truths we sometimes find his worst errors, contradictions, and paradoxes; that his eloquent utterances about God often degenerate into a vague Pantheism; and that even on the doctrine of immortality his hold is too slight to save him from waverings and contradictions;[51] yet as a moral teacher he is full of real greatness, and was often far in advance of the general opinion of his age. Few men have written more finely, or with more evident sincerity, about truth and courage, about the essential equality of man,[52] about the duty of kindness and consideration to slaves,[53] about tenderness even in dealing with sinners,[54] about the glory of unselfishness,[55] about the great idea of humanity[56] as something which transcends all the natural and artificial prejudices of country and of caste. Many of his writings are Pagan sermons and moral essays of the best and highest type. The style, as Quintilian says, "abounds in delightful faults," but the strain of sentiment is never otherwise than high and true.

He is to be regarded rather as a wealthy, eminent, and successful Roman, who devoted most of his leisure to moral philosophy, than as a real philosopher by habit and profession. And in this point of view his very inconsistencies have their charm, as illustrating his ardent, impulsive, imaginative temperament. He was no apathetic, self-contained, impassible Stoic, but a passionate, warm-hearted man, who could break into a flood of unrestrained tears at the death of his friend Annaeus Serenus,[57] and feel a trembling solicitude for the welfare of his wife and little ones. His was no absolute renunciation, no impossible perfection;[58] but few

---

[51] Consol. ad Polyb. 27; Ad Helv. 17; Ad Marc. 24, seqq
[52] Ep. 32; De Benef. iii. 2.
[53] De Irâ, iii. 29, 32.
[54] Ibid. i. 14; De Vit. beat. 24.
[55] Ep. 55, 9.
[56] Ibid. 28; De Oti Sapientis, 31.
[57] Ep. 63.
[58] Martha, Les Moralistes, p. 61.

men have painted more persuasively, with deeper emotion, or more entire conviction, the pleasures of virtue, the calm of a well-regulated soul, the strong and severe joys of a lofty self-denial. In his youth, he tells us, he was preparing himself for a righteous life, in his old age for a noble death.[59] And let us not forget, that when the hour of crisis came which tested the real calm and bravery of his soul, he was not found wanting. "With no dread," he writes to Lucilius, "I am preparing myself for that day on which, laying aside all artifice or subterfuge, I shall be able to judge respecting myself whether I merely speak or really feel as a brave man should; whether all those words of haughty obstinacy which I have hurled against fortune were mere pretence and pantomime.... Disputations and literary talks, and words collected from the precepts of philosophers, and eloquent discourse, do not prove the true strength of the soul. For the mere speech of even the most cowardly is bold; what you have really achieved will then be manifest when your end is near. I accept the terms, I do not shrink from the decision."[60]

"Accipio conditionem, non reformido judicrum." They were courageous and noble words, and they were justified in the hour of trial. When we remember the sins of Seneca's life, let us recall also the constancy of his death; while we admit the inconsistencies of his systematic philosophy, let us be grateful for the genius, the enthusiasm, the glow of intense conviction, with which he clothes his repeated utterance of truths, which, when based upon a surer basis, were found adequate for the moral regeneration of the world. Nothing is more easy than to sneer at Seneca, or to write clever epigrams on one whose moral attainments fell infinitely short of his own great ideal. But after all he was not more inconsistent than thousands of those who condemn him. With all his faults he yet lived a nobler and a better life, he had loftier aims, he was braver, more self-denying—nay, even more consistent—than the majority of professing Christians. It would be well for us all if those who pour such scorn upon his memory attempted to achieve one tithe of the good which he achieved for humanity and for Rome. His thoughts deserve our imperishable gratitude: let him who is without sin among us be eager to fling stones at his failures and his sins!

---

[59] Ep. 61.
[60] Ep. 26.

EPICTETUS

CHAPTER I

THE LIFE OF EPICTETUS, AND HOW HE REGARDED IT

In the court of Nero, Seneca must have been thrown into more or less communication with the powerful freedmen of that Emperor, and especially with his secretary or librarian, Epaphroditus. Epaphroditus was a constant companion of the Emperor; he was the earliest to draw Nero's attention to the conspiracy in which Seneca himself perished. There can be no doubt that Seneca knew him, and had visited at his house. Among the slaves who thronged that house, the natural kindliness of the philosopher's heart may have drawn his attentions to one little lame Phrygian boy, deformed and mean-looking, whose face—if it were any index of the mind within—must even from boyhood have worn a serene and patient look. The great courtier, the great tutor of the Emperor, the great Stoic and favourite writer of his age, would indeed have been astonished if he had been suddenly told that that wretched-looking little slave-lad was destined to attain purer and clearer heights of philosophy than he himself had ever done, and to become quite as illustrious as himself, and far more respected as an exponent of Stoic doctrines. For that lame boy was Epictetus—Epictetus for whom was written the memorable epitaph: "I was Epictetus, a slave, and maimed in body, and a beggar for poverty, and dear to the immortals."

Although we have a clear sketch of his philosophical doctrines, we have no materials whatever for any but the most meagre description of his life. The picture of his mind—an effigy of that which he alone regarded as his true self—may be seen in his works, and to this we can add little except a few general facts and uncertain anecdotes.

Epictetus was probably born in about the fiftieth year of the Christian era; but we do not know the exact date of his birth, nor do we even know his real name. "Epictetus" means "bought" or "acquired," and is simply a servile designation. He was born at Hierapolis, in Phrygia, a town between the rivers Lycus and

Meander, and considered by some to be the capital of the province. The town possessed several natural wonders—sacred springs, stalactite grottoes, and a deep cavern remarkable for its mephitic exhalations. It is more interesting to us to know that it was within a few miles of Colossae and Laodicea, and is mentioned by St. Paul (Col. iv. 13) in connexion with those two cities. It must, therefore, have possessed a Christian Church from the earliest times, and, if Epictetus spent any part of his boyhood there, he might have conversed with men and women of humble rank who had heard read in their obscure place of meeting the Epistle of St. Paul to the Colossians, and the other, now lost, which he addressed to the Church of Laodicea.[61]

It is probable, however, that Hierapolis and its associations produced very little influence on the mind of Epictetus. His parents were people in the very lowest and humblest class, and their moral character could hardly have been high, or they would not have consented under any circumstance to sell into slavery their sickly child. Certainly it could hardly have been possible for Epictetus to enter into the world under less enviable or less promising auspices. But the whole system of life is full of divine and memorable compensations, and Epictetus experienced them. God kindles the light of genius where He will, and He can inspire the highest and most regal thoughts even into the meanest slave:—

> "Such seeds are scattered night and day
>   By the soft wind from Heaven,
> And in the poorest human clay
>   Have taken root and thriven."

What were the accidents—or rather, what was "the unseen Providence, by man nicknamed chance"—which assigned Epictetus to the house of Epaphroditus we do not know. To a heart refined and noble there could hardly have been a more trying position. The slaves of a Roman familia were crowded together in immense gangs; they were liable to the most violent and capricious punishments; they might be subjected to the most degraded and brutalising influences. Men sink too often to the level to which they are supposed to belong. Treated with infamy for long years, they are apt to deem themselves worthy of infamy—to lose that self-respect which is the invariable concomitant of religious feeling, and which, apart from religious feeling, is the sole preventive of personal degradation. Well may St. Paul say, "Art thou called, being a

---

[61] Col. iv. 16.

servant? care not for it: but if thou mayest be made free, use it rather."[62]

It is true that even in the heathen world there began at this time to be disseminated among the best and wisest thinkers a sense that slaves were made of the same clay as their masters, that they differed from freeborn men only in the externals and accidents of their position, and that kindness to them and consideration for their difficulties was a common and elementary duty of humanity. "I am glad to learn," says Seneca, in one of his interesting letters to Lucilius, "that you live on terms of familiarity with your slaves; it becomes your prudence and your erudition. Are they slaves? Nay, they are men. Slaves? Nay, companions. Slaves? Nay, humble friends. Slaves? Nay, fellow-slaves, if you but consider that fortune has power over you both." He proceeds, in a passage to which we have already alluded, to reprobate the haughty and inconsiderate fashion of keeping them standing for hours, mute and fasting, while their masters gorged themselves at the banquet. He deplores the cruelty which thinks it necessary to punish with terrible severity an accidental cough or sneeze. He quotes the proverb—a proverb which reveals a whole history—"So many slaves, so many foes," and proves that they are not foes, but that men made them so; whereas, when kindly treated, when considerately addressed, they would be silent, even under torture, rather than speak to their master's disadvantage. "Are they not sprung," he asks, "from the same origin, do they not breathe the same air, do they not live and die just as we do?" The blows, the broken limbs, the clanking chains, the stinted food of the ergastula or slave-prisons, excited all Seneca's compassion, and in all probability presented a picture of misery which the world has rarely seen surpassed, unless it were in that nefarious trade which England to her shame once practised, and, to her eternal glory, resolutely swept away.

But Seneca's inculcation of tenderness towards slaves was in reality one of the most original of his moral teachings; and, from all that we know of Roman life, it is to be feared that the number of those who acted in accordance with it was small. Certainly Epaphroditus, the master of Epictetus, was not one of them. The historical facts which we know of this man are slight. He was one of the four who accompanied the tragic and despicable flight of Nero from Rome in the year 69, and when, after many waverings of cowardice, Nero at last, under imminent peril of being captured and executed, put the dagger to his breast, it was Epaphroditus who helped the tyrant to drive it home into his heart, for which he was

---

[62] 1 Cor. vii. 21.

subsequently banished, and finally executed by the Emperor Domitian.

Epictetus was accustomed to tell one or two anecdotes which, although given without comment, show the narrowness and vulgarity of the man. Among his slaves was a certain worthless cobbler named Felicio; as the cobbler was quite useless, Epaphroditus sold him, and by some chance he was bought by some one of Caesar's household, and made Caesar's cobbler. Instantly Epaphroditus began to pay him the profoundest respect, and to address him in the most endearing terms, so that if any one asked what Epaphroditus was doing, the answer, as likely as not, would be, "He is holding an important consultation with Felicio."

On one occasion, some one came to him bewailing, and weeping, and embracing his knees in a paroxysm of grief, because of all his fortune little more than 50,000l. was left! "What did Epaphroditus do?" asks Epictetus; "did he laugh at the man as we did? Not at all; on the contrary, he exclaimed, in a tone of commiseration and surprise, 'Poor fellow! how could you possibly keep silence and endure such a misfortune?'"

How brutally he could behave, and how little respect he inspired, we may see in the following anecdote. When Plautius Lateranus, the brave nobleman whose execution during Piso's conspiracy we have already related, had received on his neck an ineffectual blow of the tribune's sword, Epaphroditus, even at that dread moment, could not abstain from pressing him with questions. The only reply which he received from the dying man was the contemptuous remark, "Should I wish to say anything, I will say it (not to a slave like you, but) to your master."

Under a man of this calibre it is hardly likely that a lame Phrygian boy would experience much kindness. An anecdote, indeed, has been handed down to us by several writers, which would show that he was treated with atrocious cruelty. Epaphroditus, it is said, once gratified his cruelty by twisting his slave's leg in some instrument of torture. "If you go on, you will break it," said Epictetus. The wretch did go on, and did break it. "I told you that you would break it," said Epictetus quietly, not giving vent to his anguish by a single word or a single groan. Stories of heroism no less triumphant have been authenticated both in ancient and modern times; but we may hope for the sake of human nature that this story is false, since another authority tells us that Epictetus became lame in consequence of a natural disease. Be that however as it may, some of the early writers against Christianity—such, for instance, as the physician Celsus—were fond of adducing this anecdote in proof of a magnanimity which not even Christianity

106

could surpass; to which use of the anecdote Origen opposed the awful silence of our Saviour upon the cross, and Gregory of Nazianzen pointed out that, though it was a noble thing to endure inevitable evils, it was yet more noble to undergo them voluntarily with an equal fortitude. But even if Epaphroditus were not guilty of breaking the leg of Epictetus, it is clear that the life of the poor youth was surrounded by circumstances of the most depressing and miserable character; circumstances which would have forced an ordinary man to the low and animal level of existence which appears to have contented the great majority of Roman slaves. Some of the passages in which he speaks about the consideration due to this unhappy class show a very tender feeling towards them. "It would be best," he says, "if, both while making your preparations and while feasting at your banquets, you distribute among the attendants some of the provisions. But if such a plan, at any particular time, be difficult to carry out, remember that you who are not fatigued are being waited upon by those who are fatigued; you who are eating and drinking by those who are not eating and drinking; you who are conversing by those who are mute—you who are at your ease by people under painful constraint. And thus you will neither yourself be kindled into unseemly passion, nor will you in a fit of fury do harm to any one else." No doubt Epictetus is here describing conduct which he had often seen, and of which he had himself experienced the degradation. But he had early acquired a loftiness of soul and an insight into truth which enabled him to distinguish the substance from the shadow, to separate the realities of life from its accidents, and so to turn his very misfortunes into fresh means of attaining to moral nobility. In proof of this let us see some of his own opinions as to his state of life.

At the very beginning of his Discourses he draws a distinction between the things which the gods have and the things which they have not put in our own power, and he held (being deficient here in that light which Christianity might have furnished to him) that the blessings denied to us are denied not because the gods would not, but because they could not grant them to us. And then he supposes that Jupiter addresses him:—

"O Epictetus, had it been possible, I would have made both your little body and your little property free and unentangled; but now, do not be mistaken, it is not yours at all, but only clay finely kneaded. Since, however, I could not do this, I gave you a portion of ourselves, namely, this power of pursuing and avoiding, of desiring and of declining, and generally the power of dealing with appearances: and if you cultivate this power, and regard it as that which constitutes your real possession, you will never be hindered or impeded, nor will you groan or find fault with, or flatter any one. Do these advantages then appear to you to be trifling? Heaven forbid! Be content therefore with these, and thank the gods."

And again in one of his Fragments (viii. ix.):—

"Freedom and slavery are but names, respectively, of virtue and of vice: and both of them depend upon the will. But neither of them have anything to do with those things in which the will has no share. For no one is a slave whose will is free."

"Fortune is an evil bond of the body, vice of the soul; for he is a slave whose body is free but whose soul is bound, and, on the contrary, he is free whose body is bound but whose soul is free."

Who does not catch in these passages the very tone of St, Paul when he says, "He that is called in the Lord, being a servant, is the Lord's freeman: likewise also he that is called, being free, is Christ's servant?"

Nor is his independence less clearly express when he speaks of his deformity. Being but the deformity of a body which he despised, he spoke of himself as "an ethereal existence staggering under the burden of a corpse." In his admirable chapter on Contentment, he very forcibly lays down that topic of consolation which is derived from the sense that "the universe is not made for our individual satisfaction." "Must my leg be lame?" he supposes some querulous objector to inquire. "Slave!" he replies, "do you then because of one miserable little leg find fault with the universe? Will you not concede that accident to the existence of general laws? Will you not dismiss the thought of it? Will you not cheerfully assent to it for the sake of him who gave it. And will you be indignant and displeased at the ordinances of Zeus, which he ordained and appointed with the Destinies, who were present and wove the web of your being? Know you not what an atom you are compared with the whole?—that is, as regards your body, since as regards your reason you are no whit inferior to, or less than the gods. For the greatness of reason is not estimated by size or height, but by the doctrines which it embraces. Will you not then lay up your treasure in those matters wherein you are equal to the gods?" And, thanks to such principles, a poor and persecuted slave was able to raise his voice in sincere and eloquent thanksgiving to that God to whom he owed his "creation, preservation, and all the blessings of this life."

Speaking of the multitude of our natural gifts, he says, "Are these the only gifts of Providence towards us? Nay, what power of speech suffices adequately to praise, or to set them forth? for, had we but true intelligence, what duty would be more perpetually incumbent on us than both in public and in private to hymn the Divine, and bless His name and praise His benefits? Ought we not, when we dig, and when we plough, and when we eat, to sing this hymn to God? 'Great is God, because He hath given us these implements whereby we may till the soil; great is God, because He hath given us hands, and the means of nourishment by food, and insensible growth, and breathing sleep;' these things in each particular we ought to hymn, and to chant the greatest and the divinest hymn, because He hath given us the power to appreciate these blessings, and continuously to use them. What then? Since the most of you are blinded, ought there not to be some one to fulfil this province for you, and on behalf of all to sing his hymn to God? And what else can I do, who am a lame old man, except sing praises to God? Now, had I been a nightingale, I should have sung the songs of a nightingale, or had I been a swan the songs of a swan; but, being a reasonable being, it is my duty to hymn God. This is my task, and I accomplish it; nor, so far as may be granted to me, will I ever abandon this post, and you also do I exhort to this same song."

There is an almost lyric beauty about these expressions of resignation and faith in God, and it is the utterance of such warm feelings towards Divine Providence that constitutes the chief originality of Epictetus. It is interesting to think that the oppressed heathen philosopher found the same consolation, and enjoyed the same contentment, as the persecuted Christian Apostle. "Whether ye eat or drink," says St. Paul, "or whatsoever ye do, do all to the glory of God." "Think of God," says Epictetus, "oftener than you breathe. Let discourse of God be renewed daily more surely than your food."

Here, again, are his views about his poverty (Fragment xix.):—

"Examine yourself whether you wish to be rich or to be happy; and if you wish to be rich, know that it neither is a blessing, nor is it altogether in your own power; but if to be happy, know that it both is a blessing, and is in your own power; since the former is but a temporary loan of fortune, but the gift of happiness depends upon the will."

"Just as when you see a viper, or an asp, or a scorpion, in a casket of ivory or gold, you do not love or congratulate them on the splendour of their material, but because their nature is pernicious you turn from and loathe them, so likewise when you see vice enshrined in wealth and the pomp of circumstance do not be astounded at the glory of its surroundings, but despise the meanness of its character."

"Wealth is not among the number of good things; extravagance is among the number of evils, sober-mindedness of good things. Now sober-mindedness invites us to frugality and the acquisition of real advantages; but wealth to extravagance, and it drags us away from sober-mindedness. It is a hard matter, therefore, being rich to be sober-minded, or being sober-minded to be rich."

The last sentence will forcibly remind the reader of our Lord's own words, "How hardly shall they that have riches (or as the parallel passage less startlingly expresses it, 'Children, how hard is it for them that trust in riches to') enter into the kingdom of God."

But this is a favourite subject with the ancient philosopher, and Epictetus continues:—

"Had you been born in Persia, you would not have been eager to live in Greece, but to stay where you were, and be happy; and, being born in poverty, why are you eager to be rich, and not rather to abide in poverty, and so be happy?"

"As it is better to be in good health, being hard-pressed on a little truckle-bed, than to roll, and to be ill in some broad couch; so too it is better in a small competence to enjoy the calm of moderate desires, than in the midst of superfluities to be discontented."

This, too, is a thought which many have expressed. "Gentle sleep," says Horace, "despises not the humble cottages of rustics, nor the shaded banks, nor valleys whose foliage waves with the western wind;" and every reader will recall the magnificent words of our own great Shakespeare—

> "Why rather, Sleep, liest thou in smoky cribs,
> Upon uneasy pallets stretching thee,
> And hush'd with buzzing night-flies to thy slumber,
> Than in the perfumed chambers of the great,
> Under the canopies of costly state,
> And lull'd with sounds of sweetest melody?"

To the subject of freedom, and to the power which man possesses to make himself entirely independent of all surrounding circumstances, Epictetus incessantly recurs. With the possibility of banishment to an ergastulum perpetually before his eyes, he defines a prison as being any situation in which a man is placed against his will; to Socrates for instance the prison was no prison, for he was there willingly, and no man need be in prison, against his will if he has learnt, as one of his primary duties, a cheerful acquiescence in the inevitable. By the expression of such sentiments Epictetus had anticipated by fifteen hundred years the immortal truth so sweetly expressed by Lovelace:

> "Stone walls do not a prison make,
>   Nor iron bars a cage;

110

> Minds innocent and quiet take
> That for a hermitage."

Situated as he was, we can hardly wonder that thoughts like these occupied a large share of the mind of Epictetus, or that he had taught himself to lay hold of them with the firmest possible grasp. When asked, "Who among men is rich?" he replied, "He who suffices for himself;" an expression which contains the germ of the truth so forcibly expressed in the Book of Proverbs, "The backslider in heart shall be filled with his own ways, and a good man shall be satisfied from himself". Similarly, when asked, "Who is free?" he replies, "The man who masters his own self," with much the same tone of expressions as that of Solomon, "He that is slow to anger is better than the mighty, and he that ruleth his spirit than he that taketh a city." Socrates was one of the great models whom Epictetus constantly seats before him, and this is one of the anecdotes which he relates about him with admiration. When Archelaus sent a message to express the intention of making him rich, Socrates bade the messenger inform him that at Athens four quarts of meal might be bought for three halfpence, and the fountains flow with water. "If then my existing possessions are insufficient for me, at any rate I am sufficient for them, and so they too are sufficient for me. Do you not see that Polus acted the part of Oedipus in his royal state with no less beauty of voice than that of Oedipus in Colonos, a wanderer and beggar? Shall then a noble man appear inferior to Polus, so as not to act well every character imposed upon him by Divine Providence; and shall he not imitate Ulysses, who even in rags was no less conspicuous than in the curled nap of his purple cloak?"

Generally speaking, the view which Epictetus took of life is always simple, and always consistent; it is a view which gave him consolation among life's troubles, and strength to display some of its noblest virtues, and it may be summed up in the following passages of his famous Manual:—

"Remember," he says, "that you are an actor of just such a part as is assigned you by the Poet of the play; of a short part, if the part be short; of a long part, if it be long. Should He wish you to act the part of a beggar, take care to act it naturally and nobly; and the same if it be the part of a lame man, or a ruler, or a private man; for this is in your power, to act well the part assigned to you; but to choose that part is the function of another."

"Let not these considerations afflict you: 'I shall live despised, and the merest nobody;' for if dishonour be an evil, you cannot be involved in evil any more than you can be involved in baseness through any one else's means. Is it then at all your business to be a

111

leading man, or to be entertained at a banquet? By no means. How then can it be a dishonor not to be so? And how will you be a mere nobody, since it is your duty to be somebody only in those circumstances which are in your own power, in which you may be a person of the greatest importance?"

"Honour, precedence, confidence," he argues in another passage, "whether they be good things or evil things, are at any rate things for which their own definite price must be paid. Lettuces are sold for a penny, and if you want your lettuce you must pay your penny; and similarly, if you want to be asked out to a person's house, you must pay the price which he demands for asking people, whether the coin he requires be praise or attention; but if you do not give these, do not expect the other. Have you then gained nothing in lieu of your supper? Indeed you have; you have escaped praising a person whom you did not want to praise, and you have escaped the necessity of tolerating the upstart impertinence of his menials."

Some parts of this last thought have been so beautifully expressed by the American poet Lowell that I will conclude this chapter in his words:

"Earth hath her price for what earth gives us;
    The beggar is tax'd for a corner to die in;
The priest hath his fee who comes and shrieves us;
    We bargain for the graves we lie in:
At the devil's mart are all things sold,
Each ounce of dross costs its ounce of gold,
For a cap and bells our lives we pay.
    Bubbles we earn with our whole soul's tasking,
'Tis only God that is given away,
    'Tis only heaven may be had for the asking."

CHAPTER II

LIFE AND VIEWS OF EPICTETUS (continued)

Whether any of these great thoughts would have suggested themselves spontaneously to Epictetus—whether there was an inborn wisdom and nobleness in the mind of this slave which would have enabled him to elaborate such views from his own consciousness, we cannot tell; they do not, however, express his sentiments only, but belong in fact to the moral teaching of the great Stoic school, in the doctrines of which he had received instruction.

It may sound strange to the reader that one situated as Epictetus was should yet have had a regular tutor to train him in Stoic doctrines. That such should have been the case appears at first sight inconsistent with the cruelty with which he was treated, but it is a fact which is capable of easy explanation. In times of universal luxury and display—in times when a sort of surface-refinement is found among all the wealthy—some sort of respect is always paid to intellectual eminence, and intellectual amusements are cultivated as well as those of a coarser character. Hence a rich Roman liked to have people of literary culture among his slaves; he liked to have people at hand who would get him any information which he might desire about books, who could act as his amanuenses, who could even correct and supply information for his original compositions. Such learned slaves formed part of every large establishment, and among them were usually to be found some who bore, if they did not particularly merit, the title of "philosophers." These men—many of whom are described as having been mere impostors, ostentatious pedants, or ignorant hypocrites—acted somewhat like domestic chaplains in the houses of their patrons. They gratified an amateur taste for wisdom, and helped to while away in comparative innocence the hours which their masters might otherwise have spent in lassitude or sleep. It was no more to the credit of Epaphroditus that he wished to have a philosophic slave, than it is to the credit of an illiterate millionaire in modern times that he likes to have works of high art in his drawing-room, and books of reference in his well-furnished library.

Accordingly, since Epictetus must have been singularly useless for all physical purposes, and since his thoughtfulness and intelligence could not fail to command attention, his master determined to make him useful in the only way possible, and sent him to Caius Musonius Rufus to be trained in the doctrines of the Stoic philosophy.

Musonius was the son of a Roman knight. His learning and eloquence, no less than his keen appreciation of Stoic truths, had so deeply kindled the suspicions of Nero, that he banished him to the rocky little island of Gyaros, on the charge of his having been concerned in Piso's conspiracy. He returned to Rome after the suicide of Nero, and lived in great distinction and respect, so that he was allowed to remain in the city when the Emperor Vespasian banished all the other philosophers of any eminence.

The works of Musonius have not come down to us, but a few notices of him, which are scattered in the Discourses of his greater pupil, show us what kind of man he was. The following anecdotes will show that he was a philosopher of the strictest school.

Speaking of the value of logic as a means of training the reason, Epictetus anticipates the objection that, after all, a mere error in reasoning is no very serious fault. He points out that it is a fault, and that is sufficient. "I too," he says, "once made this very remark to Rufus when he rebuked me for not discovering the suppressed premiss in some syllogism. 'What!' said I, 'have I then set the Capitol on fire, that you rebuke me thus?' 'Slave!' he answered, 'what has the Capitol to do with it? Is there no other fault then short of setting the Capitol on fire? Yes! to use one's own mere fancies rashly, at random, anyhow; not to follow an argument, or a demonstration, or a sophism; not, in short, to see what makes for oneself or not, in questioning and answering—is none of these things a fault?'"

Sometimes he used to test the Stoical endurance of his pupil by pointing out the indignities and tortures which his master might at any moment inflict upon him; and when Epictetus answered that, after all, such treatment was what man had borne, and therefore could bear, he would reply approvingly that every man's destiny was in his own hands; that he need lack nothing from any one else; that, since he could derive from himself magnanimity and nobility of soul, he might despise the notion of receiving lands or money or office. "But," he continued, "when any one is cowardly or mean, one ought obviously in writing letters about such a person to speak of him as a corpse, and to say, 'Favour us with the corpse and blood of So-and-so,' For? in fact, such a man is a mere corpse, and nothing more; for if he were anything more, he would have perceived that no man ever suffers any real misfortunes by another's means." I do not know whether Mr. Ruskin is a student of Epictetus, but he, among others, has forcibly expressed the same truth. "My friends, do you remember that old Scythian custom, when the head of a house died? How he was dressed in his finest dress, and set in his chariot, and carried about to his friends' houses; and each of them placed him at his table's head, and all feasted in his presence? Suppose it were offered to you, in plain words, as it is offered to you in dire facts, that you should gain this Scythian honour gradually, while you yet thought yourself alive.... Would you take the offer verbally made by the death-angel? Would the meanest among us take it, think you?

114

Yet practically and verily we grasp at it, every one of us, in a measure; many of us grasp at it in the fulness of horror."

The way in which Musonius treated would-be pupils much resembled the plan adopted by Socrates. "It is not easy," says Epictetus, "to train effeminate youths, any more than it is easy to take up whey with a hook. But those of fine nature, even if you discourage them, desire instruction all the more. For which reason Rufus often discouraged pupils, using this as a criterion of fine and of common natures; for he used to say, that just as a stone, even if you fling it into the air, will fall down to the earth by its own gravitating force, so also a noble nature, in proportion as it is repulsed, in that proportion tends more in its own natural direction." As Emerson says,—

> "Yet on the nimble air benign
> Speed nimbler messages,
> That waft the breath of grace divine
> To hearts in sloth and ease.
> So nigh is grandeur to our dust,
>   So near is God to man,
> When Duty whispers low, 'THOU MUST,'
>   The youth replies, 'I CAN.'"

One more trait of the character of Musonius will show how deeply Epictetus respected him, and how much good he derived from him. In his Discourse on Ostentation, Epictetus says that Rufus was in the habit of remarking to his pupils, "If you have leisure to praise me, I can have done you no good." "He used indeed so to address us that each one of us, sitting there, thought that some one had been privately telling tales against him in particular, so completely did Rufus seize hold of his characteristics, so vividly did he portray our individual faults."

Such was the man under whose teaching Epictetus grew to maturity, and it was evidently a teaching which was wise and noble, even if it were somewhat chilling and austere. It formed an epoch in the slave's life; it remoulded his entire character; it was to him the source of blessings so inestimable in their value that it is doubtful whether they were counter-balanced by all the miseries of poverty, slavery, and contempt. He would probably have admitted that it was better for him to have been sold into cruel slavery, than it would have been to grow up in freedom, obscurity, and ignorance in his native Hierapolis. So that Epictetus might have found, and did find, in his own person, an additional argument in favour of Divine Providence: an additional proof that God is kind and merciful to all men; an additional intensity of conviction that, if our lots on earth are not equal, they are at least dominated by a principle of justice and of wisdom, and each man, on the whole, may gain that which is best for him, and that which most honestly and most heartily he desires. Epictetus reminds us again and again that we may have many, if not all, such advantages as the world has to offer, if we are willing to pay the price by which they are obtained. But if that price be a mean or a wicked one, and if we should scorn ourselves were we ever tempted to pay it, then we must not even cast one longing look of regret towards things which can only be got by that which we deliberately refuse to give. Every good and just man may gain, if not happiness, then something higher than happiness. Let no one regard this as a mere phrase, for it is capable of a most distinct and definite meaning. There are certain things which all men desire, and which all men would gladly, if they could lawfully and innocently obtain. These things are health, wealth, ease, comfort, influence, honour, freedom from opposition and from pain; and yet, if you were to place all these blessings on the one side, and on the other side to place poverty, and disease, and anguish, and trouble, and contempt,—yet, if on this side also you were to place truth and justice, and a sense that, however densely the clouds may gather about our life, the light of God will be visible beyond them, all the noblest men who ever lived would choose, as without hesitation they always have chosen, the latter destiny. It is not that they like failure, but they prefer failure to falsity; it is not that they love persecution, but they prefer persecution to meanness; it is not that they relish opposition, but they welcome opposition rather than guilty acquiescence; it is not that they do not shrink from agony, but they would not escape agony by crime. The selfishness of Dives in his purple is to them less enviable than the innocence of Lazarus in rags; they would be chained with John in prison rather than loll with Herod at the feast; they would fight with beasts with Paul in the arena rather than be steeped in the foul luxury of Nero on the throne. It is not happiness, but it is something higher than happiness; it is stillness, it is assurance, it is satisfaction, it is peace; the world can neither understand it, nor give it, nor take it away,—it is something indescribable—it is the gift of God.

"The fallacy" of being surprised at wickedness in prosperity, and righteousness in misery, "can only lie," says Mr. Froude, in words which would have delighted Epictetus, and which would express the inmost spirit of his philosophy, "in the supposed right to happiness.... Happiness is not what we are to look for. Our place is to be true to the best we know, to seek that, and do that; and if by 'virtue is its own reward' be meant that the good man cares only to continue good, desiring nothing more, then it is a true and a noble saying.... Let us do right, and then whether happiness come, or unhappiness, it is no very mighty matter. If it come, life will be sweet; if it do not come, life will be bitter—bitter, not sweet, and yet to be borne.... The well-being of our souls depends only on what we are; and nobleness of character is nothing else but steady love of good, and steady scorn of evil.... Only to those who have the heart to say, 'We can do without selfish enjoyment: it is not what we ask or desire,' is there no secret. Man will have what he desires, and will find what is really best for him, exactly as he honestly seeks for it. Happiness may fly away, pleasure pall or cease to be obtainable, wealth decay, friends fail or prove unkind; but the power to serve God never fails, and the love of Him is never rejected."

CHAPTER III

LIFE AND VIEWS OF EPICTETUS (continued.)

Of the life of Epictetus, as distinct from his opinions, there is unfortunately little more to be told. The life of

> "That halting slave, who in Nicopolis
> Taught Arrian, when Vespasian's brutal son
> Cleared Rome of what most shamed him,"

is not an eventful life, and the conditions which surrounded it are very circumscribed. Great men, it has been observed, have often the shortest biographies; their real life is in their books.

At some period of his life, but how or when we do not know, Epictetus was manumitted by his master, and was henceforward regarded by the world as free. Probably the change made little or no difference in his life. If it saved him from a certain amount of brutality, if it gave him more uninterrupted leisure, it probably did not in the slightest degree modify the hardships of his existence, and may have caused him some little anxiety as to the means of procuring the necessaries of life. He, of all men, would have attached the least importance to the external conditions under which he lived; he always regarded them as falling under the category of things which lay beyond the sphere of his own influence, and therefore as things with which he had nothing to do. Even in his most oppressed days, he considered himself, by the grace of heaven, to be more free—free in a far truer and higher sense—than thousands of those who owed allegiance to no master's will. Whether he had saved any small sum of money, or whether his needs were supplied by the many who loved and honoured him, we do not know. He was a man who was content with the barest necessaries of life, and we may be sure that he would have refused to be indebted to any one for more than these.

It is probable that he never married. This may have been due to that shade of indifference to the female character of which we detect traces here and there in his writings. In one passage he complains that women seemed to think of nothing but admiration and getting married; and, in another, he observes, almost with a sneer, that the Roman ladies were fond of Plato's Republic because he allowed some very liberal marriage regulations. We can only infer from these passages that he had been very unfortunate in the specimens of women with whom he had been thrown. The Roman ladies of his time were certainly not models of character; he was not likely to fall in with very exalted females among the slaves of Epaphroditus or the ladies of his family, and he had probably never known the love of a sister or a mother's care. He did not, however, go the length of condemning marriage altogether; on the contrary, he blames the philosophers who did so. But it is equally obvious that he approves of celibacy as a "counsel of perfection," and indeed his views on the subject have so close and remarkable a resemblance to those of St. Paul that our readers will be interested in seeing them side by side.

In 1 Cor. vii. St. Paul, after speaking of the nobleness of virginity, proceeds, nevertheless, to sanction matrimony as in itself a hallowed and honourable estate. It was not given to all, he says, to abide even as he was, and therefore marriage should be adopted as a sacred and indissoluble bond. Still, without being sure that he has any divine sanction for what he is about to say, he considers celibacy good "for the present distress," and warns those that marry that they "shall have trouble in the flesh." For marriage involves a direct multiplication of the cares of the flesh: "He that is unmarried careth for the things that belong to the Lord, how he may please the Lord: but he that is married careth for the things that are of the world, how he may please his wife.... And this I speak for your own profit, not that I may cast a snare upon you, but for that which is comely, and that ye may attend upon the Lord without distraction."

It is clear, then, that St. Paul regarded virginity as a "counsel

118

of perfection," and Epictetus uses respecting it almost identically the same language. Marriage was perfectly permissible in his view, but it was much better for a Cynic (i.e. for all who carried out most fully their philosophical obligations) to remain single: "Since the condition of things is such as it now is, as though we were on the eve of battle, ought not the Cynio to be entirely without distraction" [the Greek word being the very same as that used by St. Paul] "for the service of God? ought he not to be able to move about among mankind free from the entanglement of private relationships or domestic duties, which if he neglect he will no longer preserve the character of a wise and good man, and which if he observe he will lose the function of a messenger, and sentinel, and herald of the gods?" Epictetus proceeds to point out that if he is married he can no longer look after the spiritual interests of all with whom he is thrown in contact, and no longer maintain the rigid independence of all luxuries which marked the genuine philosopher. He must, for instance, have a bath for his child, provisions for his wife's ailments, and clothes for his little ones, and money to buy them satchels and pens, and cribs and cups; and hence a general increase of furniture, and all sorts of undignified distractions, which Epictetus enumerates with an almost amusing manifestation of disgust. It is true (he admits) that Crates, a celebrated cynic, was married, but it was to a lady as self-denying as himself, and to one who had given up wealth and friends to share hardship and poverty with him. And, if Epictetus does not venture to say in so many words that Crates in this matter made a mistake, he takes pains to point out that the circumstances were far too exceptional to be accepted as a precedent for the imitation of others.

"But," inquires the interlocutor, "how then is the world to get on?" The question seems quite to disturb the bachelor equanimity of Epictetus; it makes him use language of the strongest and most energetic contempt: and it is only when he trenches on this subject that he ever seems to lose the nobility and grace, the "sweetness and light," which are the general characteristic of his utterances. In spite of his complete self-mastery he was evidently a man of strong feelings, and with a natural tendency to express them strongly. "Heaven bless us," he exclaims in reply, "are they greater benefactors of mankind who bring into the world two or three evilly-squalling brats,[63] or those who, to the best of their power,

---

[63] [Greek: kakorrugcha paidia]. Another reading is [Greek: kokorugcha], which M. Martha renders, "Marmots à vilain petit museau!" It is evident that Epictetus did not like children, which makes his subsequently

keep a beneficent eye on the lives, and habits, and tendencies of all mankind? Were the Thebans who had large families more useful to their country than the childless Epaminondas; or was Homer less useful to mankind than Priam with his fifty good-for-nothing sons?... Why, sir, the true cynic is a father to all men; all men are his sons and all women his daughters; he has a bond of union, a lien of affection with them all." (Dissert. iii. 22.)

The whole character of Epictetus is sufficient to prove that he would only do what he considered most desirable and most exalted; and passages like these, the extreme asperity of which I have necessarily, softened down, are, I think, decisive in favour of the tradition which pronounces him to have been unmarried.

We are told that he lived in a cottage of the simplest and even meanest description: it neither needed nor possessed a fastening of any kind, for within it there was no furniture except a lamp and the poor straw pallet on which he slept. About his lamp there was current in antiquity a famous story, to which he himself alludes. As a piece of unwonted luxury he had purchased a little iron lamp, which burned in front of the images of his household deities. It was the only possession which he had, and a thief stole it. "He will be finely disappointed when he comes again," quietly observed Epictetus. "for he will only find an earthenware lamp next time." At his death the little earthenware lamp was bought by some genuine hero-worshipper for 3,000 drachmas. "The purchaser hoped," says the satirical Lucian, "that if he read philosophy at night by that lamp, he would at once acquire in dreams the wisdom of the admirable old man who once possessed it."

But, in spite of his deep poverty, it must not be supposed that there was anything eccentric or ostentatious in the life of Epictetus. On the contrary, his writings abound in directions as to the proper bearing of a philosopher in life. He warns his students that they may have ridicule to endure. Not only did the little boys in the streets, the gamins of Rome, appear to consider a philosopher "fair game," and think it fine fun to mimic his gestures and pull his beard, but he had to undergo the sneers of much more dignified people. "If," says Epictetus, "you want to know how the Romans regard philosophers, listen. Maelius, who had the highest philosophic reputation among them, once when I was present, happened to get into a great rage with his people, and as though he had received an intolerable injury, exclaimed, 'I cannot endure it; you are killing me; why, you'll make me like him! pointing to me," evidently as if Epictetus were the

mentioned compassion to the poor neglected child still more creditable to him.

merest insect in existence. And, again he says in the Manual. "If you wish to be a philosopher, prepare yourself to be thoroughly laughed at since many will certainly sneer and jeer at you, and will say, 'He has come back to us as a philosopher all of a sudden,' and 'Where in the world did he get this superciliousness?' Now do not you be supercilious, but cling to the things which appear best to you in such a manner as though you were conscious of having been appointed by God to this position." Again in the little discourse On the Desire of Admiration, he warns the philosopher "not to walk as if he had swallowed a poker" or to care for the applause of those multitudes whom he holds to be immersed in error. For all display, and pretence, and hypocrisy, and Pharisaism, and boasting, and mere fruitless book-learning he seems to have felt a genuine and profound contempt. Recommendations to simplicity of conduct, courtesy of manner, and moderation of language were among his practical precepts. It is refreshing, too, to know that with the strongest and manliest good sense, he entirely repudiated that dog-like brutality of behaviour, and repulsive eccentricity of self-neglect, which characterised not a few of the Cynic leaders. He expressly argues that the Cynic should be a man of ready tact, and attractive presence; and there is something of almost indignant energy in his words when he urges upon a pupil the plain duty of scrupulous cleanliness. In this respect our friends the Hermits would not quite have satisfied him, although he might possibly have pardoned them on the plea that they abode in desert solitudes, since he bids those who neglect the due care of their bodies to live "either in the wilderness or alone."

Late in life Epictetus increased his establishment by taking in an old woman as a servant. The cause of his doing so shows an almost Christian tenderness of character. According to the hideous custom of infanticide which prevailed in the pagan world, a man with whom Epictetus was acquainted exposed his infant son to perish. Epictetus in pity took the child home to save its life, and the services of a female were necessary to supply its wants. Such kindness and self-denial were all the more admirable because pity, like all other deep emotions, was regarded by the Stoics in the light rather of a vice than of a virtue. In this respect, however, both Seneca and Epictetus, and to a still greater extent Marcus Aurelius, were gloriously false to the rigidity of the school to which they professed to belong. We see with delight that one of the Discourses of Epictetus was On the Tenderness and Forbearance due to Sinners; and he abounds in exhortations to forbearance in judging others. In one of his Fragments he tells the following anecdote:—A person who had seen a poor ship-wrecked and almost dying pirate

121

took pity on him, carried him home, gave him clothes, and furnished him with all the necessaries of life. Somebody reproached him for doing good to the wicked—"I have honoured," he replied, "not the man, but humanity in his person."

But one fact more is known in the life of Epictetus, Domitian, the younger son of Vespasian, succeeded his far nobler brother the Emperor Titus; and in the course of his reign a decree was passed which banished all the philosophers from Italy. Epictetus was not exempted from this unjust and absurd decree. That he bore it with equanimity may be inferred from the approval with which he tells an anecdote about Agrippinus, who while his cause was being tried in the Senate went on with all his usual avocations, and on being informed on his return from bathing that he had been condemned, quietly asked, "To death or banishment?" "To banishment," said the messenger. "Is my property confiscated?" "No," "Very well, then let us go as far as Aricia" (about sixteen miles from Rome), "and dine there."

There was a certain class of philosophers whose external mark and whose sole claim to distinction rested in the length of their beards; and when the decree of Domitian was passed these gentleman contented themselves with shaving. Epictetus alludes to this in his second Discourse, "Come, Epictetus, shave off your beard," he imagines some one to say to him. "If I am a philosopher I will not," he replies. "Then I will take off your head." "By all means, if that will do you any good."

He went to Nicopolis, a town of Epirus, which had been built by Augustus in commemoration of his victory at Actium. Whether he ever revisited Rome is uncertain, but it is probable that he did so, for we know that he enjoyed the friendship of several eminent philosophers and statesmen, and was esteemed and honoured by the Emperor Hadrian himself. He is said to have lived to a good old age, surrounded by affectionate and eager disciples, and to have died with the same noble simplicity which had marked his life. The date of his death is as little known as that of his birth. It only remains to give a sketch of those thoughts which, poor though he was, and despised, and a slave, yet made him "dear to the immortals."

CHAPTER IV

THE "MANUAL" AND "FRAGMENTS" OF EPICTETUS

It is nearly certain that Epictetus never committed any of his doctrines to writing. Like his great exemplar. Socrates, he contented himself with oral instruction, and the bulk of what has come down to us in his name consists in the Discourses reproduced for us by his pupil Arrian. It was the ambition of Arrian "to be to Epictetus what Xenophon had been to Socrates," that is, to hand down to posterity a noble and faithful picture of the manner in which his master had lived and taught. With this view, he wrote four books on Epictetus,—a life, which is now unhappily lost; a book of conversation or "table talk," which is also lost; and two books which have come down to us, viz. the Discourses and the Manual. It is from these two invaluable books, and from a good many isolated fragments, that we are enabled to judge what was the practical morality of Stoicism, as expounded by the holy and upright slave.

The Manual is a kind of abstract of Epictetus's ethical principles, which, with many additional illustrations and with more expansion, are also explained in the Discourses. Both books were so popular that by their means Arrian first came into conspicuous notice, and ultimately attained the highest eminence and rank. The Manual was to antiquity what the Imitatio of Thomas à Kempis was to later times, and what Woodhead's Whole Duty of Man or Wilberforce's Practical View of Christianity have been to large sections of modern Englishmen. It was a clear, succinct, and practical statement of common daily duties, and the principles upon which they rest. Expressed in a manner entirely simple and unornate, its popularity was wholly due to the moral elevation of the thoughts which it expressed. Epictetus did not aim at style; his one aim was to excite his hearers to virtue, and Arrian tells us that in this endeavour he created a deep impression by his manner and voice. It is interesting to know that the Manual was widely accepted among Christians no less than among Pagans, and that, so late as the fifth century, paraphrases were written of it for Christian use. No systematic treatise of morals so simply beautiful was ever composed, and to this day the best Christian may study it, not with interest only, but with real advantage. It is like the voice of the Sybil, which, uttering things simple, and unperfumed, and unadorned, by

123

God's grace reacheth through innumerable years. We proceed to give a short sketch of its contents.

Epictetus began by laying down the broad comprehensive statement that there are some things which are in our power, and depend upon ourselves; other things which are beyond our power, and wholly independent of us. The things which are in our power are our opinions, our aims, our desires, our aversions—in a word, our actions. The things beyond our power are bodily accidents, possessions, fame, rank, and whatever lies beyond the sphere of our actions. To the former of these classes of things our whole attention must be confined. In that region we may be noble, unperturbed, and free; in the other we shall be dependent, frustrated, querulous, miserable. Both classes cannot be successfully attended to; they are antagonistic, antipathetic; we cannot serve God and Mammon.

Now, if we take a right view of all these things which in no way depend on ourselves we shall regard them as mere semblances—as shadows which are to be distinguished from the true substance. We shall not look upon them as fit subjects for aversion or desire. Sin and cruelty, and falsehood we may hate, because we can avoid them if we will; but we must look upon sickness, and poverty, and death as things which are not fit subjects for our avoidance, because they lie wholly beyond our control.

This, then,—endurance of the inevitable, avoidance of the evil—is the keynote of the Epictetean philosophy. It has been summed up in the three words, [Greek: Anechou kai apechou], "sustine et abstine," "Bear and forbear,"—bear whatever God assigns to you, abstain from that which He forbids.

The earlier part of the Manual is devoted to practical advice which may enable men to endure nobly. For instance, "If there be anything," says Epictetus, "which you highly value or tenderly love, estimate at the same time its true nature. Is it some possession? remember that it may be destroyed. Is it wife or child? remember that they may die." "Death," says an epitaph in Chester Cathedral—

"Death, the great monitor, comes oft to prove,
'Tis dust we dote on, when 'tis man we love."

"Desire nothing too much. If you are going to the public baths and are annoyed or hindered by the rudeness, the pushing, the abuse, the thievish propensities of others, do not lose your temper: remind yourself that it is more important that you should keep your will in harmony with nature than that you should bathe. And so with all troubles; men suffer far less from the things themselves than from the opinions they have of them."

"If you cannot frame your circumstances in accordance with your wishes, frame your will into harmony with your circumstances.[64] When you lose the best gifts of life, consider them as not lost but only resigned to Him who gave them. You have a remedy in your own heart against all trials—continence as a bulwark against passion, patience against opposition, fortitude against pain. Begin with trifles: if you are robbed, remind yourself that your peace of mind is of more value and importance than the thing which has been stolen from you. Follow the guidance of nature; that is the great thing; regret nothing, desire nothing, which can disturb that end. Behave as at a banquet—take with gratitude and in moderation what is set before you, and seek for nothing more; a higher and diviner step will be to be ready and able to forego even that which is given you, or which you might easily obtain. Sympathise with others, at least externally, when they are in sorrow and misfortune; but remember in your own heart that to the brave and wise and true there is really no such thing as misfortune; it is but an ugly semblance; the croak of the raven can portend no harm to such a man, he is elevated above its power."

"We do not choose our own parts in life, and have nothing to do with those parts; our simple duty is confined to playing them well. The slave may be as free as the consul; and freedom is the chief of blessings; it dwarfs all others; beside it all others are insignificant, with it all others become needless, without it no others are possible. No one can insult you if you will not regard his words or deeds as insults.[65] Keep your eye steadily fixed on the great reality of death, and all other things will shrink to their true proportions. As in a voyage, when a ship has come to anchor, if you have gone out to find water, you may amuse yourself with picking up a little shell or bulb, but you must keep your attention steadily fixed upon the ship, in case the captain should call, and then you must leave all such things lest you should be flung on board, bound like sheep. So in life; if, instead of a little shell or bulb, some wifeling or childling be granted you, well and good; but, if the captain call, run to the ship and leave such possessions behind you, not looking back. But if you be an old man, take care not to go a long distance from the ship at all, lest you should be called and come too late." The metaphor is a significant one, and perhaps the following

---

[64] "When what thou willest befalls not, thou then must will what befalleth."
[65] Compare Cowper's Conversation:—

> "Am I to set my life upon a throw
> Because a bear is rude and surly?—No.—
> A modest, sensible, and well-bred man
> Will not insult me, and no other can."

lines of Sir Walter Scott, prefixed anonymously to one of the chapters of the Waverley Novels, may help to throw light upon it:

> "Death finds us 'midst our playthings; snatches us,
> As a cross nurse might do a wayward child,
> From all our toys and baubles—the rough call
> Unlooses all our favourite ties on earth:
> And well if they are such as may be answered
> In yonder world, where all is judged of truly."

"Preserve your just relations to other men; their misconduct does not affect your duties. Has your father done wrong, or your brother been unjust? Still he is your father, he is your brother; and you must consider your relation to him, not whether he be worthy of it or no.

"Your duty towards the gods is to form just and true opinions respecting them. Believe that they do all things well, and then you need never murmur or complain."

"As rules of practice," says Epictetus, "prescribe to yourself an ideal, and then act up to it. Be mostly silent; or, if you converse, do not let it be about vulgar and insignificant topics, such as dogs, horses, racing, or prize-fighting. Avoid foolish and immoderate laughter, vulgar entertainments, impurity, display, spectacles, recitations, and all egotistical remarks. Set before you the examples of the great and good. Do not be dazzled by mere appearances. Do what is right quite irrespective of what people will say or think. Remember that your body is a very small matter and needs but very little; just as all that the foot needs is a shoe, and not a dazzling ornament of gold, purple, or jewelled embroidery. To spend all one's time on the body, or on bodily exercises, shows a weak intellect. Do not be fond of criticising others, and do not resent their criticisms of you. Everything," he says, and this is one of his most characteristic precepts, "has two handles! one by which it may be borne, the other by which it cannot. If your brother be unjust, do not take up the matter by that handle—the handle of his injustice—for that handle is the one by which it cannot be taken up; but rather by the handle that he is your brother and brought up with you; and then you will be taking it up as it can be borne."

All these precepts have a general application, but Epictetus adds others on the right bearing of a philosopher; that is, of one whose professed ideal is higher than the multitude. He bids him above all things not to be censorious, and not to be ostentatious. "Feed on your own principles; do not throw them up to show how much you have eaten. Be self-denying, but do not boast of it. Be independent and moderate, and regard not the opinion or censure of others, but keep a watch upon yourself as your own most dangerous enemy. Do not plume yourself on an intellectual knowledge of philosophy, which is in itself quite valueless, but on a consistent nobleness of action. Never relax your efforts, but aim at perfection. Let everything which seems best be to you a law not to be transgressed; and whenever anything painful, or pleasurable, or glorious, or inglorious, is set before you, remember that now is the struggle, now is the hour of the Olympian contest, and it may not be put off, and that by a single defeat or yielding your advance in virtue may be either secured or lost. It was thus that Socrates attained perfection, by giving his heart to reason, and to reason only. And thou, even if as yet thou art not a Socrates, yet shouldst live as though it were thy wish to be one." These are noble words, but who that reads them will not be reminded of those sacred and far more deeply-reaching words, "Be ye perfect, even as your Father which is in heaven is perfect" Behold, now is the accepted time; behold, now is the day of salvation.

In this brief sketch we have included all the most important thoughts in the Manual. It ends in these words. "On all occasions we may keep in mind these three sentiments:—"

'Lead me, O Zeus, and thou, Destiny, whithersoever ye have appointed me to go, for I will follow, and that without delay. Should I be unwilling, I shall follow as a coward, but I must follow all the same.' (Cleanthes.)

'Whosoever hath nobly yielded to necessity, I hold him wise, and he knoweth the things of God.' (Euripides.)

And this third one also, 'O Crito, be it so, if so be the will of heaven. Anytus and Melitus can indeed slay me, but harm me they cannot.' (Socrates.)

To this last conception of life; quoted from the end of Plato's Apology, Epictetus recurs elsewhere: "What resources have we," he asks, "in circumstances of great peril? What other than the remembrance of what is or what is not in our own power; what is possible to us and what is not? I must die. Be it so; but need I die groaning? I must be bound; but must I be bound bewailing? I must be driven into exile, well, who prevent me then from going with laughter, and cheerfulness, and calm of mind?

"'Betray secrets.'

"'Indeed I will not, for that rests in my own hands.'

"'Then I will put you in chains.'

"'My good sir, what are you talking about? Put me in chains? No, no! you may put my leg in chains, but not even Zeus himself can master my will.'

"'I will throw you into prison.'

"'My poor little body; yes, no doubt.'

"'I will cut off your head.'

"'Well did I ever tell you that my head was the only one which could not be cut off?'

"Such are the things of which philosophers should think, and write them daily, and exercise themselves therein."

There are many other passages in which Epictetus shows that the free-will of man is his noblest privilege, and that we should not "sell it for a trifle;" or, as Scripture still more sternly expresses it, should not "sell ourselves for nought." He relates, for instance, the complete failure of the Emperor Vespasian to induce Helvidius Priscus not to go to the Senate. "While I am a Senator," said Helvidius, "I must go." "Well, then, at least be silent there." "Ask me no questions, and I will be silent." "But I must ask your opinion." "And I must say what is right." "But I will put you to death." "Did I ever tell you I was immortal? Do your part, and I will do mine. It is yours to kill me, mine to die untrembling; yours to banish me, mine to go into banishment without grief."

We see from these remarkable extracts that the wisest of the heathen had, by God's grace, attained to the sense that life was subject to a divine guidance. Yet how dim was their vision of this truth, how insecure their hold upon it, in comparison with that which the meanest Christian may attain! They never definitely grasped the doctrine of immortality. They never quite got rid of a haunting dread that perhaps, after all, they might be nothing better than insignificant and unheeded atoms, swept hither and thither in the mighty eddies of an unseen, impersonal, mysterious agency, and destined hereafter "to be sealed amid the iron hills," or

> "To be imprisoned in the viewless winds.
> And blown with reckless violence about
> The pendent world."

Their belief in a personal deity was confused with their belief in nature, which, in the language of a modern sceptic, "acts with fearful uniformity: stern as fate, absolute as tyranny, merciless as death; too vast to praise, too inexorable to propitiate, it has no ear for prayer, no heart for sympathy, no arm to save." How different the soothing and tender certainty of the Christian's hope, for whom Christ has brought life and immortality to light! For "chance" is not only "the daughter of forethought," as the old Greek lyric poet calls her, but the daughter also of love. How different the prayer of David, even in the hours of his worst agony and shame, "Let Thy

loving Spirit lead me forth into the land of righteousness."
Guidance, and guidance by the hand of love, was—as even in that
dark season he recognised—the very law of his life; and his soul,
purged by affliction, had but a single wish—the wish to be led, not
into prosperity, not into a recovery of his lost glory, not even into
the restoration of his lost innocence; but only,—through paths
however hard—only into the land of righteousness. And because he
knew that God would lead him thitherward, he had no wish, no care
for anything beyond. We will end this chapter by translating a few of
the isolated fragments of Epictetus which have been preserved for
us by other writers. The wisdom and beauty of these fragments will
interest the reader, for Epictetus was one of the few "in the very
dust of whose thoughts was gold."

"A life entangled with accident is like a wintry torrent, for it is
turbulent, and foul with mud, and impassable, and tyrannous, and
loud, and brief."

"A soul that dwells with virtue is like a perennial spring; for it
is pure, and limpid, and refreshful, and inviting, and serviceable,
and rich, and innocent, and uninjurious."

"If you wish to be good? first believe that you are bad."

Compare Matt. ix. 12, "They that be whole need not a
physician, but they that are sick;" John ix. 41, "Now ye say, We see,
therefore your sin remaineth;" and 1 John i. 8, "If we say that we
have no sin, we deceive ourselves, and the truth is not in us."

"It is base for one who sweetens that which he drinks with the
gifts of bees, to embitter by vice his reason, which is the gift of God."

"Nothing is meaner than the love of pleasure, the love of gain,
and insolence: nothing nobler than high-mindedness, and
gentleness, and philanthropy, and doing good."

"The vine bears three clusters: the first of pleasure; the second
of drunkenness; the third of insult."

"He is a drunkard who drinks more than three cups; even if he
be not drunken, he has exceeded moderation."

Our own George Herbert has laid down the same limit:—

"Be not a beast in courtesy, but stay,
    Stay at the third cup, or forego the place,
    Wine above all things doth God's stamp deface."

"Like the beacon-lights in harbours, which, kindling a great
blaze by means of a few fagots, afford sufficient aid to vessels that
wander over the sea, so, also, a man of bright character in a storm-
tossed city, himself content with little, effects great blessings for his
fellow-citizens."

129

The thought is not unlike that of Shakespeare:

"How far yon little candle throws its beams,
So shines a good deed in a naughty world."

But the metaphor which Epictetus more commonly adopts is one no less beautiful. "What good," asked some one, "did Helvidius Priscus do in resisting Vespasian, being but a single person?" "What good," answers Epictetus, "does the purple do on the garment? Why, it is splendid in itself, and splendid also in the example which it affords."

"As the sun does not wait for prayers and incantations that he may rise, but shines at once, and is greeted by all; so neither wait thou for applause, and shouts, and eulogies, that thou mayst do well;—but be a spontaneous benefactor, and thou shalt be beloved like the sun."

"Thales, when asked what was the commonest of all possessions, answered, 'Hope; for even those who have nothing else have hope.'"

"Lead, lead me on, my hopes," says Mr. Macdonald; "I know that ye are true and not vain. Vanish from my eyes day after day, but arise in new forms. I will follow your holy deception; follow till ye have brought me to the feet of my Father in heaven, where I shall find you all, with folded wings, spangling the sapphire dusk whereon stands His throne which is our home.

"What ought not to be done do not even think of doing."
Compare

"Guard well your thoughts for thoughts are heard in heaven."'

Epictetus, when asked how a man could grieve his enemy, replied, "By preparing himself to act in the noblest way."

Compare Rom. xii. 20, "If thine enemy hunger, feed him; if he thirst, give him drink: for in so doing thou shall heap coals of fire on his head"

"If you always remember that in all you do in soul or body God stands by as a witness, in all your prayers and your actions you will not err; and you shall have God dwelling with you."

Compare Rev. iii. 30, "Behold I stand at the door and knock: if any man hear my voice, and open the door, I will come in to him and will sup with him, and he with me."

In the discourse written to prove that God keeps watch upon human actions, Epictetus touches again on the same topic, saying that God has placed beside each one of us his own guardian spirit—a

130

spirit that sleeps not and cannot be beguiled—and has handed us each over to that spirit to protect us. "And to what better or more careful guardian could He have entrusted us? So that when you have closed your doors and made darkness within, remember never to say that you are alone. For you are not alone. God, too, is present there, and your guardian spirit; and what need have they of light to see what you are doing."

There is in this passage an almost startling coincidence of thought with those eloquent words in the Book of Ecclesiasticus: "A man that breaketh wedlock, saying thus in his heart, Who seeth me? I am compassed about with darkness, the walls cover me, and nobody seeth me: what need I to fear? the Most Highest will not remember my sins: such a man only feareth the eyes of man, and knoweth not that the eyes of the Lord are ten thousand times brighter than the sun, beholding all the ways of men, and considering the most secret parts. He knew all things ere ever they were created: so also after they were perfected He looked upon all. This man shall be punished in the streets of the city, and where he expecteth not he shall be taken." (Ecclus. xxiii. 11-21.)

"When we were children, our parents entrusted us to a tutor who kept a continual watch that we might not suffer harm; but, when we grow to manhood, God hands us over to an inborn conscience to guard us. We must, therefore, by no means despise this guardianship, since in that case we shall both be displeasing to God and enemies to our own conscience."

Beautiful and remarkable as these fragments are we have no space for more, and must conclude by comparing the last with the celebrated lines of George Herbert:—

> "Lord! with what care hast Thou begirt us round;
>   Parents first season us. Then schoolmasters
> Deliver us to laws. They send us bound
>   To rules of reason. Holy messengers;
> Pulpits and Sundays, sorrow dogging sin;
>   Afflictions sorted; anguish of all sizes;
> Fine nets and stratagems to catch us in!
>   Bibles laid open; millions of surprises;
> Blessings beforehand; ties of gratefulness;
>   The sound of glory ringing in our ears;
> Without one shame; within our consciences;
>   Angels and grace; eternal hopes and fears!
> Yet all these fences and their whole array,
>   One cunning bosom sin blows quite away."

131

CHAPTER V

THE DISCOURSES OF EPICTETUS

The Discourses of Epictetus, as originally published by Arrian, contained eight books, of which only four have come down to us. They are in many respects the most valuable expression of his views. There is something slightly repellent in the stern concision, the "imperious brevity," of the Manual. In the Manual, says M. Martha,[66] "the reason of the Stoic proclaims its laws with an impassibility which is little human; it imposes silence on all the passions, even the most respectable; it glories in waging against them an internecine war, and seems even to wish to repress the most legitimate impulses of generous sensibility. In reading these rigorous maxims one might be tempted to believe that this legislator of morality is a man without a heart, and, if we were not touched by the original sincerity of the language, one would only see in this lapidary style the conventional precepts of a chimerical system or the aspirations of an impossible perfection." The Discourses are more illustrative, more argumentative, more diffuse, more human. In reading them one feels oneself face to face with a human being, not with the marble statue of the ideal wise man. The style, indeed, is simple, but its "athletic nudity" is well suited to this militant morality; its picturesque and incisive character, its vigorous metaphors, its vulgar expressions, its absence of all conventional elegance, display a certain "plebeian originality" which gives them an almost autobiographic charm. With trenchant logic and intrepid conviction "he wrestles with the passions, questions them, makes them answer, and confounds them in a few words which are often sublime. This Socrates without grace does not amuse us by making his adversary fall into the long entanglement of a captious dialogue, but he rudely seizes and often finishes him with two blows. It is like the eloquence of Phocion, which Demosthenes compares to an axe which is lifted and falls."

Epictetus, like Seneca, is a preacher; a preacher with less wealth of genius, less eloquence of expression, less width of culture, but with far more bravery, clearness, consistency, and grasp of his subject. His doctrine and his life were singularly homogeneous, and his views admit of brief expression, for they are not weakened by any fluctuations, or chequered with any lights and shades. The

---

[66] Moralistes sous l'Empire, p. 200.

Discourses differ from the Manual only in their manner, their frequent anecdotes, their pointed illustrations, and their vivid interlocutory form. The remark of Pascal, that Epictetus knew the grandeur of the human heart, but did not know its weakness, applies to the Manual but can hardly be maintained when we judge him by some of the answers which he gave to those who came to seek for his consolation or advice.

The Discourses are not systematic in their character, and, even if they were, the loss of the last four books would prevent us from working out their system with any completeness. Our sketch of the Manual will already have put the reader in possession of the main principles and ideas of Epictetus; with the mental and physical philosophy of the schools he did not in any way concern himself; it was his aim to be a moral preacher, to ennoble the lives of men and touch their hearts. He neither plagiarised nor invented, but he gave to Stoicism a practical reality. All that remains for us to do is to choose from the Discourses some of his most characteristic views, and the modes by which he brought them home to his hearers.

It was one of the most essential peculiarities of Stoicism to aim at absolute independence, or self-independence. Now, as the weaknesses and servilities of men arise most frequently from their desire for superfluities, the true man must absolutely get rid of any such desire. He must increase his wealth by moderating his wishes; he must despise all the luxuries for which men long, and he must greatly diminish the number of supposed necessaries. We have already seen some of the arguments which point in this direction, and we may add another from the third book of Discourses.

A certain magnificent orator, who was going to Rome on a lawsuit, had called on Epictetus. The philosopher threw cold water on his visit, because he did not believe in his sincerity. "You will get no more from me," he said, "than you would get from any cobbler or greengrocer, for you have only come because it happened to be convenient, and you will only criticise my style, not really wishing to learn principles" "Well, but," answered the orator, "if I attend to that sort of thing, I shall be a mere pauper like you, with no plate, or equipage, or land." "I don't want such things," replied Epictetus; "and, besides, you are poorer than I am, after all." "Why, how so?" "You have no constancy, no unanimity with nature, no freedom from perturbations. Patron or no patron, what care I? You do care. I am richer than you. I don't care what Caesar thinks of me. I flatter no one. This is what I have instead of your silver and gold plate. You have silver vessels, but earthenware reasons, principles, appetites. My mind to me a kingdom is, and it furnishes me abundant and happy occupation in lieu of your restless idleness. All your

133

possessions seem small to you, mine seem great to me. Your desire is insatiate, mine is satisfied." The comparison with which he ends the discussion is very remarkable. I once had the privilege of hearing Sir William Hooker explain to the late Queen Adelaide the contents of the Kew Museum. Among them was a cocoa-nut with a hole in it, and Sir William explained to the Queen that in certain parts of India, when the natives want to catch the monkeys they make holes in cocoa-nuts, and fill them with sugar. The monkeys thrust in their hands and fill them with sugar; the aperture is too small to draw the paws out again when thus increased in size; the monkeys have not the sense to loose their hold of the sugar, and so they are caught. This little anecdote will enable the reader to relish the illustration of Epictetus. "When little boys thrust their hands into narrow-mouthed jars full of figs and almonds, when they have filled their hands they cannot draw them out again, and so begin to howl. Let go a few of the figs and almonds, and you'll get your hand out. And so you, let go your desires. Don't desire many things, and you'll get what you do desire." "Blessed is he that expecteth nothing, for he shall not be disappointed!"

Another of the constant precepts of Epictetus is that we should aim high; we are not to be common threads in the woof of life, but like the laticlave on the robe of a senator, the broad purple stripe which gave lustre and beauty to the whole. But how are we to know that we are qualified for this high function? How does the bull know, when the lion approaches, that it is his place to expose himself for all the herd? If we have high powers we shall soon be conscious of them, and if we have them not we may gradually acquire them. Nothing great is produced at once,—the vine must blossom, and bear fruit, and ripen, before we have the purple clusters of the grape,—"first the blade, then the ear, after that the full corn in the ear."

But whence are we to derive this high sense of duty and possible eminence? Why, if Caesar had adopted you, would you not show your proud sense of ennoblement in haughty looks; how is it that you are not proud of being sons of God? You have, indeed, a body, by virtue of which many men sink into close kinship with pernicious wolves, and savage lions, and crafty foxes, destroying the rational within them, and so becoming greedy cattle or mischievous vermin; but above and beyond this, "If," says Epictetus, "a man have once been worthily interpenetrated with the belief that we all have been in some special manner born of God, and that God is the Father of gods and men, I think that he will never have any ignoble, any humble thoughts about himself." Our own great Milton has hardly expressed this high truth more nobly when he says, that "He that holds himself in reverence and due esteem, both for the dignity of God's image upon him, and for the price of his redemption, which he thinks is visibly marked upon his forehead, accounts himself both a fit person to do the noblest and godliest deeds, and much better worth than to deject and defile, with such a debasement and pollution as sin is, himself so highly ransomed, and ennobled to a new friendship and filial relation with God."

"And how are we to know that we have made progress? We may know it if our own wills are bent to live in conformity with nature; if we be noble, free, faithful, humble; if desiring nothing, and shunning nothing which lies beyond our power, we sit loose to all earthly interests; if our lives are under the distinct governance of immutable and noble laws.

"But shall we not meet with troubles in life? Yes, undoubtedly; and are there none at Olympia? Are you not burnt with heat, and pressed for room, and wetted with showers when it rains? Is there not more than enough clamour, and shouting, and other troubles? Yet I suppose you tolerate and endure all these when you balance them against the magnificence of the spectacle? And, come now, have you not received powers wherewith to bear whatever occurs? Have you not received magnanimity, courage, fortitude? And why, if I am magnanimous, should I care for anything that can possibly happen? what shall alarm or trouble me, or seem painful? Shall I not use the faculty for the ends for which it was granted me, or shall I grieve and groan at all the accidents of life? On the contrary, these troubles and difficulties are strong antagonists pitted against us, and we may conquer them, if we will, in the Olympic game of life.

"But if life and its burdens become absolutely intolerable, may we not go back to God, from whom we came? may we not show thieves and robbers, and tyrants who claim power over us by means of our bodies and possessions, that they have no power? In a word, may we not commit suicide?" We know how Shakespeare treats this question:—

> "For who would bear the whips and scorns of time,
> Th' oppressor's wrong, the proud man's contumely,
> The pangs of despised love, the law's delay,
> The insolence of office, and the spurns
> Which patient merit of the unworthy takes,
> When he himself might his quietus make
> With a bare bodkin? Who would these fardels bear,
> To grunt and sweat under a weary life,
> But that the dread of something after death,
> The undiscovered country from whose bourne

No traveller returns, puzzles the will:
And makes us rather bear those ills we have
Than fly to others that we know not of?"

But Epictetus had no materials for such an answer. I do not remember a single passage in which he refers to immortality or the life to come, and it is therefore probable either that he did not believe in it at all, or that he put it aside as one of those things which are out of our own power. Yet his answer is not that glorification of suicide which we find throughout the tragedies of Seneca, and which was one of the commonplaces of Stoicism. "My friends," he says, "wait God's good time till He gives you the signal, and dismisses you from this service; then dismiss yourself to go to Him. But for the present restrain yourselves, inhabiting the spot which He has at present assigned you. For, after all, this time of your sojourn here is short, and easy for those who are thus disposed; for what tyrant, or thief, or judgment-halls, are objects of dread to those who thus absolutely disesteem the body and its belongings? Stay, then, and do not depart without due cause."

It will be seen that Epictetus permits suicide without extolling it, for in another place (ii. 1) he says: "What is pain? A mere ugly mask; turn it, and see that it is so. This little flesh of ours is acted on roughly, and then again smoothly. If it is not for your interest to bear it, the door is open; if it is for your interest—endure. It is right that under all circumstances the door should be open, since so men end all trouble."

This power of endurance is completely the keynote of the Stoical view of life, and the method of attaining to it, by practising contempt for all external accidents, is constantly inculcated. I have already told the anecdote about Agrippinus by which Epictetus admiringly shows that no extreme of necessary misfortune could wring from the true Stoic a single expression of indignation or of sorrow.

The inevitable, then, in the view of the Stoics, comes from God, and it is our duty not to murmur against it. But this being the guiding conception as regards ourselves, how are we to treat others? Here, too, our duties spring directly from our relation to God. It is that relation which makes us reverence ourselves, it is that which should make us honour others. "Slave! will you not bear with your own brother, who, has God for his father no less than you? But they are wicked, perhaps—thieves and murderers. Be it so, then they deserve all the more pity. You don't exterminate the blind or deaf because of their misfortunes, but you pity them: and how much

136

more to be pitied are wicked men? Don't execrate them. Are you yourself so very wise?"

Nor are the precepts of Epictetus all abstract principles; he often pauses to give definite rules of conduct and practice. Nothing, for instance, can exceed the wisdom with which he speaks of habits (ii. 18), and the best means of acquiring good habits and conquering evil ones. He points out that we are the creatures of habit; that every single act is a definite grain in the sand-multitude of influences which make up our daily life; that each time we are angry or evil-inclined we are adding fuel to a fire, and virulence to the seeds of a disease. A fever may be cured, but it leaves the health weaker; and so also is it with the diseases of the soul. They leave their mark behind them.

Take the instance of anger. "Do you wish not to be passionate? do not then cherish the habit within you, and do not add any stimulant thereto. Be calm at first, and then number the days in which you have not been in a rage. I used to be angry every day, now it is only every other day, then every third, then every fourth day. But should you have passed even thirty days without a relapse, then offer a sacrifice to God. For the habit is first loosened, then utterly eradicated. 'I did not yield to vexation today, nor the next day, nor so on for two or three months, but I restrained myself under various provocations.' Be sure, if you can say that, that it will soon be all right with you."

But how is one to do all this? that is the great question, and Epictetus is quite ready to give you the best answer he can. We have, for instance, already quoted one passage in which (unlike the majority of Pagan moralists) he shows that he has thoroughly mastered the ethical importance of controlling even the thought of wickedness. Another anecdote about Agrippinus will further illustrate the same doctrine. It was the wicked practice of Nero to make noble Romans appear on the stage or in gladiatorial shows, in order that he might thus seem to have their sanction for his own degrading displays. On one occasion Florus, who was doubting whether or not he should obey the mandate, consulted Agrippinus on the subject. "Go by all means," replied Agrippinus. "But why don't you go, then?" asked Florus. "Because", said Agrippinus, "I do not deliberate about it." He implied by this answer that to hesitate is to yield, to deliberate is to be lost; we must act always on principles, we must never pause to calculate consequences. "But if I don't go," objected Florus, "I shall have my head cut off." "Well, then, go, but I won't." "Why won't you go?" "Because I do not care to be of a piece with the common thread of life; I like to be the purple sewn upon it."

And if we want a due motive for such lofty choice Epictetus will supply it. "Wish," he says, "to win the suffrages of your own inward approval, wish to appear beautiful to God. Desire to be pure with your own pure self, and with God. And when any evil fancy assails you, Plato says, 'Go to the rites of expiation, go as a suppliant to the temples of the gods, the averters of evil.' But it will be enough should you even rise and depart to the society of the noble and the good, to live according to their examples, whether you have any such friend among the living or among the dead. Go to Socrates, and gaze on his utter mastery over temptation and passion; consider how glorious was the conscious victory over himself! What an Olympic triumph! How near does it place him to Hercules himself.' So that, by heaven, one might justly salute him, 'Hail, marvellous conqueror, who hast conquered, not these miserable boxers and athletes, nor these gladiators who resemble them.' And should you thus be accustomed to train yourself, you will see what shoulders you will get, what nerves, what sinews, instead of mere babblements, and nothing more. This is the true athlete, the man who trains himself to deal with such semblances as these. Great is the struggle, divine the deed; it is for kingdom, for freedom, for tranquillity, for peace. Think on God; call upon Him as thine aid and champion, as sailors call on the Great Twin Brethren in the storm. And indeed what storm is greater than that which rises from powerful semblances that dash reason out of its course? What indeed but semblance is a storm itself? Since, come now, remove the fear of death, and bring as many thunders and lightnings as thou wilt, and thou shalt know how great is the tranquillity and calm in that reason which is the ruling faculty of the soul. But should you once be worsted, and say that you will conquer hereafter, and then the same again and again, know that thus your condition will be vile and weak, so that at the last you will not even know that you are doing wrong, but you will even begin to provide excuses for your sin; and then you will confirm the truth of that saying of Hesiod,—

"'The man that procrastinates struggles ever with ruin.'"

Even so! So early did a heathen moralist learn the solemn fact that "only this once" ends in "there is no harm in it." Well does Mr. Coventry Patmore sing:—

"How easy to keep free from sin;
  How hard that freedom to recall;
For awful truth it is that men

138

Forget the heaven from which they fall."

In another place Epictetus warns us, however, not to be too easily discouraged in our attempts after good;—and, above all, never to despair. "In the schools of the wrestling master, when a boy falls he is bidden to get up again, and to go on wrestling day by day till he has acquired strength; and we must do the same, and not be like those poor wretches who after one failure suffer themselves to be swept along as by a torrent. You need but will" he says, "and it is done; but if you relax your efforts, you will be ruined; for ruin and recovery are both from within.—And what will you gain by all this? You will gain modesty for inpudence, purity for vileness, moderation for drunkenness. If you think there are any better ends than these, then by all means go on in sin, for you are beyond the power of any god to save."

But Epictetus is particularly in earnest about warning us that to profess these principles and talk about them is one thing—to act up to them quite another. He draws a humorous picture of an inconsistent and unreal philosopher, who—after eloquently proving that nothing is good but what pertains to virtue, and nothing evil but what pertains to vice, and that all other things are indifferent— goes to sea. A storm comes on, and the masts creak, and the philosopher screams; and an impertinent person stands by and asks in surprise, "Is it then vice to suffer shipwreck? because, if not, it can be no evil;" a question which makes our philosopher so angry that he is inclined to fling a log at his interlocutor's head. But Epictetus sternly tells him that the philosopher never was one at all, except in name; that as he sat in the schools puffed up by homage and adulation, his innate cowardice and conceit were but hidden under borrowed plumes; and that in him the name of Stoic was usurped.

"Why," he asks in another passage, "why do you call yourself a Stoic? Why do you deceive the multitude? Why do you act the Jew when you are a Greek? Don't you see on what terms each person is called a Jew? or a Syrian? or an Egyptian? And when we see some mere trimmer we are in the habit of saying, 'This is no Jew; he is only acting the part of one,' but when a man takes up the entire condition of a proselyte, thoroughly imbued with Jewish doctrines, then he both is in reality and is called a Jew. So we philosophers too, dipped in a false dye, are Jews in name, but in reality are something else.... We call ourselves philosophers when we cannot even play the part of men, as though a man should try to heave the stone of Ajax who cannot lift ten pounds." The passage is interesting not only on its own account, but because of its curious similarity

139

both with the language and with the sentiment of St. Paul—"He is not a Jew who is one outwardly, neither is that circumcision which is outward in the flesh, but he is a Jew who is one inwardly; and circumcision is that of the heart, in the spirit and not in the latter; whose praise is not of men, but of God."

The best way to become a philosopher in deed is not by a mere study of books and knowledge of doctrines, but by a steady diligence of actions and adherence to original principles, to which must be added consistency and self control. "These principles," says Epictetus, "produce friendship in a house, unanimity in a city, peace in nations; they make a man grateful to God, bold under all circumstances, as though dealing with things alien and valueless. Now we are capable of writing these things, and reading them, and praising them when they are read, but we are far enough off following them. Hence comes it that the reproach of the Lacedaemonians, that they are 'lions at home, foxes at Ephesus,' will also apply to us; in the school we are lions, out of it foxes."

These passages include, I think, all the most original, important, and characteristic conceptions which are to be found in the Discourses. They are most prominently illustrated in the long and important chapter on the Cynic philosophy. A genuine Cynic— one who was so, not in brutality of manners or ostentation of rabid eccentricity, but a Cynic in life and in his inmost principles—was evidently in the eyes of Epictetus one of the loftiest of human beings. He drew a sketch of his ideal conception to one of his scholars who inquired of him upon the subject.

He begins by saying that a true Cynic is so lofty a being that he who undertakes the profession without due qualifications kindles against him the anger of heaven. He is like a scurrilous Thersites, claiming the imperial office of an Agamemnon. "If you think," he tells the young student, "that you can be a Cynic merely by wearing an old cloak, and sleeping on a hard bed, and using a wallet and staff, and begging, and rebuking every one whom you see effeminately dressed or wearing purple, you don't know what you are about—get you gone; but if you know what a Cynic really is, and think yourself capable of being one, then consider how great a thing you are undertaking.

"First as to yourself. You must be absolutely resigned to the will of God. You must conquer every passion, abrogate every desire. Your life must be transparently open to the view of God and man. Other men conceal their actions with houses, and doors, and darkness, and guards; your house, your door, your darkness, must be a sense of holy shame. You must conceal nothing; you must have nothing to conceal. You must be known as the spy and messenger of God among mankind.

"You must teach men that happiness is not there, where in their blindness and misery they seek it. It is not in strength, for Myro and Ofellius were not happy: not in wealth, for Croesus was not happy: not in power, for the Consuls are not happy: not in all these together, for Nero, and Sardanapalus, and Agamemnon sighed, and wept, and tore their hair, and were the slaves of circumstances and the dupes of semblances. It lies in yourselves: in true freedom, in the absence or conquest of every ignoble fear; in perfect self-government; in a power of contentment and peace, and the 'even flow of life' amid poverty, exile, disease, and the very valley of the shadow of death. Can you face this Olympic contest? Are your thews and sinews strong enough? Can you face the fact that those who are defeated are also disgraced and whipped?

"Only by God's aid can you attain to this. Only by His aid can you be beaten like an ass, and yet love those who beat you, preserving an unshaken unanimity in the midst of circumstances which to other men would cause trouble, and grief, and disappointment, and despair.

"The Cynic must learn to do without friends, for where can he find a friend worthy of him, or a king worthy of sharing his moral sceptre? The friend of the truly noble must be as truly noble as himself, and such a friend the genuine Cynic cannot hope to find. Nor must he marry; marriage is right and honourable in other men, but its entanglements, its expenses, its distractions, would render impossible a life devoted to the service of heaven.

"Nor will he mingle in the affairs of any commonwealth: his commonwealth is not Athens or Corinth, but mankind.

"In person he should be strong, and robust, and hale, and in spite of his indigence always clean and attractive. Tact and intelligence, and a power of swift repartee, are necessary to him. His conscience must be clear as the sun. He must sleep purely, and wake still more purely. To abuse and insult he must be as insensible as a stone, and he must place all fears and desires beneath his feet. To be a Cynic is to be this: before you attempt it deliberate well, and see whether by the help of God you are capable of achieving it."

I have given a sketch of the doctrines of this lofty chapter, but fully to enjoy its morality and eloquence the reader should study it entire, and observe its generous impatience, its noble ardour, its vivid interrogations, "in which," says M. Martha, "one feels as it were a frenzy of virtue and of piety, and in which the plenitude of a great heart tumultuously precipitates a torrent of holy thoughts."

Epictetus was not a Christian. He has only once alluded to the

Christians in his works, and there it is under the opprobrious title of "Galileans," who practised a kind of insensibility in painful circumstances and an indifference to worldly interests which Epictetus unjustly sets down to "mere habit." Unhappily it was not granted to these heathen philosophers in any true sense to know what Christianity was. They ignorantly thought that it was an attempt to imitate the results of philosophy, without having passed through the necessary discipline. They viewed it with suspicion, they treated it with injustice. And yet in Christianity, and in Christianity alone, they would have found an ideal which would have surpassed their loftiest conceptions. Nor was it only an impossible ideal; it was an ideal rendered attainable by the impressive sanction of the highest authority, and one which supported men to bear the difficulties of life with fortitude, with peacefulness, and even with an inward joy; it ennobled their faculties without overstraining them; it enabled them to disregard the burden of present trials, not by vainly attempting to deny their bitterness or ignore their weight, but in the high certainty that they are the brief and necessary prelude to "a far more exceeding and eternal weight of glory."

MARCUS AURELIUS

CHAPTER I

THE EDUCATION OF AN EMPEROR

The life of the noblest of Pagan Emperors may well follow that of the noblest of Pagan slaves. Their glory shines the purer and brighter from the midst of a corrupt and deplorable society. Epictetus showed that a Phrygian slave could live a life of the loftiest exaltation; Aurelius proved that a Roman Emperor could live a life of the deepest humility. The one—a foreigner, feeble, deformed, ignorant, born in squalor, bred in degradation, the despised chattel of a despicable freedman, surrounded by every depressing, ignoble, and pitiable circumstance of life—showed how one who seemed born to be a wretch could win noble happiness and immortal memory; the other—a Roman, a patrician, strong, of heavenly beauty, of noble ancestors, almost born to the purple, the favourite of Emperors, the greatest conquerer, the greatest philosopher, the greatest ruler of his time-proved for ever that it is possible to be virtuous, and tender, and holy, and contented in the midst of sadness, even on an irresponsible and imperial throne. Strange that, of the two, the Emperor is even sweeter, more simple, more admirable, more humbly and touchingly resigned, than the slave. In him, Stoicism loses all its haughty self-assertion, all its impracticable paradox, for a manly melancholy which at once troubles and charms the heart. "It seems," says M. Martha, "that in him the philosophy of heathendom grows less proud, draws nearer and nearer to a Christianity which it ignored or which it despised, and is ready to fling itself into the arms of the 'Unknown God.' In the sad Meditations of Aurelius we find a pure serenity, sweetness, and docility to the commands of God, which before him were unknown, and which Christian grace has alone surpassed. If he has not yet attained to charity in all that fulness of meaning which Christianity has given to the word he has already gained its unction, and one cannot read his book, unique in the history of Pagan philosophy, without thinking of the sadness of Pascal and the gentleness of Fénelon. We must pause before this soul, so lofty and so pure, to contemplate ancient virtue in its softest brilliancy, to see the moral delicacy to which profane doctrines have attained—how they laid down their pride, and how penetrating a grace they have found in their new simplicity. To make the example yet more striking, Providence, which, according to the Stoics, does nothing by chance, determined that the example of these simple virtues should bloom in the midst of all human grandeur—that charity should be taught by the successor of blood stained Caesars, and humbleness of heart by an Emperor."

Aurelius has always exercised a powerful fascination over the minds of eminent men "If you set aside, for a moment, the contemplation of the Christian verities," says the eloquent and thoughtful Montesquieu, "search throughout all nature, and you will not find a grander object than the Antonines.... One feels a secret pleasure in speaking of this Emperor; one cannot read his life without a softening feeling of emotion. He produces such an effect upon our minds that we think better of ourselves, because he inspires us with a better opinion of mankind." "It is more delightful," says the great historian Niebuhr, "to speak of Marcus Aurelius than of any man in history; for if there is any sublime human virtue it is his. He was certainly the noblest character of his time, and I know no other man who combined such unaffected kindness, mildness, and humility, with such conscientiousness and severity towards himself. We possess innumerable busts of him, for every Roman of his time was anxious to possess his portrait, and if there is anywhere an expression of virtue it is in the heavenly features of Marcus Aurelius."

Marcus Aurelius was born on April 26, A.D. 121. His more correct designation would be Marcus Antoninus, but since he bore several different names at different periods of his life, and since at that age nothing was more common than a change of designation, it is hardly worth while to alter the name by which he is most popularly recognised. His father, Annius Verus, who died in his Praetorship, drew his blood from a line of illustrious men who claimed descent from Numa, the second King of Rome. His mother, Domitia Calvilla, was also a lady of consular and kingly race. The character of both seems to have been worthy of their high dignity. Of his father he can have known little, since Annius died when Aurelius was a mere infant; but in his Meditations he has left us a grateful memorial of both his parents. He says that from his grandfather he learned (or, might have learned) good morals and the government of his temper; from the reputation and remembrance of his father, modesty and manliness; from his mother, piety, and beneficence, and abstinence not only from evil deeds, but even from evil thoughts; and, further, simplicity of life far removed from the habits of the rich.

The childhood and boyhood of Aurelius fell during the reign of Hadrian. The times were better than those which we have contemplated in the reigns of the Caesars. After the suicide of Nero and the brief reigns of Galba and Otho, the Roman world had breathed more freely for a time under the rough good humour of Vespasian and the philosophic virtue of Titus. The reign of Domitian, indeed, who succeeded his brother Titus, was scarcely less terrible and infamous than that of Caius or of Nero; but that prince, shortly before his murder, had dreamt that a golden neck had grown out of his own, and interpreted the dream to indicate that a better race of princes should follow him. The dream was fulfilled. Whatever may have been their other faults, Nerva, Trajan, Hadrian, were wise and kind-hearted rulers; Antoninus Pius and Marcus Aurelius were among the very gentlest and noblest sovereigns whom the world has ever seen.

Hadrian, though an able, indefatigable, and, on the whole, beneficial Emperor, was a man whose character was stained with serious faults. It is, however, greatly to his honour that he recognized in Aurelius, at the early age of six years, the germs of those extraordinary virtues which afterwards blessed the empire and elevated the sentiments of mankind. "Hadrian's bad and sinful habits left him," says Niebuhr, "when he gazed on the sweetness of that innocent child. Playing on the boy's paternal name of Verus, he called him Verissimus, 'the most true.'" It is interesting to find that this trait of character was so early developed in one who thought that all men "should speak as they think, with an accent of heroic verity."

Toward the end of his long reign, worn out with disease and weariness, Hadrian, being childless, had adopted as his son L. Ceionius Commodus, a man who had few recommendations but his personal beauty. Upon his death, which took place a year afterwards, Hadrian, assembling the senators round his sick bed, adopted and presented to them as their future Emperor Arrius Antoninus, better known by the surname of Pius, which he won by his gratitude to the memory of his predecessor. Had Aurelius been older—he was then but seventeen—it is known that Hadrian would have chosen him, and not Antoninus, for his heir. The latter, indeed, who was then fifty-two years old, was only selected on the express condition that he should in turn adopt both Marcus Aurelius and the son of the deceased Ceionius. Thus, at the age of seventeen, Aurelius, who, even from his infancy, had been loaded with

145

conspicuous distinctions, saw himself the acknowledged heir to the empire of the world.

We are happily able, mainly from his own writings, to give some sketch of the influences and the education which had formed him for this exalted station.

He was brought up in the house of his grandfather, a man who had been three times consul. He makes it a matter of congratulation, and thankfulness to the gods, that he had not been sent to any public school, where he would have run the risk of being tainted by that frightful corruption into which, for many years, the Roman youth had fallen. He expresses a sense of obligation to his great-grandfather for having supplied him with good teachers at home, and for the conviction that on such things a man should spend liberally. There was nothing jealous, barren, or illiberal, in the training he received. He was fond of boxing, wrestling, running; he was an admirable player at ball, and he was fond of the perilous excitement of hunting the wild boar. Thus, his healthy sports, his serious studies, his moral instruction, his public dignities and duties, all contributed to form his character in a beautiful and manly mould. There are, however, three respects in which his education seems especially worthy of notice;—I mean the diligence, the gratitude, and the hardiness in which he was encouraged by others, and which he practised with all the ardour of generous conviction.

1. In the best sense of the word, Aurelius was diligent. He alludes more than once in his Meditations to the inestimable value of time, and to his ardent desire to gain more leisure for intellectual pursuits. He flung himself with his usual undeviating stedfastness of purpose into every branch of study, and though he deliberately abandoned rhetoric, he toiled hard at philosophy, at the discipline of arms, at the administration of business, and at the difficult study of Roman jurisprudence. One of the acquisitions for which he expresses gratitude to his tutor Rusticus, is that of reading carefully, and not being satisfied with the superficial understanding of a book. In fact, so strenuous was his labour, and so great his abstemiousness, that his health suffered by the combination of the two.

2. His opening remarks show that he remembered all his teachers—even the most insignificant—with sincere gratitude. He regarded each one of them as a man from whom something could be learnt, and from whom he actually did learn that something. Hence the honourable respect—a respect as honourable to himself as to them—which he paid to Fronto, to Rusticus, to Julius Proculus, and others whom his noble and conscientious gratitude raised to the

highest dignities of the State. He even thanks the gods that "he made haste to place those who brought him up in the station of honour which they seemed to desire, without putting them off with mere hopes of his doing it some time after, because they were then still young." He was far the superior of these men, not only socially but even morally and intellectually; yet from the height of his exalted rank and character he delighted to associate with them on the most friendly terms, and to treat them, even till his death, with affection and honour, to place their likenesses among his household gods, and visit their sepulchres with wreaths and victims.

3. His hardiness and self-denial were perhaps still more remarkable. I wish that those boys of our day, who think it undignified to travel second-class, who dress in the extreme of fashion, wear roses in their buttonholes, and spend upon ices and strawberries what would maintain a poor man for a year, would learn how infinitely more noble was the abstinence of this young Roman, who though born in the midst of splendour and luxury, learnt from the first to loathe the petty vice of gluttony, and to despise the unmanliness of self-indulgence. Very early in life he joined the glorious fellowship of those who esteem it not only a duty but a pleasure

"To scorn delights, and live laborious days,"

and had learnt "endurance of labour, and to want little, and to work with his own hands." In his eleventh year he became acquainted with Diognetus, who first introduced him to the Stoic philosophy, and in his twelfth year he assumed the Stoic dress. This philosophy taught him "to prefer a plank bed and skin, and whatever else of the kind belongs to the Grecian discipline." It is said that "the skin" was a concession to the entreaties of his mother, and that the young philosopher himself would have chosen to sleep on the bare boards or on the ground. Yet he acted thus without self-assertion and without ostentation. His friends found him always cheerful; and his calm features,—in which a dignity and thoughtfulness of spirit contrasted with the bloom and beauty of a pure and honourable boyhood,—were never overshadowed with ill-temper or with gloom.

The guardians of Marcus Aurelius had gathered around him all the most distinguished literary teachers of the age. Never had a prince a greater number of eminent instructors; never were any teachers made happy by a more grateful, a more humble, a more blameless, a more truly royal and glorious pupil. Long years after his education had ceased, during his campaign among the Quadi, he wrote a sketch of what he owed to them. This sketch forms the first book of his Meditations, and is characterised throughout by the most unaffected simplicity and modesty.

The Meditations of Marcus Aurelius were in fact his private diary, they are a noble soliloquy with his own heart, an honest examination of his own conscience; there is not the slightest trace of their having been intended for any eye but his own. In them he was acting on the principle of St. Augustine: "Go up into the tribunal of thy conscience, and set thyself before thyself." He was ever bearing about—

"A silent court of justice in himself,
Himself the judge and jury, and himself
The prisoner at the bar."

And writing amid all the cares and distractions of a war which he detested, he averted his eyes from the manifold wearinesses which daily vexed his soul, and calmly sat down to meditate on all the great qualities which he had observed, and all the good lessons that he might have learnt from those who had instructed his boyhood, and surrounded his manly years.

And what had he learnt?—learnt heartily to admire, and (we may say) learnt to practise also? A sketch of his first book will show us. What he had gained from his immediate parents we have seen already, and we will make a brief abstract of his other obligations.

From "his governor"—to which of his teachers this name applies we are not sure—he had learnt to avoid factions at the races, to work hard, and to avoid listening to slander; from Diognetus, to despise frivolous superstitions, and to practise self-denial; from Apollonius, undeviating steadiness of purpose, endurance of misfortune, and the reception of favours without being humbled by them; from Sextus of Chaeronea (a grandson of the celebrated Plutarch), tolerance of the ignorant, gravity without affectation, and benevolence of heart; from Alexander, delicacy in correcting others; from Severus, "a disposition to do good, and to give to others readily, and to cherish good hope, and, to believe that I am beloved of my friends;" from Maximus, "sweetness and dignity, and to do what was set before me without complaining;" from Alexander the Platonic, "not frequently to say to any one, nor to write in a letter, that I have no leisure; nor continually to excuse the neglect of ordinary duties by alleging urgent occupations."

To one or two others his obligations were still more characteristic and important. From Rusticus, for instance, an excellent and able man, whose advice for years he was accustomed to respect, he had learnt to despise sophistry and display, to write with simplicity, to be easily pacified, to be accurate, and—an inestimable benefit this, and one which tinged the colour of his whole life—to become acquainted with the Discourses of Epictetus. And from his adoptive father, the great Antoninus Pius, he had derived advantages still more considerable. In him he saw the example of a sovereign and statesman firm, self-controlled, modest, faithful, and even tempered; a man who despised flattery and hated meanness; who honoured the wise and distinguished the meritorious; who was indifferent to contemptable trifles, and indefatigable in earnest business; one, in short, "who had a perfect and invincible soul," who, like Socrates, "was able both to abstain from and to enjoy those things which many are too weak to abstain from and cannot enjoy without excess."[67] Piety, serenity, sweetness, disregard of empty fame, calmness, simplicity, patience, are virtues which he attributes to him in another full-length portrait (vi. 30) which he concludes with the words, "Imitate all this, that thou mayest have as good a conscience when thy last hour comes as he had."

He concludes these reminiscenses of thankfulness with a summary of what he owed to the gods. And for what does he thanks the gods? for being wealthy, and noble, and an emperor? Nay, for no vulgar or dubious blessings such as these, but for the guidance which trained him in philosophy, and for the grace which kept him from sin. And here it is that his genuine modesty comes out. As the excellent divine used to say when he saw a criminal led past for execution, "There, but for the grace of God, goes John Bradford," so, after thanking the gods for the goodness of all his family and relatives, Aurelius says, "Further, I owe it to the gods that I was not hurried into any offence against any of them, though I had a disposition which, if opportunity had offered, might have led me to do something of this kind; but through their favour there never was such a concurrence of circumstances as put me to the trial. Further, that I was subjected to a ruler and father who took away all pride from me, and taught me that it was possible to live in a palace without guards, or embroidered dresses, or torches, and statues, and such-like show, but to live very near to the fashion of a private person, without being either mean in thought or remiss in action; that after having fallen into amatory passions I was cured; that

[67] My quotations from Marcus Aurelius will be made (by permission) from the forcible and admirably accurate translation of Mr. Long. In thanking Mr. Long, I may be allowed to add that the English reader will find in his version the best means of becoming acquainted with the purest-and noblest book of antiquity.

though it was my mother's fate to die young, she spent the last years of her life with me; that whenever I wished to help any man, I was never told that I had not the means of doing it;—that I had abundance of good masters for my children: for all these thing require the help of the gods and fortune."

The whole of the Emperor's Meditations deserve the profound study of this age. The self-denial which they display is a rebuke to our ever-growing luxury; their generosity contrasts favourably with the increasing bitterness of our cynicism; their contented acquiescence in God's will rebukes our incessant restlessness; above all, their constant elevation shames that multitude of little vices, and little meannesses, which lie like a scurf over the conventionality of modern life. But this earlier chapter has also a special value for the young. It offers a picture which it would indeed be better for them and for us if they could be induced to study. If even under

"That fierce light that beats upon the throne,"

the life of Marcus Aurelius shows no moral stain, it is still more remarkable that the free and beautiful boyhood of this Roman prince had early learnt to recognise only the excellences of his teachers, their patience and firmness, their benevolence and sweetness, their integrity and virtue. Amid the frightful universality of moral corruption he preserved a stainless conscience and a most pure soul; he thanked God in language which breathes the most crystalline delicacy of sentiment and language, that he had preserved uninjured the flower of his early life, and that under the calm influences of his home in the country, and the studies of philosophy, he had learnt to value chastity as the sacred girdle of youth, to be retained and honoured to his latest years. "Surely," says Mr. Carlyle, "a day is coming when it will be known again what virtue is in purity and continence of life; how divine is the blush of young human cheeks; how high, beneficent, sternly inexorable is the duty laid on every creature in regard to these particulars. Well, if such a day never come, then I perceive much else will never come. Magnanimity and depth of insight will never come; heroic purity of heart and of eye; noble pious valour to amend us and the age of bronze and lacquers, how can they ever come? The scandalous bronze-lacquer age of hungry animalisms, spiritual impotencies, and mendacities will have to run its course till the pit swallow it."

CHAPTER II

THE LIFE AND THOUGHTS OF MARCUS AURELIUS

On the death of Hadrian in A. D. 138, Antoninus Pius succeeded to the throne, and, in accordance with the late Emperor's conditions, adopted Marcus Aurelius and Lucius Commodus. Marcus had been betrothed at the age of fifteen to the sister of Lucius Commodus, but the new Emperor broke off the engagement, and betrothed him instead to his daughter Faustina. The marriage, however, was not celebrated till seven years afterwards, A.D. 146.

The long reign of Antoninus Pius is one of those happy periods that have no history. An almost unbroken peace reigned at home and abroad. Taxes were lightened, calamities relieved, informers discouraged; confiscation were rare, plots and executions were almost unknown. Throughout the whole extent of his vast domain the people loved and valued their Emperor, and the Emperor's one aim was to further, the happiness of his people. He, too, like Aurelius, had learnt that what was good for the bee was good for the hive. He strove to live as the civil administrator, of an unaggressive and united republic; he disliked war, did not value the military title of Imperator, and never deigned to accept a triumph.

With this wise and eminent prince, who was as amiable in his private relations as he was admirable in the discharge of his public duties, Marcus Aurelius spent the next twenty-three years of his life. So close and intimate was their union, so completely did they regard each other as father and son, that during all that period Aurelius never slept more than twice away from the house of Antoninus. There was not a shade of jealousy between them; each was the friend and adviser of the other, and, so far from regarding his destined heir with suspicion, the Emperor gave him the designation "Caesar," and heaped upon him all the honours of the Roman Commonwealth. It was in vain that the whisper of malignant tongues attempted to shake this mutual confidence. Antoninus once saw the mother of Aurelius in earnest prayer before the statue of Apollo. "What do you think she is praying for so intently?" asked a wretched mischief-maker of the name of Valerius Omulus: "it is that you may die, and her son reign." This wicked suggestion might have driven a prince of meaner character into violence and disgust, but Antoninus passed it over with the silence of contempt.

It was the main delight of Antoninus to enjoy the quiet of his

151

country villa. Unlike Hadrian, who traversed immense regions of his vast dominion, Antoninus lived entirely either at Rome, or in his beautiful villa at Lorium, a little seacoast village about twelve miles from the capital. In this villa he had been born, and here he died, surrounded by the reminiscences of his childhood. In this his real home it was his special pleasure to lay aside the pomp and burden of his imperial rank. "He did not," says Marcus, "take the bath at unseasonable hours; he was not fond of building houses, nor curious about what he eat, nor about the texture and colour of his clothes, nor about the beauty of his slaves." Even the dress he wore was the work of the provincial artist in his little native place. So far from checking the philosophic tastes of his adopted son he fostered them, and sent for Apollonius of Chalcis to be his teacher in the doctrines of Stoicism. In one of his notes to Fronto, Marcus draws the picture of their simple country occupations and amusements. Hunting, fishing, boxing, wrestling, occupied the leisure of the two princes, and they shared the rustic festivities of the vintage. "I have dined," he writes, "on a little bread.... We perspired a great deal, shouted a great deal, and left some gleanings of the vintage hanging on the trellis work.... When I got home I studied a little, but not to much advantage I had a long talk with my mother, who was lying on her couch." Who knows how much Aurelius and how much the world may have gained from such conversation as this with a mother from whom he had learnt to hate even the thought of evil? Nor will any one despise the simplicity of heart which made him mingle with the peasants as an amateur vintager, unless he is so tasteless and so morose as to think with scorn of Scipio and Laelius as they gathered shells on the seashore, or of Henry IV. as he played at horses with his little boys on all-fours. The capability of unbending thus, the genuine cheerfulness which enters at due times into simple amusements, has been found not rarely in the highest and purest minds.

For many years no incident of importance broke the even tenor of Aurelius's life. He lived peaceful, happy, prosperous, and beloved, watching without envy the increasing years of his adopted father. But in the year 161, when Marcus was now forty years old, Antoninus Pius, who had reached the age of seventy-five, caught a fever at Lorium. Feeling that his end was near, he summoned his friends and the chief men of Rome to his bedside, and there (without saying a word about his other adopted son, who is generally known by the name of Lucius Verus) solemnly recommended Marcus to them as his successor; and then, giving to the captain of the guard the watchword of "Equanimity," as though his earthly task was over he ordered to be transferred to the bedroom of Marcus the little golden statue of Fortune, which was kept in the private chamber of the Emperors as an omen of public prosperity.

The very first public act of the new Emperor was one of splendid generosity, namely, the admission of his adoptive brother Lucius Verus into the fullest participation of imperial honours, the Tribunitian and proconsular powers, and the titles Caesar and Augustus. The admission of Lucius Verus to a share of the empire was due to the innate modesty of Marcus. As he was a devoted student, and cared less for manly exercises, in which Verus excelled, he thought that his adoptive brother would be a better and more useful general than himself, and that he could best serve the State by retaining the civil administration, and entrusting to his brother the management of war. Verus, however, as soon as he got away from the immediate influence and ennobling society of Marcus, broke loose from all decency, and showed himself to be a weak and worthless personage, as unfit for war as he was for all the nobler duties of peace, and capable of nothing but enormous gluttony and disgraceful self-indulence. Two things only can be said in his favour; the one, that, though depraved, he was wholly free from cruelty; and the other, that he had the good sense to submit himself entirely to his brother, and to treat him with the gratitude and deference which were his due.

Marcus had a large family by Faustina, and in the first year of his reign his wife bore twins, of whom the one who survived became the wicked and detested Emperor Commodus. As though the birth of such a child were in itself an omen of ruin, a storm of calamity began at once to burst over the long tranquil State. An inundation of the Tiber flung down houses and streets over a great part of Rome, swept away multitudes of cattle, spoiled the harvests, devastated the fields, and caused a distress which ended in wide-spread famine. Men's minds were terrified by earthquakes, by the burning of cities, and by plagues or noxious insects. To these miseries, which the Emperors did their best to alleviate, was added the horrors of wars and rumours of wars. The Partians, under their king Vologeses, defeated and all but destroyed a Roman army, and devastated with impunity the Roman province of Syria. The wild tribes of the Catti burst over Germany with fire and sword; and the news from Britain was full of insurrection and tumult. Such were the elements of trouble and discord which overshadowed the reign of Marcus Aurelius from its very beginning down to its weary close.

As the Partian war was the most important of the three, Verus was sent to quell it, and but for the ability of his generals—the greatest of whom was Avidius Cassius—would have ruined irretrievably the fortunes of the Empire. These generals, however, vindicated the majesty of the Roman name, and Verus returned in triumph, bringing back with him from the East the seeds of a terrible pestilence which devastated the whole Empire and by which, on the outbreak of fresh wars, Verus himself was carried off at Aquileia.

Worthless as he was, Marcus, who in his lifetime had so often pardoned and concealed his faults, paid him the highest honours of sepulcre, and interred his ashes in the mausoleum of Hadrian. There were not wanting some who charged him with the guilt of fratricide, asserting that the death of Verus had been hastened by his means!

I have only one reason for alluding to atrocious and contemptible calumnies like these, and that is because—since no doubt such whispers reached his ears—they help to account for that deep unutterable melancholy which breathes through the little golden book of the Emperor's Meditations. We find, for instance, among them this isolated fragment:—

"A black character, a womanish character, a stubborn character, bestial, childish, animal, stupid, counterfeit, scurrilous, fraudulent, tyrannical."

We know not of whom he was thinking—perhaps of Nero, perhaps of Caligula, but undoubtedly also of men whom he had seen and known, and whose very existence darkened his soul. The same sad spirit breathes also through the following passages:—

"Soon, very soon, thou wilt be ashes, or a skeleton, and either a name, or not even a name; but name is sound and echo. And the things which are much valued in life are empty, and rotten, and trifling, and little dogs biting one another, and little children quarrelling, laughing, and then straightway weeping. But fidelity, and modesty, and justice, and truth are fled

"'Up to Olympus from the wide-spread earth.'"

(v. 33.)

"It would be a man's happiest lot to depart from mankind without having had a taste of lying, and hypocrisy, and luxury, and pride. However to breathe out one's life when a man has had enough of those things is the next best voyage, as the saying is." (ix.2.)

"Enough of this wretched life, and murmuring, and apish trifles. Why art thou thus disturbed? What is there new in this? What unsettles thee?... Towards the gods, then, now become at last more simple and better." (ix. 37.) The thought is like that which

154

dominates through the Penitential Psalms of David,—that we may take refuge from men, their malignity and their meanness, and find rest for our souls in God. From men David has no hope; mockery, treachery, injustice, are all that he expects from them,—the bitterness of his enemies, the far-off indifference of his friends. Nor does this greatly trouble him, so long as he does not wholly lose the light of God's countenance. "I had no place to flee unto, and no man cared for my soul. I cried unto thee, O Lord, and said, Thou art my hope, and my portion in the land of the living." "Cast me not away from Thy presence, and take not Thy Holy Spirit from me."

But whatever may have been his impulse at times to give up in despair all attempt to improve the "little breed" of men around him, Marcus had schooled his gentle spirit to live continually in far other feelings. Were men contemptible? It was all the more reason why he should himself be noble. Were men petty, and malignant, and passionate and unjust? In that proportion were they all the more marked out for pity and tenderness, and in that proportion was he bound to the utmost of his ability to show himself great, and forgiving, and calm, and true. Thus Marcus turns his very bitterest experience to gold, and from the vilenesses of others, which depressed his lonely life, so far from suffering himself to be embittered as well as saddened, he only draws fresh lessons of humanity and love.

He says, for instance, "Begin the morning by saying to thyself, I shall meet with the busybody, the ungrateful, arrogant, deceitful, envious, unsocial. All these things happen to them by reason of their ignorance of what is good and evil. But I who have seen the nature of the good that it is beautiful, and of the bad that it is ugly, and the nature of him that does wrong that is akin to me,... and that it partakes of the same portion of the divinity, I can neither be injured by any of them, for no one can fix on me what is ugly, nor can I be angry with my kinsman, nor hate him. For we are made for co-operation, like feet, like hands, like eyelids, like the rows of the upper and lower teeth. To act against one another then is contrary to nature; and it is acting against one another to be vexed and turn away." (ii. 1.) Another of his rules, and an eminently wise one, was to fix his thoughts as much as possible on the virtues of others, rather than on their vices. "When thou wishest to delight thyself, think of the virtues of those who live with thee—the activity of one, the modesty of another, the liberality of a third, and some other good quality of a fourth." What a rebuke to the contemptuous cynicism which we are daily tempted to display! "An infinite being comes before us," says Robertson, "with a whole eternity wrapt up in his mind and soul, and we proceed to classify him, put a label

155

upon him, as we would upon a jar, saying, This is rice, that is jelly, and this pomatum; and then we think we have saved ourselves the necessity of taking off the cover, How differently our Lord treated the people who came to Him!... consequently, at His touch each one gave out his peculiar spark of light."

Here, again, is a singularly pithy, comprehensive, and beautiful piece of advice:—

"Men exist for the sake of one another. Teach them or bear with them" (viii. 59.)

And again: "The best way of revenging thyself is not to become like the wrong doer."

And again, "If any man has done wrong, the harm is his own. But perhaps he has not done wrong." (ix. 38.)

Most remarkable, however, are the nine rules which he drew up for himself, as subjects for reflection when any one had offended him, viz.—

1. That men were made for each other: even the inferior for the sake of the superior, and these for the sake of one another.

2. The invincible influences that act upon men, and mould their opinions and their acts.

3. That sin is mainly error and ignorance,—an involuntary slavery.

4. That we are ourselves feeble, and by no means immaculate; and that often our very abstinence from faults is due more to cowardice and a care for our reputation than to any freedom from the disposition to commit them.

5. That our judgments are apt to be very rash and premature. "And in short a man must learn a great deal to enable him to pass a correct judgment on another man's acts."

6. When thou art much vexed or grieved, consider that man's life is only a moment, and after a short time we are all laid out dead.

7. That no wrongful act of another can bring shame on us, and that it is not men's acts which disturb us, but our own opinions of them.

8. That our own anger hurts us more than the acts themselves.

9. That benevolence is invincible, if it be not an affected smile, nor acting a part. "For what will the most violent man do to thee if thou continuest benevolent to him? gently and calmly correcting him, admonishing him when he is trying to do thee harm, saying, 'Not so, my child: we are constituted by nature for something else: I shall certainly not be injured, but thou art injuring thyself, my child' And show him with gentle tact and by general principles that this is so, and that even bees do not do as he does, nor any gregarious animal. And this you must do simply, unreproachfully,

affectionately; without rancour, and if possible when you and he are alone." (xi. 18.)

"Not so, my child; thou art injuring thyself, my child." Can all antiquity show anything tenderer than this, or anything more close to the spirit of Christian teaching than these nine rules? They were worthy of the men who, unlike the Stoics in general, considered gentleness to be a virtue, and a proof at once of philosophy and of true manhood. They are written with that effusion of sadness and benevolence to which it is difficult to find a parallel. They show how completely Marcus had triumphed over all petty malignity, and how earnestly he strove to fulfil his own precept of always keeping the thoughts so sweet and clear, that "if any one should suddenly ask, 'What hast thou now in thy thoughts?' with perfect openness thou mightest immediately answer, 'This or That,'" In short, to give them their highest praise, they would have delighted the great Christian Apostle who wrote,—

"Warn them that are unruly, comfort the feeble-minded, support the weak, be patient towards all men. See that none render evil for evil unto any man; but ever follow that which is good, both among yourselves, and to all men." (1 Thess. iv. 14. 15.)

"Count him not as an enemy, but admonish him as a brother." (2. Thess. iv. 15.)

"Forbearing one another, and forgiving one another, if any man have a quarrel against any." (Col. iii. 13.)

Nay, are they not even in full accordance with the mind and spirit of Him who said,—

"If thy brother trespass against thee, go and tell him his fault between thee and him alone: if he shall hear thee thou hast gained thy brother."

In the life of Marcus Aurelius, as in so many lives, we are able to trace the great law of compensation. His exalted station, during the later years of his life, threw him among many who were false and Pharisaical and base; but his youth had been spent under happier conditions, and this saved him from falling into the sadness of those whom neither man nor woman please. In his earlier years it had been his lot to see the fairer side of humanity, and the recollection of those pure and happy days was like a healing tree thrown into the bitter and turbid waters of his reign.

CHAPTER III

THE LIFE AND THOUGHTS OF MARCUS AURELIUS (continued)

Marcus was now the undisputed lord of the Roman world. He was seated on the dizziest and most splendid eminence which it was possible for human grandeur to obtain.

But this imperial elevation kindled no glow of pride or self-satisfaction in his meek and chastened nature. He regarded himself as being in fact the servant of all. It was his duty, like that of the bull in the herd, or the ram among the flocks, to confront every peril in his own person, to be foremost in all the hardships of war and the most deeply immersed in all the toils of peace. The registry of the citizens, the suppression of litigation, the elevation of public morals, the restraining of consanguineous marriages, the care of minors, the retrenchment of public expenses, the limitation of gladitorial games and shows, the care of roads, the restoration of senatorial privileges, the appointment of none but worthy magistrates—even the regulation of street traffic—these and numberless other duties so completely absorbed his attention that, in spite of indifferent health, they often kept him at severe labour from early morning till long after midnight. His position indeed often necessitated his presence at games and shows, but on these occasions he occupied himself either in reading, or being read to, or in writing notes. He was one of those who held that nothing should be done hastily, and that few crimes were worse than the waste of time. It is to such views and such habits that we owe the compositions of his works. His Meditations were written amid the painful self-denial and distracting anxieties of his wars with the Quadi and the Marcomanni, and he was the author of other works which unhappily have perished. Perhaps of all the lost treasures of antiquity there are few which we should feel a greater wish to recover than the lost autobiography of this wisest of Emperors and holiest of Pagan men.

As for the external trappings of his rank,—those gorgeous adjuncts and pompous circumstances which excite the wonder and envy of mankind,—no man could have shown himself more indifferent to them. He recognized indeed the necessity of maintaining the dignity of his high position. "Every moment," he

158

says, "think steadily as a Roman and a man to do what thou hast in hand with perfect and simple dignity, and affection, and freedom, and justice" (ii. 5); and again, "Let the Deity which is in thee be the guardian of a living being, manly and of ripe age, and engaged in matters political, and a Roman, and a ruler, who has taken his post like a man waiting for the signal which summons him from life" (iii. 5). But he did not think it necessary to accept the fulsome honours and degrading adulations which were so dear to many of his predecessors. He refused the pompous blasphemy of temples and altars, saying that for every true ruler the world was a temple, and all good men were priests. He declined as much as possible all golden statues and triumphal designations. All inevitable luxuries and splendour, such as his public duties rendered indispensable, he regarded as a mere hollow show. Marcus Aurelius felt as deeply as our own Shakespeare seems to have felt the unsubstantiality, the fleeting evanescence of all earthly things: he would have delighted in the sentiment that,

> "We are such stuff
> As dreams are made on, and our little life
> Is rounded by a sleep."

"When we have meat before us," he says, "and such eatables, we receive the impression that this is the dead body of a fish, and this is the dead body of a bird, or of a pig; and, again, that this Falerian is only a little grape-juice, and this purple robe some sheep's wool dyed with the blood of a shellfish: such then are these impressions, and they reach the things themselves and penetrate them, and so we see what kind of things they are. Just in the same way.... where there are things which appear most worthy of our approbation, we ought to lay them bare, and look at their worthlessness, and strip them of all the words by which they are exalted." (vi. 13.)

"What is worth being valued? To be received with clapping of hands? No. Neither must we value the clapping of tongues, for the praise which comes from the many is a clapping of tongues." (vi.16.)

"Asia, Europe, are corners of the universe; all the sea is a drop in the universe; Athos a little clod of the universe; all the present time is a point in eternity. All things are little, changeable, perishable" (vi. 36.)

And to Marcus too, no less than to Shakespeare, it seemed that—

"All the world's a stage,
And all the men and women merely players;"

for he writes these remarkable words:—

"The idle business of show, plays on the stage, flocks of sheep, herds, exercises with spears, a bone cast to little dogs, a bit of bread in fishponds, labourings of ants, and burden-carrying runnings about of frightened little mice, puppets pulled by strings—this is what life resembles. It is thy duty then in the midst of such things to show good humour, and not a proud air; to understand however that every man is worth just so much as the things are worth about which he busies himself."

In fact, the Court was to Marcus a burden; he tells us himself that Philosophy was his mother, Empire only his stepmother; it was only his repose in the one that rendered even tolerable to him the burdens of the other. Emperor as he was, he thanked the gods for having enabled him to enter into the souls of a Thrasea, an Helvidius, a Cato, a Brutus. Above all, he seems to have had a horror of ever becoming like some of his predecessors; he writes:—

"Take care that thou art not made into a Caesar;[68] take care thou art not dyed with this dye. Keep thyself then simple, good, pure, serious, free from affectation, a friend of justice, a worshipper of the gods, kind, affectionate, strenuous in all proper acts. Reverence the gods and help men. Short is life. There is only one fruit of this terrene life; a pious disposition and social acts." (iv. 19,)

It is the same conclusion as that which sorrow forced from another weary and less admirable king: "Let us hear the conclusion of the whole matter: Fear God, and keep His commandments; for this is the whole duty of man."

But it is time for us to continue the meagre record of the life of Marcus, so far as the bare and gossiping compilations of Dion Cassius,[69] and Capitolinus, and the scattered allusions of other writers can enable us to do so.

It must have been with a heavy heart that he set out once more for Germany to face the dangerous rising of the Quadi and Marcomanni. To obtain soldiers sufficient to fill up the vacancies in his army which had been decimated by the plague, he was forced to enrol slaves; and to obtain money he had to sell the ornaments of the palace, and even some of the Empress's jewels. Immediately

---

[68] Marcus here invents what M. Martha justly calls "an admirable barbarism" to express his disgust towards such men—[Greek: ora mae apukaidaoosaes]—"take care not to be Caesarised."
[69] As epitomised by Xiphilinus.

before he started his heart was wrung by the death of his little boy, the twin-brother of Commodus, whose beautiful features are still preserved for us on coins. Early in the war, as he was trying the depth of a ford, he was assailed by the enemy with a sudden storm of missiles, and was only saved from imminent death by being sheltered beneath the shields of his soldiers. One battle was fought on the ice of the wintry Danube. But by far the most celebrated event of the war took place in a great victory over the Quadi which he won in A.D. 174, and which was attributed by the Christians to what is known as the "Miracle of the Thundering Legion."

Divested of all extraneous additions, the fact which occurred,—as established by the evidence of medals, and by one of the bass-relievi on the "Column of Antonine,"—appears to have been as follows. Marcus Aurelius and his army had been entangled in a mountain defile, into which they had too hastily pursued a sham retreat of the barbarian archers. In this defile, unable either to fight or to fly, pent in by the enemy, burned up with the scorching heat and tormented by thirst, they lost all hope, burst into wailing and groans, and yielded to a despair from which not even the strenuous efforts of Marcus could arouse them. At the most critical moment of their danger and misery the clouds began to gather, and heavy shows of rain descended, which the soldiers caught in their shields and helmets to quench their own thirst and that of their horses. While they were thus engaged the enemy attacked them; but the rain was mingled with hail, and fell with blinding fury in the faces of the barbarians. The storm was also accompanied with thunder and lightning, which seems to have damaged the enemy, and filled them with terror, while no casualty occured in the Roman ranks. The Romans accordingly regarded this as a Divine interposition, and achieved a most decisive victory, which proved to be the practical conclusion of a hazardous and important war.

The Christians regarded the event not as providential but as miraculous, and attributed it to the prayers of their brethren in a legion which, from this circumstance, received the name of the "Thundering Legion." It is however now known that one of the legions, distinguished by a flash of lightning which was represented on their shields, had been known by this name since the time of Augustus; and the Pagans themselves attributed the assistance which they had received sometimes to a prayer of the pious Emperor and sometimes to the incantations of an Egyptian sorcerer named Arnuphis.

One of the Fathers, the passionate and eloquent Tertullian, attributes to this deliverance an interposition of the Emperor in favour of the Christians, and appeals to a letter of his to the Senate in which he acknowledged how effectual had been the aid he had received from Christian prayers, and forbade any one hereafter to molest the followers of the new religion, lest they should use against him the weapon of supplication which had been so powerful in his favour. This letter is preserved at the end of the Apology of Justin Martyr, and it adds that, not only are no Christians to be injured or persecuted, but that any one who informed against them is to be burned alive! We see at once that this letter is one of those impudent and transparent forgeries in which the literature of the first five centuries unhappily abounds. What was the real relation of Marcus to the Christians we shall consider hereafter.

To the gentle heart of Marcus, all war, even when accompanied with victories, was eminently distasteful; and in such painful and ungenial occupations no small part of his life was passed. What he thought of war and of its successes is graphically set forth in the following remark:—

"A spider is proud when it has caught a fly, and another when he has caught a poor hare, and another when he has taken a little fish in a net, and another when he has taken wild boars or bears, and another when he has taken Sarmatians. Are not these robbers, when thou examinest their principles?" He here condemns his own involuntary actions; but it was his unhappy destiny not to have trodden out the embers of this war before he was burdened with another far more painful and formidable.

This was the revolt of Avidius Cassius, a general of the old blunt Roman type, whom, in spite of some ominous warnings, Marcus both loved and trusted. The ingratitude displayed by such a man caused Marcus the deepest anguish; but he was saved from all dangerous consequences by the wide-spread affection which he had inspired by his virtuous reign.

The very soldiers of the rebellious general fell away from him; and, after he had been a nominal Emperor for only three months and six days, he was assassinated by some of his own officers. His head was sent to Marcus, who received it with sorrow, and did not hold out to the murderers the slightest encouragement. The joy of success was swallowed up in regret that his enemy had not lived to allow him the luxury of a genuine forgiveness. He begged the Senate to pardon all the family of Cassius, and to suffer this single life to be the only one forfeited in consequence of civil war. The Fathers received these proofs of clemency with the rapture which they deserved, and the Senate-house resounded with acclamations and blessings.

Never had a formidable conspiracy been more quietly and effectually crushed. Marcus travelled through the provinces which had favoured the cause of Avidius Cassius, and treated them all with the most complete and indulgent forbearance. When he arrived in Syria, the correspondence of Cassius was brought to him, and, with a glorious magnanimity of which history affords but few examples, he consigned it all to the flames unread.

During this journey of pacification, he lost his wife Faustina, who died suddenly in one of the valleys of Mount Taurus. History, or the collection of anecdotes which at this period often passes as history, has assigned to Faustina a character of the darkest infamy, and it has even been made a charge against Aurelius that he overlooked or condoned her offences. As far as Faustina is concerned, we have not much to say, although there is strong reason to believe that many of the stories told of her are scandalously exaggerated, if not absolutely false. Certain it is, that most of the imputations upon her memory rest on the malignant anecdotes recorded by Dion, who dearly loved every piece of scandal which degraded human nature. The specific charge brought against her of having tempted Cassius from his allegiance is wholly unsupported, even if it be not absolutely incompatible with what we find in her own existent letters; and, finally, Marcus himself not only loved her tenderly, as the kind mother of his eleven children, but in his Meditations actually thanks the gods for having granted him "such a wife, so obedient so affectionate, and so simple." No doubt Faustina was unworthy of her husband; but surely it is the glory and not the shame of a noble nature to be averse from jealousy and suspicion, and to trust to others more deeply than they deserve.

So blameless was the conduct of Marcus Aurelius that neither the malignity of contemporaries nor the sprit of posthumous scandal has succeeded in discovering any flaw in the extreme integrity of his life and principles. But meanness will not be baulked of its victims. The hatred of all excellence which made Caligula try to put down the memory of great men rages, though less openly, in the minds of many. They delight to degrade human life into that dull and barren plain "in which every molehill is a mountain, and every thistle a forest-tree." Great men are as small in their eyes as they are said to be in the eyes of their valets; and there are multitudes who, if they find

> "Some stain or blemish in a name of note,
> Not grieving that their greatest are so small,
> Innate themselves with some insane delight,
> And judge all nature from her feet of clay,
> Without the will to lift their eyes, and see

163

Her godlike head crown'd with spiritual fire,
And touching other worlds."

This I suppose is the reason why, failing to drag down Marcus Aurelius from his moral elevation, some have attempted to assail his reputation because of the supposed vileness of Faustina and the actual depravity of Commodus. Of Faustina I have spoken already. Respecting Commodus, I think it sufficient to ask with Solomon: "Who knoweth whether his son shall be a wise man or a fool?" Commodus was but nineteen when his father died; for the first three years of his reign he ruled respectably and acceptably. Marcus Aurelius had left no effort untried to have him trained aright by the first teachers and the wisest men whom the age produced; and Herodian distinctly tells us that he had lived virtuously up to the time of his father's death. Setting aside natural affection altogether, and even assuming (as I should conjecture from one or two passages of his Meditations) that Marcus had misgivings about his son, would it have been easy, would it have been even possible, to set aside on general grounds a son who had attained to years of maturity? However this may be, if there are any who think it worth while to censure Marcus because, after all, Commodus turned out to be but "a warped slip of wilderness," their censure is hardly sufficiently discriminating to deserve the trouble of refutation.

"But Marcus Aurelius cruelly persecuted the Christians." Let us briefly consider this charge. That persecutions took place in his reign is an undeniable fact, and is sufficiently evidenced by the Apologies of Justin Martyr, of Melito Bishop of Sardis, of Athenagoras, and of Apollinarius, as well as by the Letter of the Church of Smyrna describing the martyrdom of Polycarp, and that of the Churches of Lyons and Vienne to their brethren in Asia Minor. It is fair, however, to mention that there is some documentary evidence on the other side; Lactantius clearly asserts that under the reigns of those excellent princes who succeeded Domitian the Church suffered no violence from her enemies, and "spread her hands towards the East and the West:" Tertullian, writing but twenty years after the death of Marcus, distinctly says (and Eusebius quotes the assertion), that there were letters of the Emperor, in which he not only attributed his delivery among the Quadi to the prayers of Christian soldiers in the "Thundering Legion," but ordered any who informed against the Christians to be most severely punished; and at the end of the works of Justin Martyr is found a letter of similar purport, which is asserted to have been addressed by Marcus to the Senate of Rome. We may set aside these peremptory testimonies, we may believe that Tertullian and

Eusebius were mistaken, and that the documents to which they referred were spurious; but this should make us also less certain about the prominent participation of the Emperor in these persecutions. My own belief is (and it is a belief which could be supported by many critical arguments), that his share in causing them was almost infinitesimal. If those who love his memory reject the evidence of Fathers in his favour, they may be at least permitted to withhold assent from some of the assertions in virtue of which he is condemned.

Marcus in his Meditations alludes to the Christians once only, and then it is to make a passing complaint of the indifference to death, which appeared to him, as it appeared to Epictetus, to arise, not from any noble principles, but from mere obstinacy and perversity. That he shared the profound dislike with which Christians were regarded is very probable. That he was a cold-blooded and virulent persecutor is utterly unlike his whole character, essentially at variance with his habitual clemency, alien to the spirit which made him interfere in every possible instance to mitigate the severity of legal punishments, and may in short be regarded as an assertion which is altogether false. Who will believe that a man who during his reign built and dedicated but one single temple, and that a Temple to Beneficence; that a man who so far from showing any jealousy respecting foreign religions allowed honour to be paid to them all; that a man whose writings breathe on every page the inmost spirit of philanthropy and tenderness, went out of his way to join in a persecution of the most innocent, the most courageous, and the most inoffensive of his subjects?

The true state of the case seems to have been this. The deep calamities in which, during the whole reign of Marcus the Empire was involved, caused widespread distress, and roused into peculiar fury the feelings of the provincials against men whose atheism (for such they considered it to be) had kindled the anger of the gods. This fury often broke out into paroxisms of popular excitement, which none but the firmest-minded governers were able to moderate or to repress. Marcus, when appealed to, simply let the existing law take its usual course. That law was as old as the time of Trajan. The young Pliny, Governor of Bithynia, had written to ask Trajan how he was to deal with the Christians, whose blamelessness of life he fully admitted, but whose doctrines, he said, had emptied the temples of the gods, and exasperated their worshippers. Trajan in reply had ordered that the Christians should not be sought for, but that, if they were brought before the governor, and proved to be contumacious in refusing to adjure their religion, they were then to be put to death. Hadrian and Antoninus Pius had continued the same policy, and Marcus Aurilius saw no reason to alter it. But this law, which in quiet times might become a mere dead letter, might at more troubled periods be converted into a dangerous engine of persecution, as it was in the case of the venerable Polycarp, and in the unfortunate Churches of Lyons and Vienne. The Pagans believed that the reason why their gods were smiling in secret,—

> "Looking over wasted lands,
> Blight and famine, plague and earthquake, roaring deeps
> and fiery sands,—

> "Clanging fights, and flaming towns, and sinking ships, and
> praying hands,—"

was the unbelief and impiety of these hated Galileans, causes of offence which could only be expiated by the death of the guilty. "Their enemies," says Tertullian, "call aloud for the blood of the innocent, alleging this vain pretext for their hatred, that they believe the Christians to be the cause of every public misfortune. If the Tiber has overflowed its banks, or the Nile has not overflowed, if heaven has refused its rain, if famine or the plague has spread its ravages, the cry is immediate, 'The Christians to the lions.'" In the first three centuries the cry of "No Christianity" became at times as brutal, as violent, and as unreasoning as the cry of "No Popery" has often been in modern days. It was infinitely less disgraceful to Marcus to lend his ear to the one than it has been to some eminent modern statesmen to be carried away by the insensate fury of the other.

To what extent is Marcus Aurelius to be condemned for the martyrdoms which took place in his reign? Not, I think, heavily or indiscriminately, or with vehement sweeping censure. Common justice surely demands that we should not confuse the present with the past, or pass judgment on the conduct of the Emperor as though he were living in the nineteenth century, or as though he had been acting in full cognisance of the Gospels and the stones of the Saints. Wise and good men before him had, in their haughty ignorance, spoken of Christianity with execration and contempt. The philosophers who surrounded his throne treated it with jealousy and aversion. The body of the nation firmly believed the current rumours which charged its votaries with horrible midnight assemblies, rendered infamous by Thyestian banquets and the atrocities of nameless superstitions. These foul calumnies—these hideous charges of cannibalism and incest,—were supported by the reiterated perjury of slaves under torture, which in that age, as well as long afterwards, was preposterously regarded as a sure criterion of truth.

Christianity in that day was confounded with a multitude of debased and foreign superstitions; and the Emperor in his judicial capacity, if he ever encountered Christians at all, was far more likely to encounter those who were unworthy of the name, than to become acquainted with the meek, unworldly, retiring virtues of the calmest, the holiest, and the best. When we have given their due weight to considerations such as these we shall be ready to pardon Marcus Aurelius for having, in this matter, acted ignorantly, and to admit that in persecuting Christianity he may most honestly have thought that he was doing God service. The very sincerity of his belief, the conscientiousness of his rule, the intensity of his philanthrophy, the grandeur of his own philosophical tenets, all conspired to make him a worse enemy of the Church than a brutal Commodus or a disgusting Heliogabalus. And yet that there was not in him the least propensity to persecute; that these persecutions were for the most part spontaneous and accidental; that they were in no measure due to his direct instigation, or in special accordance with his desire, is clear from the fact that the martyrdoms took place in Gaul and Asia Minor, not in Rome. There must have been hundreds of Christians in Rome, and under the very eye of the Emperor; nay, there were even multitudes of Christians in his own army; yet we never hear of his having molested any of them. Melito, Bishop of Sardis, in addressing the Emperor, expresses a doubt as to whether he was really aware of the manner in which his Christian subjects were treated. Justin Martyr, in his Apology, addresses him in terms of perfect confidence and deep respect. In short he was in this matter "blameless, but unfortunate." It is painful to think that the venerable Polycarp, and the thoughtful Justin may have forfeited their lives for their principles, not only in the reign of so good a man, but even by virtue of his authority; but we must be very uncharitable or very unimaginative if we cannot readily believe that, though they had received the crown of martyrdom from his hands, the redeemed spirits of those great martyrs would have been the first to welcome this holiest of the heathen into the presence of a Saviour whose Church he persecuted, but to whose indwelling Spirit his virtues were due? whom ignorantly and unconsciously he worshipped, and whom had he ever heard of Him and known Him, he would have loved in his heart and glorified by the consistency of his noble and stainless life.

The persecution of the Churches in Lyons and Vienne happened in A.D. 177. Shortly after this period fresh wars recalled the Emperor to the North. It is said that, in despair of ever seeing

167

him again, the chief men of Rome entreated him to address them his farewell admonitions, and that for three days he discoursed to them on philosophical questions. When he arrived at the seat of war, victory again crowned his arms. But Marcus was now getting old, and he was worn out with the toils, trials, and travels of his long and weary life. He sunk under mental anxieties and bodily fatigues, and after a brief illness died in Pannonia, either at Vienna or Sirmium, on March 17, A.D. 180, in the fifty-ninth year of his age and the twentieth of his reign.

Death to him was no calamity. He was sadly aware that "there is no man so fortunate that there shall not be by him when he is dying some who are pleased with what is going to happen. Suppose that he was a good and wise man, will there not be at last some one to say of him, 'Let us at last breathe freely, being relieved from this schoolmaster. It is true that he was harsh to none of us, but I perceive that he tacitly condemns us.'... Thou wilt consider this when thou art dying, and wilt depart more contentedly by reflecting thus: 'I am going away from a life in which even my associates, on behalf of whom I have striven, and cared, and prayed so much, themselves wish me to depart, hoping perchance to get some little advantage by it.' Why then should a man cling to a longer stay here? Do not, however, for this reason go away less kindly disposed to them, but preserving thy own character, and continuing friendly, and benevolent, and kind" And dreading death far less than he dreaded any departure from the laws of virtue, he exclaims, "Come quickly, O Death, for fear that at last I should forget myself." This utterance has been well compared to the language which Bossuet put into the mouth of a Christian soul:—"O Death; thou dost not trouble my designs, thou accomplishest them. Haste, then, O favourable Death!... Nunc Dimittis."

A nobler, a gentler, a purer, a sweeter soul,—a soul less elated by prosperity, or more constant in adversity—a soul more fitted by virtue, and chastity, and self-denial to enter into the eternal peace, never passed into the presence of its Heavenly Father. We are not surprised that all, whose means permitted it, possessed themselves of his statues, and that they were to be seen for years afterwards among the household gods of heathen families, who felt themselves more hopeful and more happy from the glorious sense of possibility which was inspired by the memory of one who, in the midst of difficulties, and breathing an atmosphere heavy with corruption, yet showed himself so wise, so great, so good a man.

O framed for nobler times and calmer hearts!
O studious thinker, eloquent for truth!

Philosopher, despising wealth and death,
But patient, childlike, full of life and love!

CHAPTER IV

THE "MEDITATIONS" OF MARCUS AURELIUS

Emperor as he was, Marcus Aurelius found himself in a hollow and troublous world; but he did not give himself up to idle regret or querulous lamentations. If these sorrows and perturbations came from the gods, he kissed the hand that smote him; "he delivered up his broken sword to Fate the conqueror with a humble and a manly heart." In any case he had duties to do, and he set himself to perform them with a quiet heroism—zealously, conscientiously, even cheerfully.

The principles of the Emperor are not reducible to the hard and definite lines of a philosophic system. But the great laws which guided his actions and moulded his views of life were few and simple, and in his book of Meditations, which is merely his private diary written to relieve his mind amid all the trials of war and government, he recurs to them again and again. "Plays, war, astonishment, torpor, slavery," he says to himself, "will wipe out those holy principles of thine;" and this is why he committed those principles to writing. Some of these I have already adduced, and others I proceed to quote, availing myself, as before, of the beautiful and scholar-like translation of Mr. George Long.

All pain, and misfortune, and ugliness seemed to the Emperor to be most wisely regarded under a threefold aspect, namely, if considered in reference to the gods, as being due to laws beyond their control; if considered with reference to the nature of things, as being subservient and necessary; and if considered with reference to ourselves, as being dependent on the amount of indifference and fortitude with which we endure them.

The following passages will elucidate these points of view:—

"The intelligence of the Universe is social. Accordingly it has made the inferior things for the sake of the superior, and it has fitted the superior to one another." (v. 30.)

"Things do not touch the soul, for they are eternal, and remain immovable; but our perturbations come only from the opinion which is within.... The Universe is Transformation; life is opinion" (iv. 3.)

"To the jaundiced honey tastes bitter, and to those bitten by mad dogs water causes fear; and to little children the ball is a fine thing. Why then am I angry? Dost thou think that a false opinion has less power than the bile in the jaundiced, or the poison in him who is bitten by a mad dog?" (vi. 52.)

"How easy it is to repel and to wipe away every impression which is troublesome and unsuitable, and immediately to be at tranquillity." (v. 2.)

The passages in which Marcus speaks of evil as a relative thing,—as being good in the making,—the unripe and bitter bud of that which shall be hereafter a beautiful flower,—although not expressed with perfect clearness, yet indicate his belief that our view of evil things rises in great measure from our inability to perceive the great whole of which they are but subservient parts.

"All things," he says, "come from that universal ruling power, either directly or by way of consequence. And accordingly the lion's gaping jaws, and that which is poisonous, and every hurtful thing, as a thorn, as mud, are after-products of the grand and beautiful. Do not therefore imagine that they are of another kind from that which thou dost venerate, but form a just opinion of the source of all."

In another curious passage he says that all things which are natural and congruent with the causes which produce them have a certain beauty and attractiveness of their own; for instance, the splittings and corrugations on the surface of bread when it has been baked. "And again, figs when they are quite ripe gape open; and in the ripe olives the very circumstances of their being near to rottenness adds a peculiar beauty to the fruit. And the ears of corn bending down, and the lion's eyebrows, and the foam which flows from the mouth of wild boars, and many other things—though they are far from being beautiful, if a man should examine them severally—still, because they are consequent upon the things which are formed by nature, help to adorn them, and they please the mind; so that if a man should have a feeling and deeper insight about the things found in the universe there is hardly one of those which follow by way of consequence which will not seem to him to be in a manner disposed so as to give pleasure." (iv. 2.)

This congruity to nature—the following of nature, and obedience to all her laws—is the key-formula to the doctrines of the Roman Stoics.

"Everything which is in any way beautiful is beautiful in itself, and terminates in itself, not having praise as part of itself. Neither worse, then, nor better is a thing made by being praised.... Is such a thing as an emerald made worse than it was, if it is not praised? or gold, ivory, purple, a lyre, a little knife, a flower, a shrub?" (iv. 20.)

"Everything harmonizes with me which is harmonious to thee, O Universe. Nothing for me is too early nor too late, which is in due time for thee. Everything is fruit to me which thy seasons bring, O Nature! from thee are all things, in thee are all things, to thee all things return. The poet says, Dear city of Cecrops; and wilt not thou say, Dear city of God?" (iv. 23.)

"Willingly give thyself up to fate, allowing her to spin thy thread into whatever thing she pleases." (iv. 34.)

And here, in a very small matter—getting out of bed in a morning—is one practical application of the formula:—

"In the morning when thou risest unwillingly, let these thoughts be present—'I am rising to the work of a human being. Why, then, am I dissatisfied if I am going to do the things for which I exist, and for which I was brought into the world? Or have I been made for this, to lie in the bedclothes and keep myself warm?' 'But this is more pleasant.' Dost thou exist, then, to take thy pleasure, and not for action or exertion? Dost thou not see the little plants, the little birds, the ants, the spiders, the bees, working together to put in order their several parts of the universe? And art thou unwilling to do the work of a human being, and dost thou not make haste to do that which is according to thy nature?" (v. 1.) ["Go to the ant, thou sluggard; consider her ways, and be wise!"]

The same principle, that Nature has assigned to us our proper place—that a task has been given us to perform, and that our only care should be to perform it aright, for the blessing of the great Whole of which we are but insignificant parts—dominates through the admirable precepts which the Emperor lays down for the regulation of our conduct towards others. Some men, he says, do benefits to others only because they expect a return; some men even, if they do not demand any return, are not forgetful that they have rendered a benefit; but others do not even know what they have done, but are like a vine which has produced grapes, and seeks for nothing more after it has produced its proper fruit. So we ought to do good to others as simple and as naturally as a horse runs, or a bee makes honey, or a vine bears grapes season after season, without thinking of the grapes which it has borne. And in another passage, "What more dost thou want when thou hast done a service to another? Art thou not content to have done an act conformable to thy nature, and must thou seek to be paid for it, just as if the eye demanded a reward for seeing, or the feet for walking?"

"Judge every word and deed which is according to nature to

171

be fit for thee, and be not diverted by the blame which follows...but if a thing is good to be done or said, do not consider it unworthy of thee." (v. 3.)

Sometimes, indeed, Marcus Aurelius wavers. The evils of life overpower him. "Such as bathing appears to thee," he says, "oil, sweat, dirt, filthy water, all things disgusting—so is every part of life and everything" (viii. 24); and again:—"Of human life the time is a point, and the substance is in a flux, and the perception dull, and the composition of the whole body subject to putrefaction, and the soul a whirl, and fortune hard to divine, and fame a thing devoid of judgment." But more often he retains his perfect tranquillity, and says, "Either thou livest here, and hast already accustomed thyself to it, or thou art going away, and this was thine own will; or thou art dying, and hast discharged thy duty. But besides these things there is nothing. Be of good cheer, then." (x. 22.) "Take me, and cast me where thou wilt, for then I shall keep my divine part tranquil, that is, content, if it can feel and act conformably to its proper constitution." (viii. 45.)

There is something delightful in the fact that even in the Stoic philosophy there was some comfort to keep men from despair. To a holy and scrupulous conscience like that of Marcus, there would have been an inestimable preciousness in the Christian doctrine of the "forgiveness of the sins." Of that divine mercy—of that sin-uncreating power—the ancient world knew nothing; but in Marcus we find some dim and faint adumbration of the doctrine, expressed in a manner which might at least breathe calm into the spirit of the philosopher, though it could never reach the hearts of the suffering multitude. For "suppose," he says, "that thou hast detached thyself from the natural unity,—for thou wast made by nature a part, but now hast cut thyself off—yet here is the beautiful provision that it is in thy power again to unite thyself. God has allowed this to no other part—after it has been separated and cut asunder, to come together again. But consider the goodness with which He has privileged man; for He has put it in his power, when he has been separated, to return and to be reunited, and to resume his place" And elsewhere he says, "If you cannot maintain a true and magnanimous character, go courageously into some corner where you can maintain them; or if even there you fail, depart at once from life, not with passion, but with modest and simple freedom—which will be to have done at least one laudable act." Sad that even to Marcus Aurelius death should have seemed the only refuge from the despair of ultimate failure in the struggle to be wise and good!

Marcus valued temperance and self-denial as being the best means of keeping his heart strong and pure; but we are glad to learn

172

he did not value the rigours of asceticism. Life brought with it enough, and more than enough, of antagonism to brace his nerves; enough, and more than enough, of the rough wind of adversity in his face to make it unnecessary to add more by his own actions. "It is not fit," he says, "that I should give myself pain, for I have never intentionally given pain even to another." (viii. 42.)

It was a commonplace of ancient philosophy that the life of the wise man should be a contemplation of, and a preparation for, death. It certainly was so with Marcus Aurelius. The thoughts of the nothingness of man, and of that great sea of oblivion which shall hereafter swallow up all that he is and does, are ever present to his mind; they are thoughts to which he recurs more constantly than any other, and from which he always draws the same moral lesson.

"Since it is possible that thou mayest depart from life this very moment, regulate every act and thought accordingly.... Death certainly, and life, honour and dishonour, pain and pleasure, all these things happen equally to good men and bad, being things which make us neither better nor worse. Therefore they are neither good nor evil." (ii. 11.)

Elsewhere he says that Hippocrates cured diseases and died; and the Chaldaeans foretold the future and died; and Alexander, and Pompey, and Caesar killed thousands, and then died; and lice destroyed Democritus, and other lice killed Socrates; and Augustus, and his wife, and daughter, and all his descendants, and all his ancestors, are dead; and Vespasian and all his Court, and all who in his day feasted, and married, and were sick and chaffered, and fought, and flattered, and plotted, and grumbled, and wished other people to die, and pined to become kings or consuls, are dead; and all the idle people who are doing the same things now are doomed to die; and all human things are smoke, and nothing at all; and it is not for us, but for the gods, to settle whether we play the play out, or only a part of it. "There are many grains of frankincense on the same altar; one falls before, another falls after; but it makes no difference." And the moral of all these thoughts is, "Death hangs over thee while thou livest: while it is in thy power be good." (iv. 17.) "Thou hast embarked, thou hast made the voyage, thou hast come to shore; get out. If, indeed, to another life there is no want of gods, not even there. But if to a state without sensation, thou wilt cease to be held by pains and pleasures." (iii. 3.)

Nor was Marcus at all comforted under present annoyances by the thought of posthumous fame. "How ephemeral and worthless human things are," he says, "and what was yesterday a little mucus, to-morrow will be a mummy or ashes." "Many who are now praising thee, will very soon blame thee, and neither a posthumous name is of any value, nor reputation, nor anything else." What has become of all great and famous men, and all they desired, and all they loved? They are "smoke, and ash, and a tale, or not even a tale." After all their rages and envyings, men are stretched out quiet and dead at last. Soon thou wilt have forgotten all, and soon all will have forgotten thee. But here, again, after such thoughts, the same moral is always introduced again:—"Pass then through the little space of time conformably to nature, and end the journey in content, just as an olive falls off when it is ripe, blessing nature who produced it, and thanking the tree on which it grew" "One thing only troubles me, lest I should do something which the constitution of man does not allow, or in the way which it does not allow, or what it does not allow now."

To quote the thoughts of Marcus Aurelius is to me a fascinating task. But I have already let him speak so largely for himself that by this time the reader will have some conception of his leading motives. It only remains to adduce a few more of the weighty and golden sentences in which he lays down his rule of life.

"To say all in a word, everything which belongs to the body is a stream, and what belongs to the soul is a dream and vapour; and life is a warfare, and a stranger's sojourn, and after fame is oblivion. What, then, is that which is able to enrich a man? One thing, and only one—philosophy. But this consists in keeping the guardian spirit within a man free from violence and unharmed, superior to pains and pleasures, doing nothing without a purpose, nor yet falsely, and with hypocrisy... accepting all that happens and all that is allotted ... and finally waiting for death with a cheerful mind" (ii.17.)

"If thou findest in human life anything better than justice, truth, temperance, fortitude, and, in a word, than thine own soul's satisfaction in the things which it enables thee to do according to right reason, and In the condition that is assigned to thee without thy own choice; if, I say, thou seest anything better than this, turn to it with all thy soul, and enjoy that which thou hast found to be the best. But ... if thou findest everything else smaller and of less value than this, give place to nothing else.... Simply and freely choose the better, and hold to it." (iii. 6.)

"Body, soul, intelligence: to the body belong sensations, to the soul appetites, to the intelligence principles." To be impressed by the senses is peculiar to animals; to be pulled by the strings of desire belongs to effeminate men, and to men like Phalaris or Nero; to be guided only by intelligence belongs to atheists and traitors, and "men who do their impure deeds when they have shut the doors.... There remains that which is peculiar to the good man, to be pleased and content with what happens, and with the thread which is spun for him; and not to defile the divinity which is planted in his breast, nor disturb it by a crowd of images; but to preserve it tranquil, following it obediently as a god, neither saying anything contrary to truth, nor doing anything contrary to justice. (iii. 16.)

"Men seek retreats for themselves, houses in the country, sea-shores, and mountains, and thou too art wont to desire such things very much. But this is altogether a mark of the commonest sort of men, for it is in thy power whenever thou shalt chose to retire into thyself. For nowhere either with more quiet or with more freedom does a man retire than into his own soul, particularly when he has within him such thoughts that by looking into them he is immediately in perfect tranquillity,—which is nothing else than the good ordering of the mind." (iv. 3.)

"Unhappy am I, because this has happened to me? Not so, but happy am I though this has happened to me, because I continue free from pain; neither crushed by the present, nor fearing the future." (iv. 19.)

It is just possible that in some of these passages some readers may detect a trace of painful self-consciousness, and imagine that they detect a little grain of self-complacence. Something of self-consciousness is perhaps inevitable in the diary and examination of his own conscience by one who sat on such a lonely height; but self-complacency there is none. Nay, there is sometimes even a cruel sternness in the way in which the Emperor speaks of his own self. He certainly dealt not with himself in the manner of a dissembler with God. "When," he says (x. 8), "thou hast assumed the names of a man who is good, modest, rational, magnanimous, cling to those names; and if thou shouldst lose them, quickly return to them.... For to continue to be such as thou hast hitherto been, and to be torn in pieces, and defiled in such a life, is the character of a very stupid man, and one over-fond of his life, and like those half-devoured fighters with wild beasts, who, though covered with wounds and gore, still entreat to be kept till the following day, though they will be exposed in the same state to the same claws and bites. Therefore fix thyself in the possession of these few names: and if thou art able to abide in them, abide as if thou were removed to the Islands of the Blest." Alas! to Aurelius, in this life, the Islands of the Blest were very far away. Heathen philosophy was exalted and eloquent, but all its votaries were sad; to "the peace of God, which passeth all understanding," it was not given them to attain. We see Marcus "wise, self-governed, tender, thankful, blameless," says Mr. Arnold, "yet with all this agitated, stretching out his arms for something beyond—tendentemque manue ripae ulterioris amore"

175

I will quote in conclusion but three short precepts:—

"Be cheerful, and seek not external help, nor the tranquillity which others give. A man must stand erect, not be kept erect by others." (iv. 5.)

"Be like the promontory against which the waves continually break, but it stands firm and tames the fury of the water around it" (iv. 49.)

This comparison has been used many a time since the days of Marcus Aurelius. The reader will at once recall Goldsmith's famous lines:—

"As some tall cliff that rears its awful form,
Swells from the vale, and midway leaves the storm,
Though round its breast the rolling clouds are spread,
Eternal sunshine settles on its head."

"Short is the little that remains to thee of life. Live as on a mountain. For it makes no difference whether a man lives there or here, if he lives everywhere in the world as in a civil community. Let men see, let them know a real man who lives as he was meant to live. If they cannot endure him, let them kill him. For that is better than to live as men do." (x. 15.)

Such were some of the thoughts which Marcus Aurelius wrote in his diary after days of battle with the Quadi, and the Marcomanni, and the Sarmatae. Isolated from others no less by moral grandeur than by the supremacy of his sovereign rank, he sought the society of his own noble soul. I sometimes imagine that I see him seated on the borders of some gloomy Pannonian forest or Hungarian marsh; through the darkness the watchfires of the enemy gleam in the distance; but both among them, and in the camp around him, every sound is hushed, except the tread of the sentinel outside the imperial tent; and in that tent long after midnight sits the patient Emperor by the light of his solitary lamp, and ever and anon, amid his lonely musings, he pauses to write down the pure and holy thoughts which shall better enable him, even in a Roman palace, even on barbarian battlefields, daily to tolerate the meanness and the malignity of the men around him; daily to amend his own shortcomings, and, as the sun of earthly life begins to set, daily to draw nearer and nearer to the Eternal Light. And when I thus think of him, I know not whether the whole of heathen antiquity, out of its gallery of stately and royal figures, can furnish a nobler, or purer, or more lovable picture than that of this crowned philosopher and laurelled hero, who was yet one of the humblest and one of the most enlightened of all ancient "Seekers after God."

CONCLUSION

A sceptical writer has observed, with something like a sneer, that the noblest utterances of Gospel morality may be paralleled from the writings of heathen philosophers. The sneer is pointless, and Christian moralists have spontaneously drawn attention to the fact. In this volume, so far from trying to conceal that it is so, I have taken pleasure in placing side by side the words of Apostles and of Philosophers. The divine origin of Christianity does not rest on its morality alone. By the aid of the light which was within them, by deciphering the law written on their own consciences, however much its letters may have been obliterated or dimmed, Plato, and Cicero, and Seneca, and Epictetus, and Aurelius were enabled to grasp and to enunciate a multitude of great and memorable truths; yet they themselves would have been the first to admit the wavering uncertainty of their hopes and speculations, and the absolute necessity of a further illumination. So strong did that necessity appear to some of the wisest among them, that Socrates ventures in express words to prophesy the future advent of some heaven-sent Guide.[70] Those who imagine that without a written revelation it would have been possible to learn all that is necessary for man's well-being, are speaking in direct contradiction of the greatest heathen teachers, in contradiction even of those very teachers to whose writing they point as the proof of their assertion. Augustine was expressing a very deep conviction when he said that in Plato and in Cicero he met with many utterances which were beautiful and wise, but among them all he never found, "Come unto me, all ye that labour and are heavy laden, and I will refresh you." Glorious as was the wisdom of ancient thought, its knowledge respecting the indwelling of the Spirit, the resurrection of the body, and the forgiveness of sins, was but fragmentary and vague. Bishop Butler has justly remarked that "The great doctrines of a future state, the dangers of a course of wickedness, and the efficacy of repentance are not only confirmed in the Gospel, but are taught, especially the last is, with a degree of light to which that of nature is darkness."

The morality of Paganism was, on its own confession, insufficient. It was tentative, where Christianity is authoritative: it was dim and partial, where Christianity is bright and complete; it was inadequate to rouse the sluggish carelessness of mankind, where Christianity came in with an imperial and awakening power;

---

[70] Xen. Mem. 1, iv. 14; Plato, Alcib. ii.

177

it gives only a rule, where Christianity supplies a principle. And even where its teachings were absolutely coincident with those of Scripture, it failed to ratify them with a sufficient sanction; it failed to announce them with the same powerful and contagious ardour; it failed to furnish an absolutely faultless and vivid example of their practice; it failed to inspire them with an irresistible motive; it failed to support them with a powerful comfort under the difficulties which were sure to be encountered in the aim after a consistent and holy life.

The attempts of the Christian Fathers to show that the truths of ancient philosophy were borrowed from Scripture are due in some cases to ignorance and in some to a want of perfect honesty in controversial dealing. That Gideon (Jerubbaal) is identical with the priest Hierombalos who supplied information to Sanchoniathon, the Berytian; that Thales pieced together a philosophy from fragments of Jewish truth learned in Phoenicia; that Pythagoras and Democritus availed themselves of Hebraic traditions, collected during their travels; that Plato is a mere "Atticising Moses;" that Aristotle picked up his ethical system from a Jew whom he met in Asia; that Seneca corresponded with St. Paul: are assertions every bit as unhistorical and false as that Homer was thinking of Genesis when he described the shield of Achilles, or (as Clemens of Alexandria gravely informs us) that Miltiades won the battle of Marathon by copying the strategy of the battle of Beth-Horon! To say that Pagan morality "kindled its faded taper at the Gospel light, whether furtively or unconsciously taken," and that it "dissembled the obligation, and made a boast of the splendour as though it were originally her own, or were sufficient in her hands for the moral illumination of the world;" is to make an assertion wholly untenable.[71] Seneca, Epictetus, Aurelius, are among the truest and loftiest of Pagan moralists, yet Seneca ignored the Christians, Epictetus despised, and Aurelius persecuted them. All three, so far as they knew anything about the Christians at all, had unhappily been taught to look upon them as the most detestable sect of what they had long regarded as the most degraded and the most detestable of religions.

There is something very touching in this fact; but, if there be something very touching, there is also something very encouraging. God was their God as well as ours—their Creator, their Preserver, who left not Himself without witness among them; who, as they

---

[71] See for various statements in this passage, Josephus, c. Apion. ii. Section 36; Cic. De Fin. v. 25; Clem. Alex. Strom, 1, xxii. 150, xxv. v. 14; Euseb.; Prof. Evang. x. 4, ix. 5, &c.; Lactant. Inst. Div. iv. 2, &c.

blindly felt after Him, suffered their groping hands to grasp the hem of His robe; who sent them rain from heaven, and fruitful seasons, filling their hearts with joy and gladness. And His Spirit was with them, dwelling in them, though unseen and unknown, purifying and sanctifying the temple of their hearts, sending gleams of illuminating light through the gross darkness which encompassed them, comforting their uncertainties, making intercession for them with groaning which cannot be uttered. And more than all, our Saviour was their Saviour, too; He, whom they regarded as a crucified malefactor was their true invisible King; through His righteousness their poor merits were accepted; their inward sicknesses were healed; He whose worship they denounced as an "execrable superstition" stood supplicating for them at the right hand of the Majesty on high, helping them (though they knew Him not) to crush all that was evil within them, and pleading for them when they persecuted even the most beloved of His saints, "Father, forgive them; for they know not what they do."

Yes, they too were all His offspring. Even if they had not been, should we grudge that some of the children's meat should be given unto dogs? Shall we deny to these "unconscious prophecies of heathendom" their oracular significance? Shall we be jealous of the ethical loftiness of a Plato or an Aurelius? Shall we be loth to admit that some power of the Spirit of Christ, even mid the dark wanderings of Seneca's life, kept him still conscious of a nobler and a better way, or that some sweetness of a divine hope inspired the depressions of Epictetus in his slavery? Shall our eye be evil because God in His goodness granted the heathen also to know such truths as enabled them "to overcome the allurements of the visible and the terrors of the invisible world?" Yes, if we have of the Christian Church so mean a conception that we look upon it as a mere human society, "set up in the world to defend a certain religion against a certain other religion." But if on the other hand we believe "that it was a society established by God as a witness for the true condition of all human beings, we shall rejoice to acknowledge its members to be what they believed themselves to be,—confessors and martyrs for a truth which they could not fully embrace or comprehend, but which, through their lives and deaths, through the right and wrong acts, the true and false words, of those who understand them least, was to manifest and prove itself. Those who hold this conviction dare not conceal, or misrepresent, or undervalue, any one of those weighty and memorable sentences which are to be found in the Meditation of Marcus Aurelius. If they did, they would be underrating a portion of that very truth which the preachers of the Gospel were appointed to set forth; they would be adopting the error of the philosophical Emperor without his excuse for it. Nor dare they pretend that the Christian teaching had unconsciously imparted to him a portion of its own light while he seemed to exclude it. They will believe that it was God's good pleasure that a certain truth should be seized and apprehended by this age, and they will see indications of what that truth was in the efforts of Plutarch to understand the 'Daemon' which guided Socrates, in the courageous language of Ignatius, in the bewildering dreams of the Gnostics, in the eagerness of Justin Martyr to prove Christianity a philosophy ... in the apprehension of Christian principles by Marcus Aurelius, and in his hatred of the Christians. From every side they will derive evidence, that a doctrine and society which were meant for mankind cannot depend upon, the partial views and apprehensions of men, must go on justifying, reconciling, confuting, those views and apprehensions by the demonstration of facts"[72]

But perhaps some reader will say, What advantage, then, can we gain by studying in Pagan writers truths which are expressed more nobly, more clearly, and infinitely more effectually in our own sacred books? Before answering the question, let me mention the traditional anecdote[73] of the Caliph Omar. When he conquered Alexandria, he was shown its magnificent library, in which were collected untold treasures of literature, gathered together by the zeal, the labour, and the liberality of a dynasty of kings. "What is the good of all those books?" he said. "They are either in accordance with the Koran, or contrary to it. If the former they are superfluous; if the latter they are pernicious. In either case let them be burnt." Burnt they were, as legend tells; but all the world has condemned the Caliph's reasoning as a piece of stupid Philistinism and barbarous bigotry. Perhaps the question as to the use of reading Pagan ethics is equally unphilosophical; at any rate, we can spare but very few words to its consideration. The answer obviously is, that God has spoken to men, [Greek: polymeros kai polytropos], "at sundry times and in divers manners,"[74] with a richly variegated wisdom.[75] Sometimes He has taught truth by the voice of Hebrew prophets, sometimes by the voice of Pagan philosophers. And all His voices demand our listening ear. If it was given to the Jew to speak with diviner insight and intenser power, it is given to the

---

[72] Maurice, Philos. of the First Six Centuries, p. 37. We venture specially to recommend this weighty and beautiful passage to the reader's serious attention.
[73] Now known to be unhistorical.
[74] Heb. i. 1.
[75] [Greek: polypoikilos dophia].

Gentile also to speak at times with a large and lofty utterance, and we may learn truth from men of alien lips and another tongue. They, too, had the dream, the vision, the dark saying upon the harp, the "daughter of a voice," the mystic flashes upon the graven gems. And such truths come to us with a singular force and freshness; with a strange beauty as the doctrines of a less brightly illuminated manhood; with a new power of conviction from their originality of form, which, because it is less familiar to us, is well calculated to arrest our attention after it has been paralysed by familiar repetitions. We cannot afford to lose these heathen testimonies to Christian truth; or to hush the glorious utterances of Muse and Sibyl which have justly outlived "the drums and tramplings of a hundred triumphs." We may make them infinitely profitable to us. If St. Paul quotes Aratus, and Menander, and Epimenides,[76] and perhaps more than one lyrical melody besides, with earnest appreciation,—if the inspired Apostle could both learn himself and teach others out of the utterances of a Cretan philosopher and an Attic comedian, we may be sure that many of Seneca's apophthegams would have filled him with pleasure, and that he would have been able to read Epictetus and Aurelius with the same noble admiration which made him see with thankful emotion that memorable altar TO THE UNKNOWN GOD.

Let us then make a brief and final sketch of the three great Stoics whose lives we have been contemplating, with a view to summing up their specialties, their deficiencies, and the peculiar relations to, or divergences from, Christian truth, which their writings present to us.

"Seneca saepe noster," "Seneca, often our own," is the expression of Tertullian, and he uses it as an excuse for frequent references to his works. Yet if, of the three, he be most like Christianity in particular passages, he diverges most widely from it in his general spirit.

He diverges from Christianity in many of his modes of regarding life, and in many of his most important beliefs. What, for instance, is his main conception of the Deity? Seneca is generally a Pantheist. No doubt he speaks of God's love and goodness, but with him God is no personal living Father, but the soul of the universe— the fiery, primaeval, eternal principle which transfuses an inert, and no less eternal, matter, and of which our souls are, as it were, but divine particles or passing sparks. "God," he says, "is Nature, is Fate, is Fortune, is the Universe, is the all-pervading Mind. He

---

[76] See Acts xvii. 28; 1 Cor.; Tit. i. 12.

cannot change the substance of the universe, He is himself under the power of Destiny, which is uncontrollable and immutable. It is not God who rolls the thunder, it is Fate. He does not rejoice in His works, but is identical with them." In fact, Seneca would have heartily adopted the words of Pope:

"All are but parts of one stupendous whole,
Whose body nature is, and God the soul."

Though there may be a vague sense in which those words may be admitted and explained by Christians, yet, in the mind of Seneca, they led to conclusions directly opposed to those of Christianity. With him, for instance, the wise man is the equal of God; not His adorer, not His servant, not His suppliant, but His associate, His relation. He differs from God in time alone. Hence all prayer is needless he says, and the forms of external worship are superfluous and puerile. It is foolish to beg for that which you can impart to yourself. "What need is there of vows? Make yourself happy." Nay, in the intolerable arrogance which marked the worst aberration of Stoicism, the wise man is under certain aspects placed even higher than God—higher than God Himself—because God is beyond the reach of misfortunes, but the wise man is superior to their anguish; and because God is good of necessity, but the wise man from choice. This wretched and inflated paradox occurs in Seneca's treatise On Providence, and in the same treatise he glorifies suicide, and expresses a doubt as to the immortality of the soul.

Again, the two principles on which Seneca relied as the basis of all his moral system are: first, the principle that we ought to follow Nature; and, secondly, the supposed perfectibility of the ideal man.

1. Now, of course, if we explain this precept of "following Nature" as Juvenal has explained it, and say that the voice of Nature is always coincident with the voice of philosophy—if we prove that our real nature is none other than the dictate of our highest and most nobly trained reason, and if we can establish the fact that every deed of cruelty, of shame, of lust, or of selfishness, is essentially contrary to our nature—then we may say with Bishop Butler, that the precept to "follow Nature" is "a manner of speaking not loose and undeterminate, but clear and distinct, strictly just and true." But how complete must be the system, how long the preliminary training, which alone can enable us to find any practical value, any appreciable aid to a virtuous life, in a dogma such as this! And, in the hands of Seneca, it becomes a very empty formula. He entirely lacked the keen insight and dialectic subtlety of such a

writer as Bishop Butler; and, in his explanation of this Stoical shibboleth, any real meaning which it may possess is evaporated into a gorgeous mist of confused declamation and splendid commonplace.

2. Nor is he much more fortunate with his ideal man. This pompous abstraction presents us with a conception at once ambitious and sterile. The Stoic wise man is a sort of moral Phoenix, impossible and repulsive. He is intrepid in dangers, free from all passion, happy in adversity, calm in the storm; he alone knows how to live, because he alone knows how to die; he is the master of the world, because he is master of himself, and the equal of God; he looks down upon everything with sublime imperturbability, despising the sadnesses of humanity and smiling with irritating loftiness at all our hopes and all our fears. But, in another sketch of this faultless and unpleasant monster, Seneca presents us, not the proud athlete who challenges the universe and is invulnerable to all the stings and arrows of passion or of fate, but a hero in the serenity of absolute triumph, more tender, indeed, but still without desires, without passions, without needs, who can fell no pity, because pity is a weakness which disturbs his sapient calm! Well might the eloquent Bossuet exclaim, as he read of these chimerical perfections, "It is to take a tone too lofty for feeble and mortal men. But, O maxims truly pompous! O affected insensibility! O false and imaginary wisdom! which fancies itself strong because it is hard, and generous because it is puffed up! How are these principles opposed to the modest simplicity of the Saviour of souls, who, in our Gospel contemplating His faithful ones in affliction, confesses that they will be saddened by it! Ye shall weep and lament." Shall Christians be jealous of such wisdom as Stoicism did really attain, when they compare this dry and bloodless ideal with Him who wept over Jerusalem and mourned by the grave of Lazarus, who had a mother and a friend, who disdained none, who pitied all, who humbled Himself to death, even the death of the cross, whose divine excellence we cannot indeed attain because He is God, but whose example we can imitate because He was very man?[77]

The one grand aim of the life and philosophy of Seneca was Ease. It is the topic which constantly recurs in his books On a Happy Life, On Tranquility of Mind, On Anger, and On the Ease and On the Firmness of the Sage. It is the pitiless apathy, the stern repression, of every form of emotion, which was constantly glorified as the aim of philosophy. It made Stilpo exclaim, when he had lost wife, property, and children, that he had lost nothing, because he

---

[77] See Martha, Les Moralistes, p. 50; Aubertin, Sénèque et St. Paul p. 250.

carried in his own person everything which he possessed. It led Seneca into all that is most unnatural, all that is most fantastic, and all that is least sincere in his writings; it was the bitter source of disgrace and failure in his life. It comes out worst of all in his book On Anger. Aristotle had said that "Anger was a good servant but a bad master;" Plato had recognized the immense value and importance of the irascible element in the moral constitution. Even Christian writers, in spite of Bishop Butler, have often lost sight of this truth, and have forgotten that to a noble nature "the hate of hate" and the "scorn of scorn" are as indispensable as "the love of love." But Seneca almost gets angry himself at the very notion of the wise man being angry and indignant even against moral evil. No, he must not get angry, because it would disturb his sublime calm; and, if he allowed himself to be angry at wrong-doing, he would have to be angry all day long. This practical Epicureanism, this idle acquiescence in the supposed incurability of evil, poisoned all Seneca's career. "He had tutored himself," says Professor Maurice, "to endure personal injuries without indulging an anger; he had tutored himself to look upon all moral evil without anger. If the doctrine is sound and the discipline desirable, we must be content to take the whole result of them. If we will not do that, we must resolve to hate oppression and wrong, even at the cost of philosophical composure" But repose is not to be our aim:—

"We have no right to bliss,
No title from the gods to welfare and repose."

It is one of the truths which seems to me most needed in the modern religious world, that the type of a Christian's virtue must be very miserable, and ordinary, and ineffectual, if he does not feel his whole soul burn within him with an almost implacable moral indignation at the sight of cruelty and injustice, of Pharisaic faithlessness and social crimes.

I have thus freely criticised the radical defects of Stoicism, so far as Seneca is its legitimate exponent; but I cannot consent to leave him with the language of depreciation, and therefore here I will once more endorse what an anonymous writer has said of him: "An unconscious Christianity covers all his sentiments. If the fair fame of the man is sullied, the aspiration to a higher life cannot be denied to the philosopher; if the tinkling cymbal of a stilted Stoicism sometimes sounds through the nobler music, it still leaves the truer melody vibrating on the ear."

2. If Seneca sought for EASE, the grand aim of Epictetus was FREEDOM, of Marcus Aurelius was SELF-GOVERNMENT. This

difference of aim characterises their entire philosophy, though all three of them are filled with precepts which arise from the Stoical contempt of opinion, of fortune, and of death. "Epictetus, the slave, with imperturbable calm, voluntarily strikes off the desire for all those blessings of which fortune had already deprived him. Seneca, who lived in the Court, fenced himself beforehand against misfortune with the spirit of a man of the world and the emphasis of a master of eloquence. Marcus Aurelius, at the zenith of human power—having nothing to dread except his passions, and finding nothing above him except immutable necessity,—surveys his own soul and meditates especially on the eternal march of things. The one is the resigned slave, who neither desires nor fears; the other, the great lord, who has everything to lose; the third, finally, the emperor, who is dependent only on himself and upon God."

Of Epictetus and Marcus Aurelius we shall have very little to say by way of summary, for they show no inconsistencies and very few of the imperfections which characterise Seneca's ideal of the Stoic philosophy. The "moral peddling," the pedagogic display, the puerile ostentation, the antithetic brilliancy, which we have had to point out in Seneca, are wanting in them. The picture of the inner life, indeed, of Seneca, his efforts after self-discipline, his untiring asceticism, his enthusiasm for all that he esteems holy and of good report-this picture, marred as it is by rhetoric and vain self-conceit, yet "stands out in noble contrast to the swinishness of the Campanian villas, and is, in its complex entirety, very sad and affecting." And yet we must admit, in the words of the same writer, that when we go from Seneca to Epictetus and Marcus Aurelius, "it is going from the florid to the severe, from varied feeling to the impersonal simplicity of the teacher, often from idle rhetoric to devout earnestness." As far as it goes, the morality of these two great Stoics is entirely noble and entirely beautiful. If there be even in Epictetus some passing and occasional touch of Stoic arrogance and Stoic apathy; if there be in Marcus Aurelius a depth and intensity of sadness which shows how comparatively powerless for comfort was a philosophy which glorified suicide, which knew but little of immortality, and which lost in vague Pantheism the unspeakable blessing of realizing a personal relation to a personal God and Father—there is yet in both of them enough and more than enough to show that in all ages and in all countries they who have sought for God have found Him, that they have attained to high principles of thought and to high standards of action—that they have been enabled, even in the thick darkness, resolutely to place their feet at least on the lowest rounds of that ladder of sunbeams which winds up through the darkness to the great Father of Lights.

And yet the very existence of such men is in itself a significant comment upon the Scriptural decision that "the world by wisdom knew not God." For how many like them, out of all the records of antiquity, is it possible for us to count? Are there five men in the whole circle of ancient history and ancient literature to whom we could, without a sense of incongruity, accord the title of "holy?" When we have mentioned Socrates, Epictetus, and Marcus Aurelius, I hardly know of another. Just men there were in multitudes—men capable of high actions; men eminently worthy to be loved; men, I doubt not, who, when the children of the kingdom shall be rejected, shall be gathered from the east and the west with Abraham, Isaac, and Jacob, into the kingdom of heaven. Yes, just men in multitudes; but how many righteous, how many holy? Some, doubtless, whom we do not know, whose names were never written, even for a few years, on the records of mankind—men and women in unknown villages and humble homes, "the faithful who were not famous." We do not doubt that there were such—but were they relatively numerous? If those who rose above the level of the multitude—if those whom some form of excellence, and often of virtue, elevated into the reverence of their fellows—present to us a few examples of stainless life, can we hope that a tolerable ideal of sanctity was attained by any large proportion of the ordinary myriads? Seeing that the dangerous lot of the majority was cast amid the weltering sea of popular depravity, can we venture to hope that many of them succeeded in reaching some green island of purity, integrity, and calm? We can hardly think it; and yet, in the dispensation of the Kingdom of Heaven we see such a condition daily realized. Not only do we see many of the eminent, but also countless multitudes of the lowly and obscure, whose common lives are, as it were, transfigured with a light from heaven. Unhappy, indeed, is he who has not known such men in person, and whose hopes and habits have not caught some touch of radiance reflected from the nobility and virtue of lives like these. The thought has been well expressed by the author of Ecce Homo, and we may well ask with him, "If this be so, has Christ failed, or can Christianity die?"

No, it has not failed; it cannot die; for the saving knowledge which it has imparted is the most inestimable blessing which God has granted to our race. We have watched philosophy in its loftiest flight, but that flight rose as far above the range of the Pagan populace as Ida or Olympus rises above the plain: and even the topmost crests of Ida and Olympus are immeasurably below the blue vault, the body of heaven in its clearness, to which it has been granted to some Christians to attain. As regards the multitude, philosophy had no influence over the heart and character; "it was sectarian, not universal; the religion of the few, not of the many. It exercised no creative power over political or social life; it stood in no such relation to the past as the New Testament to the Old. Its best thoughts were but views and aspects of the truth; there was no centre around which they moved, no divine life by which they were impelled; they seemed to vanish and flit in uncertain succession of light." But Christianity, on the other hand, glowed with a steady and unwavering brightness; it not only swayed the hearts of individuals by stirring them to their utmost depths, but it moulded the laws of nations, and regenerated the whole condition of society. It gave to mankind a fresh sanction in the word of Christ, a perfect example in His life, a powerful motive in His love, an all sufficient comfort in the life of immortality made sure and certain to us by His Resurrection and Ascension. But if without this sanction, and example, and motive, and comfort, the pagans could learn to do His will,—if, amid the gross darkness through which glitters the degraded civilization of imperial Rome, an Epictetus and an Aurelius could live blameless lives in a cell and on a throne, and a Seneca could practise simplicity and self-denial in the midst of luxury and pride—how much loftier should be both the zeal and the attainments of us to whom God has spoken by His Son? What manner of men ought we to be? If Tyre and Sidon and Sodom shall rise in the judgment to bear witness against Chorazin and Bethsaida, may not the pure lives of these great Seekers after God add a certain emphasis of condemnation to the vice, the pettiness, the mammon-worship of many among us to whom His love, His nature, His attributes have been revealed with a clearness and fullness of knowledge for which kings and philosophers have sought indeed and sought earnestly, but sought in vain?

www.ingramcontent.com/pod-product-compliance
Lightning Source LLC
LaVergne TN
LVHW030632080426
835511LV00020B/3446

9 781647 993443